WHO NEEDS TO KNOW?

THE STATE OF PUBLIC ACCESS
TO FEDERAL GOVERNMENT INFORMATION

Published in the United States of America
by Bernan Press, a wholly owned subsidiary of
The Rowman & Littlefield Publishing Group, Inc.
4501 Forbes Boulevard, Suite 200
Lanham, Maryland 20706

Bernan Press
800-865-3457
info@bernan.com
www.bernan.com

ISBN 10: 1-59888-307-0 (pbk.)
ISBN 13: 978-1-59888-307-7 (pbk.)
eISBN 10: 1-59888-308-9
eISBN 13: 978-1-59888-308-4

ACKNOWLEDGMENTS

I WANT TO THANK BERNAN PRESS FOR APPROACHING ME TO DO THIS BOOK AND its faith in my "voice" throughout a process that was much longer than any of us anticipated. My appreciation also goes out to Sarah Herbert, my patient editor, who shaped this into a much more readable text. I also want to thank Steve Aftergood for all his work and for his willingness to answer frantic questions from me with his always insightful and informative thoughts. The incredible work of the National Security Archive also made much of the discussion of the Freedom of Information Act possible. The experts at the Congressional Research Service, in particular, Harold Relyea, provided invaluable objective perspectives on many of the issues this book examines. And my many colleagues in the fight to protect and strengthen public access to government-held information earn my ongoing appreciation and thanks for the work they do and what I learn from and with them.

Finally, this book would not have happened without the support—and shouldering of extra household burdens during the process of writing and editing—of my husband, Glenn Harper. His support and belief in me throughout not just this project but our years together have sustained me and made my work possible.

Contents

INTRODUCTION

"Fundamental to our way of life is the belief that when information which properly belongs to the public is systematically withheld by those in power, the people soon become ignorant of their own affairs, distrustful of those who manage them, and—eventually—incapable of determining their own destinies."

—Richard Nixon, March 8, 1972[1]

Public access to information is an essential component of responsible and responsive democracy. What I mean by this is twofold. First, in order for the public to be responsibly engaged in governance and in decision-making, it needs to have meaningful access to good information. The second half of the equation is that in order for government to remain—or become—responsible and responsive to the public, it has to be open about its activities and its processes.

The overarching principles for federal government information, developed in 1996,[2] remain salient:

Principle 1: The public has the right of access to government information.

Principle 2: The government has an obligation to disseminate and provide broad public access to its information.

Principle 3: The government has an obligation to guarantee the authenticity and integrity of its information.

Principle 4: The government has an obligation to preserve its information.

Principle 5: Government information created or compiled by government employees or at government expense should remain in the public domain.

What I plan to examine in this book are two trends in the access world. The first of these has to do with e-government. E-government is the provision of government information in an electronic form, such as over the Internet. The second trend is what I see as portents of change in the wrong direction in terms of how we understand the role and the importance of access to public information.

An underlying tension can be found throughout government: the ability—and willingness—of government to harness the promise of digital information for public access and accountability while not abusing its potential for control of that information. Government, and in particular government agencies, have been quite willing to make press releases available online. They—and here I include all the branches of government—have been overall much less keen on making their functions and performance open to public scrutiny.

On the other hand, especially since the terrorist events of September 11, 2001, we have also seen the dark side of digital government—the potential for easy control of government information. As readers probably know, after the commandeering of commercial airplanes for terrorist attacks on iconic American landmarks, vast amounts of information were removed[3] from public accessibility on government Web sites. Some departments, in particular the Department of Defense, had already been removing information from public sites and were exerting greater control over what was posted. But the follow-on to September 11 was startling for those who had become accustomed to the "let a thousand flowers bloom" culture of the Clinton Administration. It was a shock how quickly documents disappeared and it confirmed our worst fears about what we had been pointing out for a number of years—we did not have a good inventory of government information and we had very little way (other than reports from individuals, primarily) of knowing how much had really disappeared or what it might be.

Not that efforts had not been made to address both the promise and the risks of digital government. Ten years ago, Senator Daniel Patrick Moynihan[4] analyzed the organizational culture regarding access to classified information. His insights provide a useful way of looking at not just classified information but our current confrontations with expanding government secrecy:

> *"If the present report is to serve any large purpose, it is to introduce the public to the thought that secrecy is a mode of regulation. In truth, it is the ultimate mode, for the citizen does not even know that he or she is being regulated. Normal regulation concerns how citizens must behave, and so regulations are widely promulgated. Secrecy, by contrast, concerns what citizens may know; and the citizen is not told what may not be known."*

Senator Moynihan noted that "overregulation" is a continuing theme in American public life and that "secrecy would be such an issue, save that secrecy is secret."

I am in total agreement with Moynihan that secrecy is "at times legitimate and necessary." His concern, and what I examine in this book, is that a culture of secrecy not remain the only norm in American government as regards national security—and we would add now, homeland security. Senator Moynihan called for "a competing culture of openness,"

> *"a climate which simply assumes that secrecy is not the starting place.... One which asks what the purpose is of the organization, and how that purpose is best served in the radically new environment of an information age, in which almost any information is open and accessible."*

A culture of secrecy, secrecy as a form of regulation—thought-provoking concepts. And, indeed, it is forms of regulation—the Freedom of Information Act (FOIA), the reauthorization of the Paperwork Reduction Act (PRA) in 1996,[5] the E-FOIA amendments of 1996, and the E-Government Act of 2002—that were explicitly intended to countervail the government culture of secrecy and obscurity.

The reality is, though, that—with or without a system to countervail that culture—we are largely at the mercy of the government as to whether or not we can find, obtain, and use government information—in the here and now, much less over time. Good intentions, good laws, good regulations—when they occur—are up against bureaucratic and political obduracy and endurance.

Still, there are committed civil servants who still believe in the public's right to know, and there are many of us who continue to try to support them and advance openness and accountability.

This book will explore the context for policies and procedures that affect the public's ability to easily search, find, retrieve (get access to), and, importantly, use all the myriad "government information" created, collected, processed, disseminated, or disposed of by or for the federal government. For the purposes of brevity, I am going to refer to "government information"— but Alasdair Roberts[6] talks about "government-held information." This locution seems much more descriptive and does not imply that ownership resides with the government, that the public are supplicants for information boons. The use of the term "government information" has itself been fraught with policy implications as I discuss in chapters to come.

This work will attempt to provide an analysis of the current state of public access to federal government information from the perspective of the person who wants to understand what her government is doing, how to interact with it, how to engage with public policy decision-making—and how to hold government, and those who act on its behalf or under its regulation, accountable. And someone who has been involved in fights to make that happen for the better part of 15 years.

Sadly, an analysis of that state requires looking at the impact of an Administration that is dedicated to advancing its power at the expense of Congress and the public, as well as its ideology over objective science, and determined to advance its positions by whatever means it has deemed necessary. While I do not address this here in more than passing, it has been aided in much of this by a supine Congress controlled by the President's party. In the Afterword (and briefly in some parts of the text), I look forward and discuss what difference the change of power in the 110th Congress is making.

The book is roughly divided into two parts. Part I has to do with public access where a "regulatory" framework exists. This first part, chapters 1–6, will lay out what is at stake for public access to government-held information, and look at the state of public access given the approaching-total conversion of the federal government to digital records in its the conduct of the public's business: digital publications, digital records, web-based government. I will discuss the statutes underlying that access (the Federal Records Act, the Federal Depository Library Program and GPO Access, the Paperwork Reduction Act, and Circular A-130) and the work to draft—and the subsequent implementation of—the E-Government Act of 2002. This section of the book looks at the impact of the Ashcroft Memo and the "Card Memo" on access to information through the FOIA, process issues with the FOIA and the 1996 amendments to the Freedom of Information Act (the E-FOIA amendments), and at the passage of protection for Critical Infrastructure Information (CII) and how that has played out.

Additionally, Part I gives a brief look at some of the history of the protection of information related to national security and defense and scans recent misuses and abuses of classification authority. In this section of the book, I also discuss the concept of "sensitive but unclassified" information and related control markings, and provide examples of the use and abuse of such markings.

Part II, chapters 8–10, examines the impact on public access to government information and government accountability where such a "regulatory" framework is lacking—or ignored. This part of the book looks at the resistance to accountability—to the Congress and to the public—through assertions and exercise of executive power. It also looks at the second Bush administration's propagandistic use of information to shape both domestic and foreign opinion, its politicization of science, and its expansive controls on access to informed government officials.

This book is not a scholarly or legal analysis of specific laws, guidance and regulations (such as the Freedom of Information Act, Circular A-130) pertaining to access. When Bernan approached me to do this book, it was because of my knowledge in the area of public access and also my willingness to express a strong opinion. This book is my informed view as someone who has been working in this area for more than 20 years (almost 15 of those as an engaged activist on these matters). It is an expression of both my outrage at many aspects of our current state of openness and accountability and my hope for the future.

July 2007, Washington, D.C.

Notes

1 Richard Nixon, "Statement on Establishing a New System for Classification and Declassification of Government Documents Relating to National Security." The American Presidency Project. March 8, 1972. http://www.presidency.ucsb.edu/ws/print.php?pid=3762.

2 As part of the *Study to Identify Measures Necessary for a Successful Transition to a More Electronic Federal Depository Library Program.* Washington, DC: U.S. Government Printing Office (GPO), 1996.

3 See "Access to Government Information Post September 11th" for a catalog of those early months of information restriction. http://www.ombwatch.org/article/articleview/213/1/104.

4 Daniel Patrick Moynihan. "Chairman's Foreword," Report of the Commission on Protecting and Reducing Government Secrecy. Washington, DC: (GPO, 1997). http://www.fas.org/sgp/library/moynihan/index.html.

5 At least the information dissemination sections of the PRA.

6 Alasdair Roberts. "Structural Pluralism and the Right to Information." School of Policy Studies Working Paper 15, February 2001.

PART I

THERE OUGHT TO BE A LAW

THE NEED FOR FINDABLE AND USABLE INFORMATION

In the Introduction to the book, I talked about two trends in access to federal government information. Part I examines the first of these, the march toward electronic government and the kinds of problems that exist with finding and using government information, particularly digital information. In both the executive and legislative branches (more the former than the latter, sadly) government "transformation" toward e-government is proceeding, sometimes with advance thinking about what government in the digital age should entail. Often, however, what is on offer is not a comprehensive ability for the public—whether individuals, business owners, or regulated entities—to comprehensively locate and interact with the federal government information, but, rather, to do this and that discrete task, find this and that particular piece of information.

No member of the public, though, should have to know how government organizes itself and its information in order to learn about its activities and to transact business with, participate in, and be involved as a citizen with it. One of the apparent outcomes of e-government so far is that more people are realizing how much information government has collected in databases that are inconsistently defined and difficult to access. It is only a matter of time until more and more people are going to ask for meaningful access to them. And less and less is the public—including the business world and Congress—going to accept that the burden falls *outside* government to make its information accessible and useful.

Indeed, surveys taken toward the end of the Clinton Administration showed just such an interest by the public. In several Hart-Teeter polls[1] commissioned by the Council for Excellence in Government from August 2000 to February 2002, a plurality of respondents said greater government accountability was among the most significant benefits that e-government could confer. This was chosen by a considerable margin over convenient services. In a 2000 poll, a majority found greater government accountability combined with "greater public access to information" as the most significant benefits. Even after September 11, 2001 the percentages stayed high in these areas, relative to providing for homeland and national security.

Government officials were also surveyed. The 2000 survey report notes that government officials regard public access to information as the greatest benefit (34 percent) but rank accountability much lower (19 percent).[2] As the pollsters comment, the government and the public apparently are in synch in valuing e-government's ability to produce a more informed citizenry, but the public is much more focused on its empowering potential.

Question: What is the most important positive thing that may result from e-gov?	All Adults			E-Government Users	
	2/02	1/01	8/00	2/02	1/01
Government that is more accountable to its citizens	28	30	36	26	29
More efficient and cost-effective government	19	14	21	22	17
Greater public access to information	18	17	23	25	20
Government that is better able to provide for national and homeland security	16	18	NA	9	13
More convenient government services	13	15	13	15	16

I Know It's Here Somewhere, but . . .

The federal government creates and collects huge amounts of information. Too frequently, though, the government stores this information in databases that are inconsistently defined and difficult to use—assuming that you can find them. And even when you can find and use the databases, the information in them may well be incomplete or out of date. Worse, correlating the meaning of findings from a number of databases requires (in the words of the President's Information Technology Advisory Committee (PITAC) Panel on Transforming Government) "deep knowledge of the existence, content, and management schemes of those databases."[3]

Database compatibility, interoperable standards, and *searchability* may sound like rather obscure technical concepts, but you should care about them because they affect your ability to find and use government information. Take the compatibility of databases across government agencies, for example. The ability to work across agencies is critical to any possibility of a meaningful e-government. You, as a parent or a researcher, might want to take information from a number of Environmental Protection Agency (EPA) databases on water and toxic releases. You might then want to take the information you find on these EPA databases (which would include names of companies in the Toxic Release Inventory) and combine those data with Securities and Exchange Commission (SEC) data on that company. Good luck. EPA's databases are not interoperable among themselves.

And as for the ability to find, access, and use government information—take a quick look at the seven scenarios listed in the box called "Seven Scenarios of Search: Why We Need Better Data Access." If you haven't found yourself in one of these, you probably will. (These scenarios come from a Request for Information (RFI) issued by the Office of Management and Budget/General Services Administration (OMB) and (GSA)[4] that I will discuss in more detail below.)

Seven Scenarios of Search: Why We Need Better Data Access

In fall 2005, the OMB and GSA issued a Request for Information (see the discussion of this RFI on page XX). The scenarios laid out for potential respondents in the RFI usefully frame the discussion of data integration and access to records and publications (both electronic and nonelectronic). They describe various common information discovery, retrieval, aggregation, and sharing needs. While they are a bit lengthy, they are thoughtful and identify the issues facing government and the public. They merit reading.

1. Researching unexplained illnesses among defense contractors supporting U.S. military operations. A primary care physician is treating a patient suffering from an unexplained illness. He learns this patient was a defense contractor, having supported U.S. military operations in various countries worldwide. The physician suspects that his illness might be linked to his participation in these operations but needs to perform detailed research in a fairly short period of time to confirm or deny that hypothesis.

Given the relatively small population sample involved, there is little research available in academic or commercial medical literature definitively addressing the patient's symptoms. Therefore, the physician needs to perform a fairly exhaustive search for government information on the topic of unexplained illnesses among U.S. military veterans, the hypothesis being that illnesses impacting veterans will also likely impact the contractors deployed with them.

The physician knows intuitively that the Department of Defense (DoD) and the Department of Veterans Affairs (VA) are two good potential sources of information on this topic. What he does not know is that there are also government information holdings addressing this topic at other agencies, including the National Archives and Records Administration (NARA), the National Institutes of Health (NIH), and the Centers for Disease Control (CDC), as well as the legislative branch (the House, Senate, Library of Congress, and Government Accountability Office) and some state and local governments.

Relevant information is also potentially available from nongovernmental sources, such as commercial entities (e.g., insurance companies) and academic organizations (e.g., research universities). Relevant information exists in a wide variety of formats: electronic documents (plain text, HTML, XML, Adobe PDF, and other formats), tabular data (spreadsheets, databases, etc.), multimedia (sound, video, etc.), and biometric (gene databases, etc.). Some of these information resources are "deep web" or "hidden web" assets, not easily accessible from typical Internet search engines.

When conducting his search, the physician needs to be able to aggregate, analyze, and manipulate the information relevant to the topic. For example, he needs to correlate general symptoms with information found in his patient's medical records. These records are mostly hand-written forms that have been digitized. He might also need to correlate data geospatially (i.e., compare his patient's overseas travels with overlays showing disease patterns in various locales worldwide). Since time is of the essence, he needs to have the ability to analyze large data sets quickly and accurately. Once he is completed with his research, the physician will probably want to publish a paper to share his findings with the medical community.

This scholarly paper will contain citations to electronic government records available on the Internet. The physician will want to ensure that his citations will still be attainable at some arbitrary point in the future. Finally, the physician will want to be automatically notified if any new government or other information concerning unexplained military service-connected illnesses is published.

2. Performing a search for an expert. The government needs to rapidly set up a work group to study an urgent, complex, yet relatively obscure technical issue. The government wants to identify personnel throughout the federal government (civil servants, military personnel, retirees, and contractors) who are true experts in this area, and for that reason it does not want to rely solely on self-selection (volunteers) or manager selection. Since the technical issue is relatively obscure, it is unlikely (but still possible) that the skills related to it have been captured in human resources (HR)/personnel management systems.

A more likely source of identifying experts in this field will be through an analysis of subject matter-related work products or websites the individuals or their employing organizations have created or helped to create. Many of these work products are published on agency public websites, but some are located on internal federal government information systems or elsewhere outside the government. Some of these information resources are "deep web" or "hidden web" assets, not easily accessible from typical Internet search engines. Depending on how many federal experts are found, the government might also want to broaden the search to include experts from state/local/tribal governments and the private sector, especially academic and nonprofit organizations.

3. Performing academic research. A student is preparing a class report on Poland's involvement in the Cold War, including the extent to which the Poles, their leaders, and security services were reluctant or willing participants with the Soviet Union. In addition, the student seeks to discover the significant impact that Pope John Paul and Lech Walesa had in contributing to the end of the Cold War. As a part of his research for this report, he wants to locate and quickly analyze all government and other information resources covering this topic.

As a part of this analysis, he wants to be able to

1. Identify all government and other resources related to the Cold War pertaining specifically to Poland, with a preference for primary sources (reports, photos, maps, military unit histories, etc.) over secondary sources (textbooks, encyclopedias, etc.).

2. Sort through all available information and retrieve those information resources most pertinent to his specific area of interest.

3. Translate any multi-lingual content into English.

4. Derive an outline (taxonomy) describing Poland's involvement in the Cold War at a high level through an analysis of these resources.

5. Extract relevant facts, summaries, and text passages from these resources—including some facts about Poland's involvement in the Cold War that have not been widely reported and therefore providing a unique and valuable insight into this important period of history.

6. Download maps of various Cold War hotspots, and add overlays to these maps to provide additional description and clarity.

7. Organize everything using the outline created in step 4 above.

8. Publish this information as both a paper and a Web site.

4. Conducting an information audit trail. An individual or organization (policy official, land developer, commercial entity, etc.) must identify and track the flow of electronic information on a specific topic between government agencies to understand how and where that information was processed. This individual also wants to identify the extent to which the information is accurate, relevant, timely, and complete. This requirement may be driven by a routine or nonroutine process such as an application filing, environmental findings, historical research, or a need to find more authoritative sources on this information.

5. Sharing law enforcement information across jurisdictional boundaries. A small local police department raids an apartment on a tip from a citizen alleging drug trafficking and other illegal activities. A search of the apartment reveals documents containing handwritten notes in a foreign language, as well as a ledger documenting what appear to be financial transactions. The investigators are able to lift numerous usable fingerprints from the apartment. Moreover, the walls of the apartment are decorated with fresh graffiti (they are unfamiliar with gang tagging and thus unequipped to decipher it).

The investigating officer processing the crime scene collects and inventories the documents and fingerprints, takes photos of the graffiti, and then submits these materials to the desk sergeant at the precinct, who digitizes everything and posts the materials to the appropriate regional law enforcement information sharing exchange. An investigator in a large municipality receives a notification that these documents, fingerprints, and photos have been posted to the regional information exchange. The investigator translates/interprets the documents and photos, analyzes the materials, and correlates the information with other relevant information obtained from various law enforcement organizations at the federal, state, local, and tribal levels. The investigator's analysis reveals the local investigation is related to broader national-level gang-related activities being investigated at the federal level.

6. Discovering possible forged identity. A credit card company has discovered a series of accounts that were fraudulently established on behalf of a group of unaware individual victims. The credit card company notifies these victims who in turn must notify all pertinent organizations with which they have a financial relationship and governmental agencies they currently or potentially receive services from, including federal agencies.

7. Looking for all online government information regarding a unique topic. A citizen is searching for all available federal government information about a particular topic, including information located on government websites. A successful search will help her avoid using the complex, lengthy, and potentially costly Freedom of Information Act process. There is no way to know in advance what any single individual citizen may be interested in but invariably the same, similar, or related government information is located at more than one Federal agency and comes in various types of online information. Some of these information resources are "deep web" or "hidden web" assets, not easily accessible from typical Internet search engines.

For example, say you were faced with scenario number 4: Conducting an information audit trail. If you to wanted to find out if government information—on which, say, your business might rely—is accurate and to see how it is processed across the government, you would need to be able to actually track it, perhaps by a common identifier (one hopes not your Social Security number!). That is not now possible. You would want to be able to pull information out of the many databases in the potentially multiple agencies to which your information (or the information of some other party that you need to be able to see and use) may have been submitted. That, too, is generally not possible—you probably could not find all the *major information systems* used by the agencies involved and the information would not likely be usable in any easy way, because each of the information systems probably uses different (and proprietary) standards. (Think MS Word and how well it works with other word processing programs and then multiply it a hundredfold.) The scenario also says you might need to look at "historical research" or "need to find more authoritative sources on this information;" none of this is likely to be findable online across the government, especially if it does not exist in a digital format.

So you will have a very difficult and frustrating job ahead of you. But as you will see in Chapter 2, OMB thinks strong search engines will generally solve the problem. But unfortunately for you, even if OMB's "strong search engines" do succeed in being able to search the *deep web* (the things that are not findable by normal search engines), that is only the tip of the iceberg for your problems.

In short, providing real, meaningful, useful, ongoing access to—and across—the vast array of information created or collected or maintained by or for the federal government is complex. The advance of the digital revolution within the federal government has made meeting the challenge both possible (because it is now possible to electronically collect and correlate information across different record sources) and more difficult (because of widely disparate practices and standards—including those proprietary to companies providing services to and for agencies).

Managing Government Information

The problems with federal information management have been acknowledged at the highest levels of government. In August 2000, the [4] Panel on Transforming Government issued a report called "Transforming Access to Government through Information Technology." The panel issuing the report had been specifically tasked to identify the key technical challenges and to develop a long-range technology-based strategy to harness the power of advanced information systems to make the government's vast stores of information and its vital services easily accessible to and usable by all U.S. citizens "regardless of their physical location, level of computer literacy, or physical capacity."

As noted above, the PITAC report emphasized that finding information in the government's many databases is difficult, and that "correlating the meaning of findings from a number of inconsistently defined databases requires deep knowledge of the existence, content, and management schemes of those databases." Two key findings of the report were no surprise:

- Major technological barriers prevent citizens from easily accessing government information resources vital to their well being; and

- Government information is often unavailable, inadequate, out of date, and needlessly complicated.

To address this problem, the PITAC panel's recommended effort focused on "government-specific capabilities" such as "metadata creation, and comprehensive searchable catalogs of information and services." (For more on what PITAC was talking about, see "Metadata and a Few Other IT Terms.")

Metadata and a Few Other IT Terms

You will find it helpful to be familiar with a few terms that information technology (IT) folks use for some concepts that are quite familiar in a library context. *Metadata*—data about data—include data categories such as Author, Subject Headings, Publisher ("Agency of Creation" in government talk), and Date. Metadata can also include information about restrictions on information: Is it classified? And if so, why and for how long? Does it contain information to personally identify individuals? Does it contain trade secrets?

A *catalog* is just what you think it is: a list or record systematically arranged, often including descriptive material (which might be or include metadata), such as a library catalog.

Without these tools, imagine trying to find a book about what you want in the library. Even if all the books were online, doing a keyword search would yield a lot of information but most of it would be irrelevant. This is one step beyond dumping all the books on the floor and letting you dig through them; it is that, just aided by a computer. It is a good way to hide information, but not a good way to make it findable by the public. And it is no way to enable the public to be assured that they have found all the information on a topic.

As for *interoperability*, think of train tracks: trains can run efficiently only when all the tracks they must use are the same gauge. If information tracks are of different gauges—that is, if they use incompatible and, worse, proprietary standards for describing and providing access and use—the information will not flow or will flow to and from only those sites that use the same gauge. Hardly what we have in mind for finding and using government information.

The truth is, though, that these sorts of finding tools are already supposed to be in existence in federal agencies. They are required by the *Paperwork Reduction Act, the E-Government Act,* and the *E-FOIA* amendments. As you will see in the following chapters, although laws are on the books that would address these problems and impose some management on government information, they are not well or fully implemented So, despite their being legally mandated, these tools to help the public find and use government information don't exist much of anywhere in the federal government.

One of the common metaphors in the 1990s about the government's ability to share information—with itself or the public—was stovepipes. I actually prefer Vice-President Gore's earlier metaphor: silos of rotting information. Some of the information is locked away—for safekeeping or safeguarding, to use a new locution—from those who don't "have a need" for it, who might misuse it, or put it together with other bits of information. The silo-keepers claim that they know best who should, and should not, get into those silos.

We also have a few mice—or "spiders"—that will crawl around in "open" silos, find, and bring—if you say the right words—lots of bits of information to a grain depository where you can sift through it yourself. That is not my vision of access to information in a digital government, and my guess is that it is not anyone else's either.

The federal government—both government-wide and agency by agency—needs to get its information under control and beginning to manage it so all of it can be identified, located and used over time. That takes leadership committed to meaningful access, it takes commitment of serious resources, and it takes a coherent and comprehensively applied information policy—at least for each of the branches if not for all of them at the same time. None is in the offing.

E-government is an exciting frontier. But technology alone is not going to get us there. Bigger and faster servers or more powerful search engines are not all that it is going to take to move to the kind of government that uses technology as a tool to provide greater accountability through better and more meaningful public access to government information. As I argue later, the technology exists to make government information easier to find and use, but technology is a tool, not an answer. Unfortunately, when the government has turned to technology—which is something it should be doing—it has been *in place of* policy. We need a government-wide information policy that sets the guidelines for the use of technology to promote public access to government information. Despite all the laws discussed in Part I of this book, this kind of policy is still missing.

We are a long way from government that is truly e-government or from an ability to easily search, find, retrieve, and use all government information—including records held by agencies or print publications. (We are excluding, of course, information that is not so secret that public information about its very existence is prohibited.) Even with FirstGov/USA.gov and search engines on agency sites, we are still a very long way from the ability to achieve results with high precision and low recall, which is how librarians say "getting what you are looking for without being overwhelmed by extraneous returns."

But it would be nice.

Notes

1 "September 28, 2000—e-Government: The Next American Revolution." http://www.excel-gov.org/admin/FormManager/filesuploading/2000egovtopline.pdf; "e-Government: The Next American Revolution, January 2001 Supplemental Poll." http://www.excelgov.org/admin/FormManager/filesuploading/egovsupdata.pdf; "February 26, 2002—e-Government to Connect, Protect, and Serve Us." http://www.excelgov.org/admin/FormManager/filesuploading/egovconnectprotectdata2.pdf.

2 "September 28, 2000—e-Government: The Next American Revolution." http://www.excelgov.org/admin/FormManager/filesuploading/2000egovtopline.pdf.

3 President's Information Technology Advisory Committee Panel on Transforming Government. "Report to the President: Transforming Access to Government Through Information Technology," September 2000. http://www.nitrd.gov/pubs/pitac/pres-trans gov-11sep00.pdf.

4 The President's Information Technology Advisory Committee was authorized by Congress under the High-Performance Computing Act of 1991 (Pub. L. 102-194) and the Next Generation Internet Act of 1998 (Pub. L. 105-305) as a Federal Advisory Committee. Executive Order 13385 assigned the role and responsibilities of PITAC to the President's Council of Advisors on Science and Technology (PCAST), http://www.nitrd.gov/pitac/ (National Coordination Office for Networking and Information Technology Research and Development). Its report, "Report to the President: Transforming Access to Government Through Information Technology," September 2000, is available at http://www.nitrd.gov/pubs/pitac/pres-transgov-11sep00.pdf.

CHAPTER 1

TRACKING THE WILD GOVERNMENT:

THE FEDERAL RECORDS ACT AND GOVERNMENT PUBLICATIONS

An informed public needs to know what its government is doing and should have access to all of its records (apart from properly classified or confidential material—a topic for Chapter 6). But in the current state of federal record-keeping, that is harder than it should be. This chapter will

- discuss the importance of good government records;
- examine how the Federal Records Act requires the government to preserve its electronic records, such as government e-mail and Web site information; and
- review the state of government publications (as managed by the GPO).

Getting information about the ways the government organizes itself and the records of its activities—whether those records reflect information it created (letters, memoranda, policy papers) or that it collected from the public or industry (the records of citizen tax payment, corporate environmental compliance, scientific research, and so on)—should be a fairly easy first step. It *should* be, but it isn't—because federal agencies ignore with impunity the requirements of E-FOIA and other statutes. And obtaining access to the records *themselves*—in a government that has gone digital without thinking through where the technology was taking it and what the impacts were likely to be—is possibly as difficult as finding the important information stored in the government's many databases.

The Vanishing Trail

You will recall from the introduction to Part I that the President's Information Technology Advisory Committee panel said correlating findings from a number of inconsistently defined databases requires deep knowledge of the existence, contents, and management schemes of those databases. I don't want to push the analogy too far, but in the move from typewriters and then dumb terminals to desktop computers, and the parallel downsizing of support and clerical staff, we are not far from a situation where providing full and accurate access to records—especially as these migrate out of current use and are not migrated to new operating systems and new software regimes—requires deep knowledge of their existence, their contents, and the structures of the formats in which they were created. What used to be created in multicolor carbons and filed by support staff for years were allowed to reside on someone's desktop. Now they are likely to reside on a storage server but are unlikely to be indexed or be in any sort of a records-management system. The one official copy may get printed out and filed, but the drafts and the shared versions that would help a student, a historian, or a reporter trace the development of a program or a policy rarely will be saved systematically.

The National Academy of Public Administration, in a report prepared for the National Archives and Records Administration (NARA), identified a critical problem related to future historical research: We are losing our access to the history of our government.

> *"As more and more computers move into the workplace, as greater numbers of professional staff adopt electronic technologies, as the uses and variety of electronic media expand, and as electronic signatures become acceptable, paper retention will become less important. Not everything will be printed out; not everything will be retained on disk or tape; not all disks and tape will survive; not everything retained will be accessible—and the electronic media will not always be inviolable. Thus, in the future, historians may often have to be satisfied with final documents, focusing on what was agreed upon or on important disagreements, and thus losing vital information about how a policy or action developed."* [1]

The False Reassurance of Backups

And, lest you think that backup tapes solve the dilemma of federal record-keeping, I would say to you: Vice President Gore's e-mail. For those readers too young to remember, in 2000, in response to various congressional investigations of the White House (including Vice President Gore's meeting with Chinese visitors who may have made campaign contributions), the White House discovered that an entire year's worth of the Vice President's e-mail and that of his staff was never put on backup tapes and most of it had been irretrievably lost. The White House embarked on a $10 million-plus effort to retrieve hundreds of thousands of other e-mails from backup tapes that *were* made, put them in a searchable system, and scour them for evidence.[2] And, of course, now I must reference Karl Rove's e-mail—for the same reasons (and worse—possible *intentional* erasure of government records).[3]

As this demonstrates, a backup tape is not an electronic records management system—it does not provide for search and retrieval of individual documents by known search terms. Nor do document management systems meet the needs for specialized electronic records management. Commercially available document management systems can generally search and retrieve simple electronic records by particular search terms; they support an institution's *immediate* operational requirements for electronic information. A government agency needs a far more complex records management system. Electronic records management (ERM), however, supports the medium- to long-term requirements for information management by capturing electronic records and managing them from creation to disposal. Typical components of an ERM include

- Capture, storage, indexing, and retrieval of all elements of a record as a complex unit, for all types of record.
- Maintenance of links between records within a filing structure throughout lifecycle management.
- Metadata at record level providing contextual information.
- Integration of paper and electronic records.
- Secure storage and management ensuring authenticity and accountability.
- Appraisal, selection, and export or migration of records for permanent preservation in an archive.
- A systematic retention and disposal mechanism.[4]

At the point of their creation, records need to be tagged for different kinds of information: for example, information that is privacy-protected; confidential business information; properly classified information (and the duration of that classification); or information subject to other nondiscretionary exemptions under the Freedom of Information Act (FOIA). And we need to know and be able to see to whom a record circulated.

So Just What Is a Record, Anyway?

What, technically, is a record that the federal government is obligated to retain? And, of the myriad e-documents that a digitized government produces, what qualifies as a record? The Federal Records Act[5] is the starting place for this analysis. It gives a broad definition of retainable records, saying:

> *"As used in this chapter, 'records' includes all books, papers, maps, photographs, machine readable materials, or other documentary materials, regardless of physical form or characteristics, made or received by an agency of the United States Government under Federal law or in connection with the transaction of public business and preserved or appropriate for preservation by that agency or its legitimate successor as evidence of the organization, functions, policies, decisions, procedures, operations, or other activities of the Government or because of the informational value of data in them."*[6]

Every record of the federal government must be identified and kept as part of a records series, a group of documents filed or maintained together because of subject, function, physical form, or some other factor related to their creation, receipt, or use. Agencies must then get each record series appraised by the National Archives to determine the long-term importance of the information in the series. The next step creates a records schedule for each records series, which specifies where and how long records need to be retained and what their final disposition will be. Finally, each records schedule must get the blessing of the Archivist of the United States. No federal records—including electronic—may be destroyed without the permission of the Archivist; this is conveyed through the approved records schedule. E-FOIA requires this information about record series and schedules to be posted online—although this requirement is often honored more in the breach than in the observance.

The Thorny Problem of E-mail

Some of the thorniest questions in recent history have involved e-mail. A number of court cases have explored the question. Perhaps the most important of these is the so-called PROFS case, which concerned an electronic mail system, PROFS, used during the Reagan-Bush Administrations. When the Bush Administration attempted to exclude these as a category of public record in investigations of the Iran-Contra scandal, public access advocates sued. In that litigation, the court overturned an agreement between the U.S.

Archivist, Don Wilson, and George H. W. Bush that would have allowed the former president to destroy electronic federal and presidential records on computer tapes, including the e-mails exchanged by Oliver North, John Poindexter, and Robert McFarlane in the Iran-Contra scandal.[7] Judge Richey affirmed the plaintiffs' arguments and found that the government's position would "put the law back to where it was prior to 1978," when presidents successfully maintained that they could restrict access or destroy records created by officials during their administration. Judge Richey declared the Bush-Wilson Agreement null and void because it was in direct conflict with the Presidential Records Act's mandate, and because it unconstitutionally purported "to give former [first] President Bush, now a private citizen, authority to direct the 'actions of the current Executive officials.'" (Which is, of course, what the second President Bush's executive order on the Presidential Records Act, does.)

General Records Schedule 20: Obliterating the E-mail Trail

In part as a result of the PROFS litigation, in 1995 NARA issued a revision of General Records Schedule (GRS) 20. A General Records Schedule, unlike the specific records schedules required for each records series by the Federal Records Act (as discussed in the section above) is issued by the Archivist of the United States to provide authorization to dispose of records common to several or all agencies of the federal government. A GRS covers records relating to civilian personnel, fiscal accounting, procurement, communications, printing, and other common functions, as well as certain nontextual records. GRS 20 is one of the regulations implementing the Federal Records Act and provides guidance to federal agencies about the kinds of records that may be destroyed and those that must be preserved.[8]

The new guidelines of GRS 20, still in effect as of 2007, stated that individual electronic messages (but not entire electronic-mail systems in general) that meet the criteria for a federal record must be migrated to paper or an electronic storage system and scheduled for preservation. In these regulations, the Archivist stated that once electronic records are preserved in an agency's official—*print*—recordkeeping system, the versions remaining on "live" desktop computer applications "lack sufficient value to warrant further preservation." And "agencies must be able to delete electronic source documents from their 'live' systems to avoid overload."

Of course, it is precisely those electronic source documents that are likely to have the full transactional record—rather than just being the equivalent of a photocopy of the final version of a letter or memo.

It is extremely unfortunate that the GRS 20 guidelines grant the agencies themselves the authority to determine which e-mail records are of enduring historical value. The electronic source documents that often carry the most information and the most historical value are precisely those an agency is most tempted to delete, whether for reasons of space or for fear of leaving a trail. And, as noted earlier, even if such documents are kept electronically on a storage server (which agencies are very disinclined to do because of the volume), it is highly unlikely that they will be easily searched and retrieved (because they are not indexed or otherwise managed). So, effectively, the full record is easily lost or obliterated. Lost to history and lost to accountability.

But the problem isn't simply that GRS 20 is inadequate. The public access (including the historical) community considers the application of any GRS to *all* government e-mail highly inappropriate. E-mail is merely a type of information transmission; it can come from many different senders and can contain many different kinds of information. A GRS applied to e-mail treats all e-mail alike, from that of the head of a government agency down to the gardener.

Finally, given the state of government recordkeeping and the fact that even the print copies would not come to NARA for permanent preservation for years (in some cases, at least), there is no easy way to know whether even the minimal requirements of GRS 20 are being fully honored in the case of electronic mail. It is widely feared that they are largely ignored. The agencies are not meeting their obligation under E-FOIA to make their record locator systems available in their electronic reading rooms (which might give us some indication), and NARA has no history of enforcing agency compliance with its requirements. And even if and when they are observed, the "dead" recordkeeping copies retained do not, necessarily, show the development of the policy.

For these reasons, the advocacy group Public Citizen sued the National Archives over GRS 20, and many in the public access community protested it and filed comments. Ultimately, however, the National Archives prevailed.[9]

Agency Web Sites: A Path Not Taken

So what about information on agency Web sites? Again, there are regulations in place that at least make a start on the problem; the question is whether those regulations are being followed.

Starting in the mid-1990s, OMB and NARA said they were going to issue guidance reminding agencies that official information on their Web sites is record information and must be scheduled and preserved accordingly. (Of course, one might argue that anything an agency puts up on its Web site is official information.)

Finally, in January 2005, NARA issued "NARA Guidance on Managing Web Records,"[10] as required by the E-Government Act of 2002. It specifically spells out for agencies that they "must document all of their agency programs, including web sites, that are part of its overall public message." The guidance spells out that "web site-related records" include not only the information presented on the Web site, but also Web site administrative records—such as records tracking site use, file posting, and decisions about content—that provide evidence of the management and operation of the Web site. It also points out that not only federal personnel, but also federal contractors, are affected by these record management requirements.

Unfortunately, we do not know whether or how much NARA and/or the OMB are following up with the agencies to ensure compliance. This area is definitely not a strong point of either NARA or OMB. I am not reassured by a more recent (2004) speech given by the then-Archivist, John Carlin, that exemplifies NARA's change in approach to agency records in general. Mr. Carlin proclaimed NARA's willingness to give

> *"agencies the flexibility to manage their records how they use them. After all, it's more important that an agency has the records it needs when it needs them rather than a textbook records management program that may not serve its needs."*[11]

Of course, it is precisely those electronic source documents that are likely to have the full transactional record—rather than just being the equivalent of a photocopy of the final version of a letter or memo.

Your comfort level with this change will depend on how much you trust agencies not to bury inconvenient or embarrassing information. My level of trust is fairly low.

NARA's Electronic Record Archives: A Coming Solution?

NARA has, since 1999, been working on an Electronic Record Archives concept that will allow the agency to accept complex electronic records, preserve them in a platform- and software-independent form, and make them accessible and usable over time. This was an issue when NARA first started accepting electronic records for preservation; NARA would only accept flat files and ASCII text. It has come a good distance since then—but so has the complexity of records. The first iteration is supposed to be live (for a limited set of documents) in late 2007.[12] The Archives is sanguine that this technological fix will make it easier for the Archives to deal with electronic documents over time. But the technology will not solve the issues noted above, which are at heart about policy—and resources. Records that are not saved electronically will not be somehow made miraculously available next year or 100 years from now.

Government Publications—An Incomplete Solution

Our inability to find government data, documents, and records (for our purposes we can ignore any distinction or overlap between these categories) is not because of a lack of statutory requirements. Government print publications are a good example. Print publications are supposed to be locatable through several statutory mechanisms:

- They should be submitted for printing (or print file copies sent) to and catalogued by the Government Printing Office as required by law.

- They should also be described by a Government Information Locator Service (GILS) file (as required by the Paperwork Reduction Act), or—now that the GILS standard has been declared defunct—inventoried as required by the E-Government Act. (For more information on the important GILS story, see Chapter 2.)

But the reality is that these statutory requirements are often not adhered to by the agencies. Print publications become difficult to find, then, unless they are described (or at least mentioned) on an agency Web page. Government records, except for those rare ones posted in agency electronic FOIA reading rooms, are similarly difficult to find. Again, this lack of information is not from lack of a requirement to provide it—the E-FOIA amendments tell agencies that they are supposed to make descriptions of their records locators (e.g., their records schedules) available, and common sense says they should put them in their—required—electronic reading rooms. But this availability does not exist in most places in the federal government.

A Report Card for Agency Recordkeeping

The National Security Archive in its 2007 government-wide audit, "File Not Found,"[13] listed five government departments/agencies as "E-Stars:" Department of Education; Department of Justice; Federal Trade Commission; National Aeronautics and Space Administration; and National Labor Relations Board. They found that only 36 percent of agencies provide the required "indexes of records." The National Security Archives' analysis of agency sites did not distinguish the records locators requirement from the major information systems requirement, so it is hard to tell if any of the E-Stars met this requirement. I doubt that they do; no one is telling them that they have to do so.

Once Upon a Time of Paper

In the print age, federal depository libraries were the primary vehicle to ensure that the publications of the government—executive and legislative, primarily—were preserved and made available to a geographically dispersed public. (The Federal Depository Library Program (FDLP) is a venerable government institution, having its roots as far back as Congress's 1813 decision to distribute copies of House and Senate journals to select university and state libraries and historical institutions.)[14] Over the years, that initial distribution program has been expanded; now every document (with a few waivers) published by government agencies is required by law to be printed by the GPO, which then distributes copies at no cost to each Regional depository library and other depositories that elect to receive specified agency publications. These depository libraries, in turn, provide local, no-fee access to government information in an impartial environment with professional assistance. Currently, there are approximately 1,250 depository libraries participating.

The Shift to Electronic Publications: GPO Access

The ever-increasing move of the federal government away from print, though, has changed dramatically the way the GPO and the federal depository libraries do business. For many years, the number of documents submitted to the GPO for printing, as required by statute, has steadily declined. Some were printed by the agencies themselves (or by contract with other agencies); an increasing number were no longer printed at all. By October/November 2004, 95 percent of the titles in the FDLP were available electronically (even if tangible forms were also available) and only 5 percent had no electronic counterpart.

In the mid-1990s, Congress recognized this shift to electronic documents was under way and saw it, as did executive branch agencies, as a way to more cost-effectively make information available to the public. GPO Access was therefore authorized in 1993 by Public Law 103-40 in order to provide a system for online access to the *Congressional Record,* the *Federal Register,* and other documents deemed appropriate by the GPO (44 USC § 4101(a)(2)). GPO Access became operational in 1994.

GPO Access has been a mixed bag for much of its history. When GPO first decided to make the *Federal Register* available online, they attempted to charge for access. Considerable pressure from public access advocates (such as myself and James Love) made them see the error of their ways. And while a great deal of information is findable through GPO Access, the search mechanism[15] is very structured and, thus, not particularly user-friendly (for the average user). Of course, the structure of government information is also quite complex. But for a long time many of the retrieved documents were not easily searchable—possibly, some said, in order to avoid competition with commercial vendors. The issues with GPO's search mechanisms, their questionable user-friendliness, and the fact that most search engines cannot find GPO pages and documents are, we hope, being addressed by what GPO calls the "Future Digital System," still under development at the agency. Time will tell.

The GPO's Struggle Toward a Digital Future

The current plan for the digital future of the GPO and FDLP, resulting in what the GPO calls the "Future Digital System" plan, was created in 1996 as the result of the congressionally mandated "Study to Identify Measures Necessary for a Successful Transition to a More Electronic Depository Library Program."[16] The initial result of this study was direction from Congress to move rapidly, in the late 1990s, to a completely digital GPO and FDLP. After an outcry about the unfeasibility of such a preemptory move, GPO was given more time (and occasionally money) to move in that direction. The authentication of records (e.g., for documents submitted to courts) and the usability (e.g., for longitudinal comparisons of statistical records) of digital-only documents have been persistent concerns. The study continues to inform GPO's initiatives in its initiatives to move from a nineteenth century framework to a twenty-first century technology and viewpoint.

Since this 1996 report, the GPO and the depository libraries have been struggling with this notion of a digital future-mostly together but, on some key issues, *with* one another. The FDLP's basic concerns have been

- To ensure that the digital publications received from the GPO are official, verifiably government-issued publications;

- To ensure that the digital publications are publicly available permanently, at no cost, and with no restrictions; and

- To create an effective operational structure that will permit the achievement of these goals.[17]

Depository librarians have also urged GPO to direct more attention and resources to gathering "born-digital" information, such as agency Web page postings that, too often, is here today and gone tomorrow. This issue, of course, links back to the concerns with the scheduling and preservation of electronic records discussed earlier.

After years of tension between GPO and the National Archives and Records Administration (NARA), over who should maintain these records and how they should be maintained,[18] in 2003, NARA and the GPO signed an agreement to establish an affiliated relationship, the first of its kind between NARA and another government agency to specifically address electronic government records. The agreement ensures that the documents available on GPO Access will be available permanently. GPO will retain physical custody of specified permanent records that are accessioned into NARA's legal custody. GPO is responsible for providing expertise in interpretation, access, and service for the publicly accessible portions of the "Collection of Last Resort"—a complete depository collection, "consisting of multiple collections of tangible and digital publications, located at multiple sites, and operated by various partners within and beyond the U.S. Government." It is intended to serve as the dark archive (where master copies are kept) for preservation of tangible publications and digital objects as well as to provide online access.[19] GPO's practices will be guided by NARA's policies for reference, arrangement, description, preservation, and security. The problem is, of course, that the electronic records will have to have been preserved and have made it to either GPO or NARA for this agreement to have any meaning for the public. Both agencies have some distance to go to assure the public that this is consistently happening.

In Conclusion

Both the GPO and NARA face enormous challenges in meeting their respective obligations to permanently preserve valuable information (e.g., documents, records) for posterity—and for use in that posterity. Both confront the difficulties associated with digitizing information that was not "born digital." The costs to do such digitization properly are very high and the will of Congress to face up to this reality is sadly low. The temptation for many agencies (NARA included) is either to ignore the will of Congress or to heed the siren call of private sector contractors who will digitize the information—for just a few years of exclusive control of access to the digitized information (and for more discussion of that siren call, see the next chapter). Or if the agreement is written really badly, the government—the public—could lose control of the information altogether.

Once again, government-wide policy is needed—and needed yesterday, not in five or ten years' time. In any event, Congress needs to step up to the table and address the government's responsibility to make the public's information available and accessible in the form the public wants to obtain and use it.

Notes

1 National Academy of Public Administration, "Effects of Electronic Recordkeeping on the Historical Record of the U.S. Government." Prepared for NARA. Washington, D.C.: National Technical Information Service, 1989, p. 43. Cited in GODORT Whitepaper, op.cit.

2 "Gore Office E-mail Irretrievable: One-Year Lapse Blamed on Configuration Error," *Washington Post,* Friday, June 9, 2000. http://findarticles.com/p/articles/mi_qn4196/is_20000609/ai_n10598608.

3 Michael Abramowitz, "Rove E-Mail Sought by Congress May Be Missing: RNC Took Away His Access to Delete Files in 2005," *Washington Post,* Friday, April 13, 2007, p. A01. http://www.washingtonpost.com/wp-dyn/content/article/2007/04/12/AR2007041202408.html.

4 "Electronic Records Management: What Are Electronic Document Management and Electronic Records Management?" http://www.dur.ac.uk/records.management/erm/.

5 Pub. L. 90-620, Oct. 22, 1968; Pub. L. 94-575, § 4(c)(2), Oct. 21, 1976, expanded "records" to include "machine readable materials." http://assembler.law.cornell.edu/uscode/html/uscode44/usc_sec_44_00003301——000-notes.html.

6 44 U.S.C. 3301 http://assembler.law.cornell.edu/uscode/html/uscode44/usc_sec_44_00003301----000-.html.

7 *Armstrong v. Executive Office of the President,* 1 F.3d 1274 [DC Cir 1993].

8 "Electronic Mail Systems; General Records Schedule 20; Disposition of Electronic Records; Final Rule and Notice" *Federal Register,* Monday, August 28, 1995, pp. 44634-44642.

9 A brief for the case, *Public Citizen, et al. v. John Carlin, Archivist of the United States, et al.* 1996, can be found at http://www.citizen.org/litigation/briefs/ERecordsPCVCarlin/articles.cfm?ID=606. Public Citizen v. Carlin, 2 F. Supp. 2d 18, 20 (D.D.C. 1998) (Carlin II); *Public Citizen v. Carlin,* 2 F. Supp. 2d 1 (D.D.C. 1997) (Carlin I).

10 http://www.archives.gov/records-mgmt/policy/managing-web-records.html.

11 John W. Carlin, "The ERA: An Archives of the Future and for the Future," *Prologue,* Spring 2004, Vol. 36, No. 1. http://www.archives.gov/publications/prologue/2004/spring/archivist.html.

12 See Electronic Records Archives (ERA) Main Page. http://www.archives.gov/era/.

13 National Security Archive, "File Not Found: Agencies Violate Law on Freedom of Information," March 12, 2007. http://www.gwu.edu/~nsarchiv/NSAEBB/NSAEBB216/index.htm.

14 For more history of the FDLP, see "Keeping America Informed: Federal Depository Library Program." Last updated: July 13, 2000. http://www.access.gpo.gov/su_docs/fdlp/pr/keepam.html.

15 For a comparison of GPO Access and Thomas in looking for congressional information, see Peggy Garvin, "The Government Domain: GPO Access and THOMAS for Legislative Research," LLRX.com, published June 23, 2005. http://www.llrx.com/columns/govdomain6.htm.

16 In 1995, the conference committee on the FY 1996 Legislative Branch Appropriations Act directed the Public Printer to initiate a study under direction of the Committee. See Senate Report 104-114, Legislative Branch Appropriations, 1996. July 18 (legislative day, July 10), 1995. Ordered to be printed. See also, House Report 104-212, "Appropriations for the Legislative Branch for the Fiscal Year Ending September 30, 1996, and for Other Purposes."

17 See, e.g., George Barnum and Steven P. Kerchoff, "The Federal Depository Library Program Electronic Collection: Preserving a Tradition of Access to United States Government Information," Administrative Notes: Newsletter of the Federal Depository Library Program, March 15, 2001, Vol. 22, No. 5. http://www.lib.umich.edu/govdocs/adnotes/2001/220501/an2205e.txt.

CHAPTER 2

GOVERNMENT-WIDE INFORMATION POLICY

The federal government has instituted a complex system of regulation that is intended to govern how the government manages its information and the rights of the public in regard to that information. The previous chapter looked at the laws and regulations related specifically to government records and publications. This chapter will look at laws intended to more broadly govern the entire range of government information—particularly the expanding amount of electronic information—and to improve its management. Strengthening public access has been a focus in some of this legislation and regulation, but not in all. In particular, this chapter will review

- The Paperwork Reduction Act (PRA);
- Circular A-130 which is the guidance document for the PRA, the E-Government Act, and other laws; and
- The E-Government Act (and its implementing guidance, M-06-02).

My discussion will include a lot of history—because although the laws represent opportunities to improve the ability to find, gain access to, and use government information, their implementing guidance and regulations often fail to implement even what the laws do require. The key to understanding why access to government is in the state we find it, therefore, is often found in the nitty-gritty of the circulars and memoranda implementing the laws, and the follow-through with the agencies (if it exists).

The Paperwork Reduction Act and Circular A-130

The Paperwork Reduction Act is critical as the first law that affected, in a broad way, the government's collection and dissemination of electronic information. It is one of the most far-reaching, and least known, federal information laws on the books. In the PRA of 1980 (P.L. 96-511), Congress gave OMB the authority for, and charged it with, a broad range of responsibilities related to information management.

The Original 1980 Paperwork Reduction Act

A look at some of the primary purposes of the 1980 Act is revealing:

- Minimize the federal paperwork burden for individuals, small businesses, state and local governments, and other persons.

- Minimize the cost to the federal government of collecting, maintaining, using and disseminating information.

- Maximize the usefulness of information collected by the federal government.

- Ensure that automatic data processing and telecommunications technologies are acquired and used by the federal government in a manner that improves service delivery and program management, increases productivity, reduces waste and fraud, and, wherever practicable and appropriate, reduces the information-processing burden for the federal government and for persons who provide information to the federal government.

Note the emphasis on administrative efficiency and "usefulness." Information dissemination goals are pushed into the background. Indeed, as my further discussion of the PRA and the E-Government Act will show, both the Reagan and G.H.W. Bush Administrations and their congressional supporters placed general information policies in the context of a political, economic, and social philosophy that considered information an economic resource, rather than a public good.[1] Thus, what those of us in the public access community would understand as "usefulness"—i.e., the ability of the government *and* the public to use the information—was here understood *only* in terms of whether the agency needed to *collect* the information (i.e., what agency function it fulfilled and what burden it constituted on those required to respond to the government's information collection requests). Fortunately, although these requirements have been mostly maintained in later iterations of the Act, our preferred meaning of usefulness has also been represented and the balancing of burden with public benefit introduced. But still, those efficiency concerns continue to receive the lion's share of OMB's attention: that is what puts the "R" in OIRA (the Office of Information and Regulatory Affairs) at OMB, which administers the PRA and the E-Government Act.

The Original 1985 Circular A-130

To understand how the PRA (or any other federal law) works in practice, you need to know the guidance implementing the law. For the PRA and other laws relating to the management, dissemination, and security of government information, that guidance is known as "Circular A-130."

Circular A-130, "The Management of Federal Information Resources, implementing the Paperwork Reduction Act," was published by the OMB in December 1985. The circular required agencies to look first to the private sector when planning information activities, and not to disseminate information that the private sector might otherwise sell. As Tim Sprehe, then-spokesman of the OMB (and author of the original circular) has noted,[2] through A-130 the Reagan Administration conveyed the following message about information dissemination: "When in doubt, don't!"

The 1985 A-130 had a number of problematic effects that arose from its characterizing public access to information as a matter of the public's having to *request* information that belonged to the *government* (with only limited governmental obligations to disseminate information before it was requested). Of course, we in the public access community saw that as exactly the wrong attitude: public access to information should be a matter of the public's having free access to *public* information that the government ensures is well-organized and easily findable. And we did win at least parts of that battle in some later statutes and regulations—but those later changes have not been reflected in OMB guidance and the original concerns remain. This issue comes up so often in this study of public access to information that I have devoted a separate space to its discussion (see "Define Your Terms," below).

Define Your Terms: Is Government Information Public Information?

When the OMB drafted the 1985 A-130 Circular, the implementing regulation for the original 1980 PRA, it produced a regulation that epitomized its attitude: that information held by the government was *government* information—and not information that the public necessarily had a right to access. Unfortunately, despite later changes in the governing law and the 1994 improvements to the Circular, the essence of this regulation prevails at the OMB.

First, the 1985 Circular distinguished "access to information" from "dissemination of information"—the former being the process of providing information upon request and the latter referring to the legally mandated or government-initiated distribution of information to the public. In general, the Circular advocated waiting for the public to approach agencies and request information, in addition to requiring agencies to not "compete" with private sector opportunities to sell taxpayer-funded government information back to the public. It therefore discouraged the distribution of executive branch publications through the depository program of the Government Printing Office (GPO) and, in general, did not encourage openness in government.[3]

Furthermore, the Circular offered an inauspicious standard for an agency to follow if it disseminated information (and did not merely wait for its request); the standard focused on whether the activity was necessary for the proper performance of agency functions. It was left to the agency head to make that call, a problematic authority if that head does not want agency performance open to public scrutiny.

Finally, the 1985 Circular used the term "government information," rather than "public information." This implied that government publications, previously considered public information and often freely available, were now government information distributed only on request or under legal entitlement.[4] "Government information" was defined as "information created, collected, processed, disseminated, or disposed of by or for the Federal Government."

In 1993, the Clinton Administration rewrote Circular A-130 and, as I note below in the text, made important and praiseworthy changes to it. At that point, the statutory definition in the PRA was still "government information," so the Circular's definition was not changed in this rewrite. That statutory definition would change with the 1995 reauthorization of the PRA, to use the term "public information." Unfortunately, OMB has never gone back and changed the definition in Circular A-130.

This distinction between "government" and "public" information is important. We in the public access community fought hard to define information as "public," and succeeded with a definition that the 1995 reauthorization would in fact use:

> "*Public information means any information, regardless of form or format, that an agency discloses, disseminates, or makes available to the public.*"

This language, "public information," is a significant improvement over the old emphasis on "government information" found in the 1980 PRA and in the 1985 and 1993 Circulars. First, it preserves the *public's* ownership in at least the raw information. Second, it *should* mean that, even when an agency makes data accessible through proprietary software, anyone should be able to get the underlying data and make it available (or just make use of it). This is, however, an ongoing struggle and is likely to be renewed as search providers such as Google and Yahoo move to make government information on agency websites more easily found and obtained. The access community is already watching this development, as well as a related effort to digitize the records held by the National Archives.

When the E-Government Act of 2002 was being drafted, the public access community successfully argued to retain the statutory emphasis on "public information" and the public's right to access that information embodied in the PRA definition. However, the words "public information" are not magic; in the drafting of the E-Government Act, we were afraid that, because of the changed environment after September 11th, the word "public" would be read as only that information the government chooses to make public. And, as it happens, that is indeed the way OMB interpreted it (although for reasons of cost-effectiveness, which was not the reason we feared). Unfortunately, although the E-Government Act of 2002 incorporates the PRA's "public information," in its implementing guidance (Memorandum M-06-02), the OMB reverted to the old definition. The Memorandum treats as presumptively available for public access only that information "disseminated by an agency to the public."

The differences between that OMB formulation and the definition in the E-Government Act and the PRA (public information is any information "[an agency] *discloses,* disseminates, or *makes available* to the public . . .") are not trivial. On these distinctions hangs the ability of the public to know about, find, and use information *beyond* what agencies post to their Web sites. (While "disseminates" can be understood to include "publishes" in the more traditional sense, this is not the understanding that is embodied in Memorandum M-06-02. As will be discussed later in this chapter, the guidance is clearly only referring to information made available through a Web site.)

In light of Memorandum M-06-02, it is not surprising that, as noted above, OMB has never changed the definition "government information" in Circular A-130 (the OMB regulation implementing the PRA, the E-Government Act, and other statutes) to "public information," the statutory definition in the 1995 amendments to the PRA and, by reference, the E-Government Act of 2002.

1994 Circular A-130

In 1993 and 1994, the Clinton Administration rewrote Circular A-130, significantly changing information policy and practices across the executive branch.[5] They did such a good job (notwithstanding the government vs. public information issue, which has only recently become a real concern) that, although they have had to update it several times to incorporate various laws, both the public access community and the agencies urged them not to change the fundamental principles, which emphasize that the values of democracy critically rely on the public's right of access to government information. For example, the 1994 Circular states explicitly that

> *"Because the public disclosure of government information is essential to the operation of a democracy, the management of Federal information resources should protect the public's right of access to government information."*

While the 1994 A-130 principles are occasionally honored more in the breach than in observance, they have served well—and the 1994 Circular is a sea change from the 1985 Circular, which is colloquially known in public access circles as the "old, bad, Reagan-era A-130!"

1995 Paperwork Reduction Act Reauthorization

As we will see again later, elections make a difference. The Clinton Administration differed greatly from the previous Reagan and Bush Administrations in its attitude toward the government's role in the provision of information, and it showed in both the 1994 rewrite of Circular A-130 and the 1995 reauthorization of the PRA.

The PRA has been amended a number of times. In 1986, for example, amendments made agencies, in addition to the Director of OMB, responsible for implementing government-wide and agency information policies, and for periodically evaluating the accuracy and reliability of data in the federal information systems—language that came back to bite us in the Data Quality Act, which I discuss in Chapter 9. (The 1986 version was up for reauthorization in 1992, but was not finally reauthorized until 1995, the most recent reauthorization of the Act.)

The current PRA continues to concentrate wide-ranging power in OMB and, specifically, in OIRA within OMB, to

- Develop comprehensive government-wide Information Resources Management (IRM) policies and oversee their use by federal agencies;

- Control the collection of information by federal agencies and improve the management of other federal government information activities;

- Coordinate agency information practices through means such as budget review;

- Promote information sharing among agencies;

- Evaluate agency information practices and oversee planning and research related to life-cycle management; and

- Oversee governmental statistical policies and agency statistical programs.

It is instructive to compare what the 1995 revision of the PRA added to the Act's original purposes. Whereas the original purposes of the Act focused primarily on minimizing the cost of providing government information, and minimizing the collection of information by the government, the 1995 revision added the following statements of purpose:

- Improving the quality and use of federal information to strengthen decision-making, accountability, and openness in government and society;

- Providing for the dissemination of public information in a manner that promotes the utility of the information to the public; and

- Ensuring the integrity, quality, and utility of the federal statistical system.

Another important new provision refers to agency responsibility to ensure that the public has "timely and equitable access to the agency's public information." The law spells out some of the mechanisms for ensuring that access, a key one being that any agency that "provides public information maintained in electronic format" is required to provide "timely and equitable access to the underlying data (in whole or in part)." The import of this provision was to end sweetheart deals with the private sector, in which companies were given exclusive access to government information. (See the box called "Sweetheart Deals," on p. 42.) While it is necessary to allow commercial ventures to have access to government information to do value-adding (such as indexing) as needed, the public—and nonprofit intermediaries such as libraries and public interest organizations—must have access to at least the data underlying any bells and whistles the government itself may have added. We would prefer that those additions to government information not be done in proprietary format (so anyone could re-use them), but it is quite rare for this to occur.

Sweetheart Deals

In the draft of the 1995 Paperwork Reauthorization Act, Westlaw (a major computerized on-line legal research system) had inserted a provision that would have allowed it—because it corrected spelling errors in court documents and added page numbers to court documents to which it was given exclusive access—to claim ownership over the entire document and be able to prevent the government from making any use of the underlying document. The public access community mounted a campaign, the provision became known as "the Westlaw provision," and it was soon removed.

Indeed, the government's appropriate move into improving access to and usability of the public's information has created ongoing tensions with private sector companies that have established niche markets based on government information. As one lobbyist for the information industry told me in a conversation (a number of years ago), these kinds of companies would like the government to stay about 10 years behind the private sector.

Currently, we are confronting a quiet effort by companies, such as Google, to enter into memoranda of understanding (MOUs) with agencies in which the company will digitize agency documents at no expense to the agency. Sounds like a great deal! Yeah, but Google, for example, will give the agency back what is essentially a picture of the document (or a digital copy of a film, etc.) with no metadata. So, if you want to search for government information, you will have to go through Google's (or whoever's—Google is not alone in this effort) search engine. So much for anonymous viewing and using of government information, and so much for the government's obligation to make its information searchable. We never thought "searchable on government sites" would have to be added to that requirement.

The temptation for agencies is obvious, but there is a critical need for clear guidance from OMB (and Congress) before these efforts put in place privatized search engines for government information. We could end up having not only to go from agency to agency, but also search engine to search engine, as Google will have some agencies, MSN others, Yahoo still others, and so on. The bottom line for all of these companies is not public access; it is information about the public that can be used to generate revenue. There are efforts underway at this writing to put some brakes on these efforts, to urge looking at different (e.g., cooperative and open-source) models for accomplishing the important goal of getting "legacy" (or, in the parlance of another industry, "stranded") government information digitized without sacrificing the public interest to the interests of expediency and the commercial market.

Another important addition in the 1995 Amendments was the definition of the term "public information," a definition that the access community had been lobbying for. The statute defines it as "any information, regardless of form or format, that an agency discloses, disseminates, or makes available to the public." This language is a significant improvement over the statute's old emphasis on "government information," as I explain at greater length on page 37, "Define Your Terms: Is Government Information Public Information?"

Finally, to ensure meaningful public access, the law now requires that an agency "provide adequate notice when initiating, substantially modifying, or terminating significant information dissemination products." This provision has been used over the years to prevent, or try to prevent, agencies from terminating publications (or handing them over to the private sector as with the *U.S. Industrial Outlook* and *The Journal of the National Cancer Institute*) and to push for public involvement in the process (even though the provision only requires notice).[6]

GILS: A Failure of Policy Implementation

The 1980 PRA mandated the creation of a Federal Information Locator System (FILS), the purpose of which was to assist in agency and government-wide audits of all major information systems (except systems used for criminal investigations or intelligence or cryptologic activities); the elimination of any duplication of information collection requests by the government; and the identification of initiatives that might reduce the federal paperwork burden associated with federal grant programs by 10 percent. The FILS was implemented to a certain extent, but as its intent was seen—both by the public and by the affected agencies—as a means for reducing, if not outright eliminating, agency publications, it was not widely honored.

One promising provision (§ 3511) of the 1995 amendments to the PRA created the Government Information Locator Service (GILS). GILS was intended to "assist agencies and the public in locating information and to promote information sharing and equitable access by the public" through the identification of "[the] major information systems, holdings, and dissemination products of each agency." The OIRA Administrator, in cooperation with the Archivist of the United States and other key government players in information management, was supposed to establish an interagency committee to advise on technical standards for GILS that would promote interagency information sharing and public access. The outcome should have been an electronic and interoperable system of uniformly classifying and cataloging agency information, so that building efficient and effective search engines for government information could become more than a pipe dream.

The first requirement, establishing the GILS, was poorly implemented, however. For this reason and others—such as some agencies not really wanting to make their information truly visible to the public—it has been largely ignored by federal agencies. The second requirement—development of technical standards—was effectively ignored by OMB, and the standard that was deployed was resisted by many agency personnel.

OMB and many agencies have argued, since the outset, that the Internet changed everything and that, therefore, the identification and the standards requirements were (take your pick) irrelevant or already met. (See discussion below in "Implementing the E-Government Act: Another Hope Fails.") According to the OMB, the public can find anything by searching on agency Web sites—which are, of course, paragons of organization and promotion of "uniform access by the public."

Except where they aren't. And for the deep Web on agency sites, and nondigital records, and so on, I refer the reader back to the seven scenarios laid out by OMB and GSA in the Introduction to Part I for an indication of whether the current situation is adequate. (See the box "Seven Scenarios of Search").

The public access community has never considered the implementation of the GILS anywhere near adequate. Unfortunately, only one of us (me) regularly met with the agency implementors, and very few pushed OMB on the issue. In any event, the E-Government Act amended portions of the PRA, including § 3511, and established a new standard—which was also largely ignored. GILS was decommissioned as a standard in 2005 by the National Institutes of Standards and Technology. As you will see, the situation remains critical for some electronic indexing scheme that will make possible deep searching of the government's Web-based information.

Drafting the E-Government Act: An Opportunity Lost

Although the Paperwork Reduction Act made important strides, the E-Government Act of 2002 was seen as an opportunity to effect a real and lasting change in how government identifies and makes available information—and it started out with that vision in mind. However, between the changes OIRA made to the draft statute and OMB's implementation of the final Act, the opportunity has been largely squandered.

A Hope Raised (and Thwarted)

Senator Joseph Lieberman[7] (D-CT) unveiled his "E-Government Act of 2001" on May 1, 2001. The 90-page bill was the most comprehensive piece of legislation on e-government to date. It was a key step toward acknowledging and addressing the need for the government to manage its information content for access and accountability and the difficulties in doing so. The bill did not, however, rise out of a vacuum. In fact, this bill itself was developed through the use of e-government. Through a special Governmental Affairs Committee Web site, the public was able to identify issues, concerns, and recommendations for improving e-government, which Senator Lieberman used in drafting the legislation. Quite unironically, this important Web site has not been preserved and at last report could not reliably be located.

What Senators Lieberman(D-CT) and Fred Thompson (R-TN) (who was then the chairman of the Governmental Affairs Committee but played no further role in the bill) learned from that experiment is the public expects ever better and more user-friendly access to its government, but has seen its expectation disappointed because a government-wide infrastructure is lacking. The legislation therefore initially intended to set up a framework and a process for moving the executive branch forward. The bill also elevated the issue of information management and information policy. Unfortunately, the bill set the coordination and oversight responsibilities for the management of government information within the Office of Information and Regulatory Affairs (OIRA) at OMB. As noted earlier, for all of OIRA's existence, the "I" has generally been subsumed and overwhelmed by the "R." Public interest groups had been raising this issue for years. We hoped to get an office outside of OMB with responsibility for information policy and management.

A key section of the original 2001 bill, "Accessibility, Usability, and Preservation of Government Information," had several components that were key from the public access community's perspective:

- Laying the groundwork for both government and the public to know what information the government creates and collects;
- Creating standards and guidelines for permanent public accessibility of government information created and disseminated digitally;

- Improving the ability to find and use government information through the creation of common and open (nonproprietary) standards for organizing and managing data about the public information in the government's hands; and

- Inviting public participation in an open process for the creation of these standards.

A number of nonprofit public interest organizations, including the library community, had been raising these issues for many years. And, as I noted in the Introduction to Part I, even voices inside the government had begun to focus on these concerns, as in the report "Transforming Access to Government through Information Technology" from PITAC.[8]

These provisions were a good start; the senators understood that good information management is critical for access—the public cannot ask for and the government cannot disseminate what neither knows exists, or cannot find.

Moreover, the open process established in this bill was as fundamental as the end result. At every stage—in the process of identifying standards, identifying information to be inventoried (listed), to be catalogued, and to be disseminated—public participation was to be required and the results of the decisions to be posted online. An open process and public accountability are essential. Moving from the "silos of rotting information" that (in Al Gore's phrase) existed then—and continue to exist now, with some notable exceptions—to real management of government information across its life cycle (from creation/collection through its retirement from current agency use to archiving/disposition or permanent public accessibility through a repository) is not going to happen in a year or even two.

The original bill was not perfect. Key lacks were the failure to require the government to get control of and manage its electronic records, including its e-mail. It did not include legislative branch information at all, which seems a triumph of the political reality of congressional intransigence and protection of tradition and privilege. It was timid in its approach to the courts—a similar triumph. A significant gap in the bill was the lack of sustained funding for much of the information management work that was to be undertaken by the agencies. Unfortunately, not only were these gaps not addressed as the bill worked its way through Congress, but some of its most important provisions were ripped out.

Anatomy of a Gutted Bill

The administration opposed the bill as originally introduced by Senator Joseph Lieberman, but following negotiations, Senator Fred Thompson became a co-sponsor, and a compromise agreement was eventually struck, clearing the way for passage. Unfortunately, as a result of this compromise, OMB essentially gutted and rewrote the legislation. It is, thus, important to remember that the final bill was OMB's language.

While there were changes from the 2001 bill throughout what became the Act, I will focus on what are, for our purposes, the most important: those made to what became § 207, "Preserving Government Information, and Making It Accessible and Usable: Accessibility, Usability, and Preservation of Government Information." These provisions and the changes to them can be grouped under the following headings:

- Consulting with the public (or not)
- Cataloging standards—and the problem of proprietariness
- Ability to find and get access to government information
- The vanishing inventory
- Deciding what goes on the Internet
- Creating permanent public access standards
- Getting the government's phone number

Consulting with the public (or not). The 2001 bill would have established an Advisory Board, which would have included membership of and *direct participation* by representatives of the public. But, significantly, the Act established an Interagency Committee[9] on Government Information (ICGI) to make policy recommendations, after *consultation* with the public. This is not a minor distinction: the difference is between the public having a mandated role in the policy process versus what happened with the implementation[10] of the E-Government Act as discussed further in this chapter.

Cataloging standards—and the problem of proprietariness. The drafters of the original bill saw it as key that cataloging and indexing standards be interoperable and not reliant on proprietary systems. Thus the 2001 bill would have prohibited agencies from using any proprietary system, but it would have allowed the prohibition to be waived if a compelling reason to continue the use of the system was determined. Unfortunately, the Act watered down these restrictions on proprietary systems, recommending use of existing standards, and requiring the ICGI to recommend, not open standards, but standards "open to the maximum extent feasible." Again, this is not a minor change. If you use WordPerfect (as I do, when possible) and have ever imported a Word document, you understand the problem of a lack of interoperability (due to conflicting proprietary standards) on a small scale. Actually, for many years it was not functionally possible to move documents between the two without some external translation program (which now runs in the background). Multiply this several thousand times and you can get a sense of the noninteroperability of systems that describe (catalog/classify) government information but follow no widely agreed-upon standards—and don't play nicely with other systems. So you have agencies with proprietary cataloging systems and standards that either cannot or will not share data in a useful way with other agency systems—some of which are also proprietary, some of which use the interoperable standards created over many years by the library community. Moving to real interoperability was a goal of the original bill.

Ability to find and get access to government information. The existing act, does, however, still require that the ICGI recommend standards that enable the organization and categorization of government information in a way that is searchable electronically, including by *searchable identifiers*,[11] and in ways that are interoperable across agencies.

It also requires the ICGI to recommend categories of government information that should be classified under the standards, and priorities and schedules for the initial implementation of the standards by agencies.

The vanishing inventories. The drafters of the original bill stressed the importance of inventorying government information because it would have helped both governments and the public—and GPO—know what information agencies had created. Apart from classified or sensitive information, the original bill's Advisory Board would have

- Identified, for inventory purposes, all classes of government information;
- Recommended which classes should be inventoried; and
- Recommended how the information within them should be inventoried.

Each agency would also have been required to inventory agency Web sites, including all directories and subdirectories of such Web sites established by the agency or contractors of the agency. Those agency inventories would have been posted on each agency's Web site and linked to the "integrated Internet-based system" (FirstGov) to be searchable by all standard search engines. But alas—this subsection disappeared from the Act.

Deciding what goes on the Internet. The 2001 bill would have required each agency to determine which government information it would make publicly available on the Internet (and by other means), to develop priorities and schedules for creating that access, and to make its final determinations available for public comment. These determinations were to be locatable on an agency Web site with a link to the integrated Internet-based system (FirstGov, now USA.gov). Although the Act has the same essential requirements, it does not require that the final determinations be posted on a Web site linked to an integrated system, and it requires each agency to update its determinations *as needed,* after consulting with the ICGI and *soliciting public comment, if appropriate.* (Emphasis added.) The difference here recapitulates the problems identified above about mandated public participation versus optional solicitation of comment—if appropriate. The fact that the determinations, were they even done, would not be linked to an integrated, government-wide system means the public has to go agency by agency to find them and comparison is made extremely difficult. Unfortunately, none of the requirements in this subsection has consistently been observed, and neither the OMB nor Congress has taken any action regarding this lack of observance. And, even if the requirements were observed, the public might still have to look at each individual agency to find information—and hope they had found everything on a subject (and not duplicates resulting from inconsistent cataloging and indexing).

Creating permanent public access standards. The drafters of the 2001 legislation were deeply concerned about the loss of electronic records and what appeared to be the agencies' cavalier attitude toward records management and the preservation of permanently valuable information.[12] The 2001 bill would have required the original Advisory Board to recommend standards for *permanent public access to information disseminated by the federal government on the Internet and define to which types of information those standards apply.* Each agency would also have been required to report on its process for and any action taken to preserve public access, and *set standards to ensure permanent public access to information disseminated by the federal government on the Internet.* (Emphasis added.)

In contrast, under the Act the ICGI submitted recommendations to the Archivist of the United States on how agencies could ensure that they were following the relevant chapters (21, 25, 27, 29, and 31) of the Federal Records Act with respect to government information on the Internet and to other electronic records. The Archivist then issued guidance requiring the adoption and timetables by agencies of such policies. But while this is a necessary step, it is not sufficient. It does not require either NARA or the agencies to identify a process and actually take steps to preserve the information, nor does it require the development of standards for preserving such information. As noted earlier in the discussion of e-mail and the Electronic Records Archive, first the information has to be identified and preserved. The identification of the types of information to which the preservation requirement applies is critical; not all government information needs to be permanently preserved, but that decision can be quite political (and quite litigious, as we saw in Chapter 1's discussion of GRS 20 and its application to the government's e-mail).

Getting the government's phone number. Another section in the 2001 bill that was excised from the Act is that for an online federal telephone directory to have been developed by the General Services Administration (GSA) and promulgated government-wide. This section was in the draft legislation and strongly supported by the access community because it would have enhanced government transparency and accountability. Telephone contact information would have been organized and retrievable both by function and by agency name and provided to local telephone book publishers, to encourage publication and dissemination of functionally arranged directories in local federal blue pages. Each executive agency would also have been required to publish an electronically searchable online agency directory, accessible by electronic link from the online federal telephone directory, to include telephone numbers and electronic mail addresses for principal departments and principal employees, subject to security restrictions and agency judgment. While we thought the excision of this requirement had mostly to do with September 11th, we have subsequently learned[13] it had much more to do with the Bush Administration's imperative to control access to the government, discussed in more detail in Chapter 8.

Implementing the E-Government Act: Another Hope Fails

By unanimous consent, on June 27, 2002, the Senate passed the E-Government Act,[14] which was signed into law by President George W. Bush on December 12, 2002. Despite the law's being stripped of many of the most important provisions of the draft bill, a full and faithful implementation of the law could have had significant implications for improving public access to government information. I say, *could* have had; the attentive reader will note the use of the past perfect tense here. As discussed below, OMB has decided to ignore (or give only cursory attention to) many of the requirements of the E-Government Act. The public, however, has a right to expect that the executive branch "faithfully execute the laws" passed by Congress. And as long as a law is on the books, we can still use it to try to move government in the right direction—whether it wants to go there or not.

From the standpoint of public access, particularly important would have been enforcement of § 207 ("Accessibility, Usability, and Preservation of Government Information") and, especially the subsection on "categorization." For example, this section required the implementation of *searchable identifiers,* such as a facility or corporate identifier, for government information. These identifiers could have become the building blocks for searching across agencies or departments to obtain information—for example, to identify information across the government on a particular company and for companies to integrate their required reporting. This sort of linkage has been virtually impossible. The standards required by § 207 are intended to apply more broadly than just GILS (which itself was not adequately implemented, as I describe in the balance of this chapter).[15] They also related to other portions of the Act, such as § 212 requiring integrated reporting, and § 207(d) requiring standards that would strengthen the ability to search and quickly find information that is available through agency Web sites via a government-wide portal (i.e., FirstGov, now USA.gov).

Unfortunately, adequate enforcement isn't what happened. What did happen is that the OMB buried the recommendations duly submitted by the ICGI, as required by the Act, on

- A definition of which government information should be categorized;

- A standard for searchable and persistent identifiers to be applied to items of categorized government information;

- A standard set of categories (i.e., "bibliographic attributes") for categorizing government information; and

- An open standard for interoperable search of government information so categorized.[16]

Although the ICGI submitted its recommendations on time, on December 16, 2004, you would never know it; they are not to be found on OMB's e-government site nor on the site maintained by the Chief Information Officers (CIO) Council.[17] Instead, OMB ignored the recommendations in favor of a request for information (RFI) process that excluded input from the public access community, and resulted in "searchability" by commercial engines replacing the requirement that government organize and manage its information to make it findable and usable by the public. The story is worth looking at in closer detail, because it gives insight into how congressional mandates—even those rewritten by OMB to suit its goal—can be undermined, if not subverted, in the implementation.

What the OMB Should Have Done

The Work Group[17] on the Categorization of Government Information (CGI) via the Interagency Committee on Government Information (ICGI)[18] made a number of recommendations that, while not perfect, would have gone a long ways toward improving public access to federal government information. In particular, it recommended that the federal government should:

- Adopt the following broad definition of "categorizable government information:" any information product, regardless of form or format, that a U.S. Federal agency discloses, publishes, disseminates, or makes available to the public, as well as information produced for administrative or operational purposes that is of public interest or educational value. This includes information created or exchanged within or between agencies. Not included are Federal government information holdings explicitly provided in law as so constrained in access that even a reference to the holding is kept from public view for a specified period of time.[19]

- Adopt specific standards for searchable identifiers that would strengthen the ability to search, quickly find, and interoperably use information that is available through agency websites.

- Take specific actions to support standards for categorizing government information, such as requiring appropriate and consistent bibliographic treatment, supporting the automated collection of government information, and establish minimum categories for search services, so that searches could always be conducted by Identifier, Subject, Agency Creator, Title, and Publication Date—and *should* be capable of searching by Place, Audience, and Keywords.

- Adopt the ISO 23950 international standard for interoperable search.

The CGI's recommendations correctly noted that federal policy has long held that agencies must plan, in an integrated manner, for managing information throughout its life cycle.[20] They argued that their recommendations on the categorization of government information would assist agencies in meeting their obligations to manage their information resources in an efficient, effective, and economical manner. But how did the OMB react?

You might guess, from the fact that OMB has made these recommendations impossible to find on any official Web site, that maybe it did not like them. You would be right.

The OMB Buries E-Government Act Information Management

Instead of accepting the CGI's useful recommendations, in September 2005, the OMB and the General Services Administration (GSA) Office of Government-wide Policy put out a Request for Information (RFI)[21] to industry, academia, and government agencies. Note: no library associations, no public interest organizations, no members of the public. At the time that we learned of this RFI, the public access community was not able to ascertain who had been asked to respond. We asked for a chance to review and comment on the results and were told it would be offered. It was not. It is apparent, to me, that the whole effort was orchestrated, if not rigged.

We later learned, from GSA's "Response Analysis" of what the RFI produced, that the RFI "targeted representatives from industry, government and academia who are practitioners and subject matter experts in the field of information sharing."[22] Specifically,

- GSA/OMB and agency experts;

- Existing agency vendor lists;

- Market research companies;

- Government and industry councils; and

- Subject matter experts from the "Efficient and Effective Information Retrieval and Sharing (EEIRS)" RFI support team (who are nowhere identified).

But, again, there was no one who represented the interests of the public or those who serve as intermediaries to the public in the finding and use of government information.

No potential conflicts or vested interests there!

To "ensure *all points of view* were represented" (emphasis added by GSA), GSA reported that the support team solicited information "not only from the traditional IT community, but also included system integrators as well as management consulting firms, government agencies and academics." The way in which the GSA reached out to generate awareness of the RFI is also interesting. GSA conducted "a variety of outreach activities" to generate

53

awareness and interest among potential respondents"—the ones they wanted to hear from, that is. These activities included additional press coverage in government trade magazines, which was where we first learned of, not the RFI, but "RFI Practitioners' Day." This Practitioners' Day was to explain the purpose of the RFI and to provide potential respondents with an opportunity to pose clarifying questions; 86 participants attended representing 52 organizations—but none representing the interest of libraries and the public access community. Of course, the RFI *was* posted directly to FedBizOpps (www.fbo.gov); if we had looked on the right day under the right search terms, we would surely have been welcomed. (I encourage you, by the way, to try it sometime; see if you can find anything useful—if you don't already know what you are looking for. Which is, of course, why GSA had to follow up with all those other forms of notification.)

The avowed primary goal of this RFI was to evaluate various approaches and consider factors such as cost and ease of implementation in order to promote greater public access to and federal agency sharing of information. However, its stated purpose was to "identify and promote the most cost-effective means to search for ... information, and assess the net performance difference (including cost-benefits) of assigning metadata and/or a controlled vocabulary to various types of information versus not doing so." In other words, to tell OMB and GSA that, regardless of what the law requires, they should take what is ostensibly the cheaper way out by not requiring the government to manage and organize (and categorize) its information.

In addition, from the outset the RFI was encouraging the responders to give the OMB the answer it wanted: that spending money on indexing and cataloging government information, having open interoperable standards, and securing open search technology was just not necessary. As we learned in December 2005, when we finally got to see GSA's "Response Analysis" of the RFI responses,[23] the RFI support team was asking respondents the following question: "Does current search technology perform to a sufficiently high level to make an added investment in metadata tagging unnecessary in terms of cost and benefit?" This RFI came before, but not by much, OMB Memorandum M-06-02 (see discussion below), which was issued December 15, 2005—which would seem to indicate that OMB had its mind made up well before December and the process was intended to support the conclusion it already had reached.

While it is not completely unreasonable for OMB to consider cost, OMB wasn't just asking about cost: it was predetermining a decision that effective search technology was both too expensive and not effective. But that is a decision that Congress had already made. Recall that § 207 of the E-Government Act specifically *requires* recommendations to the OMB Director on the *adoption of standards*, open to the maximum extent feasible to enable the organization and categorization of government information in a way that is searchable electronically and in ways that are interoperable across agencies. Within one year of that submission, the Director of OMB was to issue policies *requiring agencies to use such policies*. (Emphasis added.)

But instead of attempting to implement these congressional instructions, the OMB used the RFI to specifically test the following hypothesis:

> *For the majority of government information, exposing it to indexing with commercial search technology is sufficient to meet the informa-tion categorization, dissemination, and sharing needs of the public and as required by law and policy.*

The RFI included the seven search scenarios I mentioned in "Seven Scenarios of Search" in the Introduction to Part I. These were actually quite interesting and, theoretically, useful. As noted previously, the scenarios were meaty stuff. Even though we were not invited to participate, the public inter-est community was intrigued. But the outcome—as you might expect, given the pointed questions the OMB was directing toward the respondents—was disappointing.

The OMB's Conclusion

GSA and OMB concluded—guess what?—that the best way to manage government information was to leave the problem to the commercial search engines. No open standards, no requirement to do metadata tagging, no inventories, no indexing. Based on this RFI study and other available litera-ture (including John Battele's book *The Search: How Google and its Rivals Rewrote the Rules of Business and Transformed Our Culture),*[24] they deter-mined that "with respect to disseminating Federal information to the public-at-large, publishing directly to the Internet all agency information intended for public use and thereby exposing it to freely available or other search func-tions is the most cost-beneficial way to enable the efficient and effective retrieval and sharing of government information."[25] (It will definitely come up again—in OMB's guidance, Memorandum M-06-02, which I discuss below.) In other words, just put the "government information" that you *want* to share up on your individual agency Web site.

GSA and OMB did concede, however, that, in some circumstances, some preparation of government information to make it more searchable might be "more cost-beneficial and even necessary." (You can ignore this phrase, though—OMB does, as you will see.) The analysis said that, as an organization moves from a passive or "casual" access model to a more active or "formal" one or from providing web pages and text to geospatial, multimedia, or structured databases, the need for advance preparation, including thorough automated or manual creation of indexes, taxonomies, or metadata tagging, begins to become apparent. This need, however, is tied to Return On Investment (ROI); the business case for advance preparation must be determined by information producers and users on a case-by-case basis.

Well, you might say, at least the GSA and OMB are prepared to direct agencies to take congressionally mandated actions to improve the searchability of government information—if and when the users say that they need better access.

And how are users supposed to let their "needs" be known and have them met? E-FOIA may require each agency to provide an online index of its major information systems—but as I explain in Chapter 3, most agencies fail to do so. So how are people who can't learn about the existence of an agency's major information systems, such as their structured databases, supposed to find out about them and ask for them? Who would they ask?

The report is illuminating:

> *Clearly it is not remotely possible for Federal agencies to engage in comprehensive interaction with all members of the public-at-large. Therefore, again, this study supports as a general principle, direct publication to the Internet is the best way to promote general dissemination and sharing of government information.*[26]

Doesn't that work out nicely?

Except that, once again, the OMB and GSA are ignoring what Congress has already decided they have to do: listen to the public. Section 207(f) of the E-Government Act directs agencies, after solicitation of public comment, to determine what types of government information they intend to make available on the Internet and by other means, and to develop timetables for doing so. As noted earlier, public comment is supposed to occur throughout the process. The Senate Committee Report made clear that the intent was "to establish a more deliberative process for agencies as they make decisions about what information should be made publicly available over the

Internet," and their belief that "[the] public comment process will be more meaningful if agencies inform the public of what government information will not be made available."[27]

Of course, the law and the Report are just what Congress said. (And as I was at the signing ceremony, I am certain that there was no signing statement saying that OMB could interpret and implement the statute in any way they saw fit.)

What the OMB Did Instead: Memorandum M-06-02 on Categorizing Government Information

So what was the outcome of all of this history I've been giving you of the OMB's approach to implementing—or, rather, *partially* implementing—the E-Government Act? On December 16, 2005, OMB issued a Memorandum (M-06-02) on "Improving Public Access to and Dissemination of Government Information and Using the Federal Enterprise Architecture Data Reference Model."[28] The Memorandum is intended to meet OMB's obligations under § 207(d) of the E-Government Act. According to OMB, "[t]his memorandum identifies procedures to organize and categorize information and make it searchable across agencies to improve public access and dissemination...." But as my discussion above indicates, in the opinion of the public access community, it does no such thing.

There were no surprises in the Memorandum for anyone familiar with the RFI. It identifies "three new requirements" in the area of "Organizing and Categorizing Government Information and Making It Searchable Across Agencies to Improve Public Access and Dissemination." Agencies must now take action in the following areas:

- *Organizing information to make it findable:* Organize and categorize their information *intended for public access, make it searchable across agencies,* and describe how they use "formal information models" to assist their dissemination activities. (Emphasis added.)

- *Having a plan and making it public, part I:* Review the performance and results of their information dissemination programs and describe the review in their Information Resources Management (IRM) Strategic Plans; and

- *Having a plan and making it public, part II:* Publish their IRM Strategic Plans on their public websites (together with their information dissemination product catalogs, directories, inventories, priorities, and schedules).[29]

Each of these requirements rhetorically meets the mandates of the law while simultaneously largely undermining them.

Organizing Information and Making It Searchable (or Not)

The Memorandum gives agencies procedures to "cost-effectively" fulfill the first requirement, to organize information and make it searchable. But OMB's primary recommendation? Not to organize it at all. Instead, the OMB recommends, in summary,

- When disseminating information to the public at large, *publish your information directly to the Internet.* This procedure exposes information to freely available and other search functions and adequately organizes and categorizes your information. (Emphasis added.)

- When interchanging data among *specific identifiable groups* or disseminating significant information dissemination products, advance preparation, such as using formal information models, may be necessary to ensure effective interchange or dissemination. (Emphasis added.)

So, as you can see, the OMB does encourage the agencies to organize their information if they are dealing with *"specific identifiable groups."* And who are these? They "can include any combination of Federal agencies, State, local, and tribal governments, industry, scientific community, academia, and *specific interested members of the general public.*" (Emphasis added.) It is a surprise to learn that the government is allowed to provide meaningful, useful access to only "specific interested members" of the general public. I won't hazard a guess as to who they might be, but it is a matter of great concern to know how they will be identified. The Memorandum contains no indication of any public involvement in that process or even a required notification that some members of the public are more equal than others.

Having a Plan and Making It Public (or Not)

The Memorandum also requires agencies to review how their information dissemination programs are working and describe the review in their Information Resources Management (IRM) Strategic Plans, and to publish their IRM Strategic Plans on their public Web sites (together with their other *information dissemination products,* e.g., catalogs, directories, and schedules). But both of these requirements fall short of the statutory mandates of the E-Government Act and the Paperwork Reduction Act.

First, it is useful to note (which OMB does not do in this guidance Memorandum) that an agency's IRM Strategic Plan is "[the] agency's" IT vision or roadmap that will align its information resources with its business strategies and investment decisions."[30] As an example, the IRM Strategic Plan might include the mission of the agency, key business processes, IT challenges, and guiding principles. It is unclear how such a Plan meets the requirements of the statute to determine "priorities and developing schedules for the initial implementation of the standards by agencies." It theoretically *could*, but there is nothing in the guidance to tell agencies to change their plans to do so. Ergo, it will not happen.

The IRM Strategic Plan is not the only information that the OMB requires agencies to publish. The OMB also requires that agencies publish information about their information dissemination products. Again, it is unclear whether the guidance even fulfills the statutory mandates on communicating with the public. Section 9 of Circular A-130 includes the requirement—from the Paperwork Reduction Act—that agencies "Establish and maintain communications with members of the public and with State and local governments so that the agency creates information dissemination products that meet their respective needs."

Oh, but perhaps the OMB and GSA are not worried about communicating with the public. As they indicated in the Analysis of the RFI responses:

> *"Clearly it is not remotely possible for Federal agencies to engage in comprehensive interaction with all members of the public-at-large. Therefore, again, this study supports as a general principle, direct publication to the Internet is the best way to promote general dissemination and sharing of government information."*

See how nicely OMB used the study to undermine the statutory requirements? If it is on the Internet, it must be what the general public wants (even if they are never asked and will probably not know what else the agency has that they might want instead or additionally).

It is also regrettable that this requirement sets agency responsibilities by using the term *"information dissemination products,"* which Circular A-130 defines as "any book, paper, map, machine-readable material, audiovisual production, or other documentary material, regardless of physical form or characteristic, *disseminated by an agency to the public.*" (Emphasis added.) Recall, however, that the CGI task force recommended a much broader term, the definition of "categorizable Government information:"

> *Categorizable Government information means any information product, regardless of form or format, that a U.S. Federal agency discloses, publishes, disseminates, or makes available to the public, as*

well as information produced for administrative or operational purposes that is of public interest or educational value. This includes information created or exchanged within or between agencies.... (Emphasis added.)

The CGI definition reflects the definition in the Paperwork Reduction Act, which the E-Government Act also references: "[the] term 'public information' means any information, regardless of form or format, that an agency discloses, disseminates, or makes available to the public." The public access community fought hard to protect this definition against those, particularly among the information industries, who sought to limit it. (See the discussion in the box, "Define Your Terms: Is Government Information Public Information?" at the opening of this chapter.)

As OMB policy guidance stands now, the public is left dangling. OMB never changed the Circular A-130 definition in response to the Paperwork Reduction Act's mandating the above, more access friendly, definition of government information. And the definition in M-06-02 makes clear they are not changing it in response to the E-Government Act (which references and reinforces the PRA's definition). The definition in these Acts is just what the law says—and who is paying any attention to that?! Not Congress. And, quite frankly, not much of anyone else—unfortunately.

In Conclusion

So, we have good laws on the books and we have a predominantly good Circular A-130 implementing the Paperwork Reduction Act, the E-Government Act, and others. The E-Government Act was the public access community's (and some members of Congress's) attempt to make the PRA into a real information management and access law. Unfortunately, OMB has throughout its history put more emphasis on the provisions of the act that control the government's collection of information from the public (10 or more persons) and, particularly, from regulated industries.

While the E-Government Act created that opportunity for real information management and access, OMB tossed the ball off court. Yes, just throwing stuff up on Web sites—the stuff an agency has decided it wants the public to know about and have access to—is cheaper than cataloging/applying metadata to, indexing, and inventorying the vast array of government information. But those are the steps needed for full accountability and access to any information the public is not specifically (by statute or regulation) prohibited from knowing about.

The laws are on the books, so hope remains that we can get the next administration to properly implement them. The PRA has been up for reauthorization since 2001. It has not happened during the Bush Administration because the folks who want to control and limit regulation control the White House (OMB) and the executive branch generally. No one on our side has wanted to open up the information management and dissemination provisions; we have feared what might be done.

Eventually, we will have another administration that wants to ensure both access and accountability. When that happens, the public access community will be in the fray—once again—to protect, expand, and strengthen public access to the information in the hands of the government.

Notes

1 Frank Reeder, cited in Holden and Hernon in Hernon, McClure, Relyea, eds. *Federal Information Policies in the 1990s: Views and Perspectives,* Greenwood Publishing Group, United Kingdom, 1996, pp. 86-88.

2 Timothy Sprehe, "OMB Revision Hammers out A-130's Kinks," *Federal Computer Week,* (July 12, 1993), Vol. 7, pp. 16, 18.

3 See Hernon & McClure, 1987.

4 Reeder, op. cit.

5 Circular No. A-130—Revised Transmittal Memorandum No. 2, effective July 15, 1994. http://clinton1.nara.gov/White_House/EOP/OMB/html/omb-a130.html. This is an interesting example of information from the Clinton Administration that was preserved when G. W. Bush took over. At a very late hour, Sally Katzen, Director of OIRA, working with NARA, was able to ensure that many agencies took "snapshots" of their websites at the last hour of the Clinton Administration. This seemed an excellent idea at the time. It has proved to be prescient, given the removal of Clinton era information from the Education Department Web site.

6 The 1995 revisions also retained some controversial provisions regarding "burden reduction" related to information collections, primarily regulatory, that are made to 10 or more persons. For discussion of this issue, I recommend OMB Watch at http://www.ombwatch.org/article/articleview/182/1/162?TopicID=2 and The Center for Regulatory Effectiveness (for an anti-regulatory view) at http://www.thecre.com.

7 Senator Lieberman was a Democrat in the time period discussed here. He is now an Independent.

8 The PITAC Panel on Transforming Government, "Report to the President: Transforming Access to Government Through Information Technology," September 2000. http://www.nitrd.gov/pubs/pitac/pres-transgov-11sep00.pdf.

9 This was one more, lost, fight in trying to get the Executive Office of the President to abide by the 1972 Federal Advisory Committee Act (FACA) (Pub. L. 92-463, 5 U.S.C., App). FACA was enacted by Congress to ensure that advice rendered to the executive branch by the various advisory committees, task forces, boards, and commissions formed over the years by Congress and the president, be both objective and accessible to the public.

10 It is important to note that the ICGI Committee on the Categorization of Government Information was completely open to the public in the process of developing its recommendations. The same cannot be said for the other implementing bodies.

11 The Senate Governmental Affairs Committee noted in its Report that the "Committee intends that the searchable identifiers—data elements created or provided at the time of origination of a record, information collection, or other information product; the identifier links the item to other common subjects which share that identifier—are essential for helping to link or integrate information from different agencies or departments, and are an important building block to sustaining meaningful public access." (Report 107-174: Report of the Committee on Governmental Affairs, United States Senate, To Accompany S. 803. 107th Congress, 2d Session. http://frwebgate.access.gpo.gov/cgi-bin/useftp.cgi?IPaddress=162.140.64.21&filename=sr174.pdf&directory=/disk3/wais/data/107_cong_reports.

12 In the Act, the title of this subsection became *Public Access to Electronic Information.*

13 Conversation with a retired senior OMB official.

14 The final version of the E-Government Act was H.R. 2458, the conference report that passed both the House and the Senate on November 15, 2002.

15 The E-Government Act amends portions of the Paperwork Reduction Act, including Sec.§ 3511. GILS was decommissioned as a standard in 2005 by the National Institutes of Standards and Technology.

16 Act, 207(d).

17 The CIO Council serves as the principal interagency forum for improving practices in the design, modernization, use, sharing, and performance of federal government agency information resources. The Council's role includes developing recommendations for information technology management policies, procedures, and standards; identifying opportunities to share information resources; and assessing and addressing the needs of the federal government's IT workforce. The Chair of the CIO Council is the Deputy Director for Management for OMB and the Vice Chair is elected by the CIO Council from its membership.

18 Categorization of Government Information Working Group of the Interagency Committee on Government Information. Recommendations on the Categorization of Government Information, December 16, 2004. http://www.ala.org/ala/washoff/Woissues/governmentinfo/ IGCIreport14dec04.pdf. Note that this report is on the ALA site, not the OMB site. OMB removed it from the various E-Government Act implementation sites maintained by OMB and the CIO Council. The earlier draft version was, however, left up. The ALA got the final version through its drafters.

19 http://www.cio.gov/documents/ICGI.html.

20 The standard definition of life cycle of government information consists of the following: Creation, use, dissemination, retention, and disposition, including permanent preservation where appropriate.

21 http://www.fbo.gov/servlet/Documents/R/1282831.

22 GSA's response analysis can be read at http://tinyurl.com/9ljc6GSA. Efficient and Effective Information Retrieval and Sharing (EEIRS) Request For Information (RFI) Response Analysis, December 2005.

23 GSA's response analysis can be read at http://tinyurl.com/9ljc6. GSA. Efficient and Effective Information Retrieval and Sharing (EEIRS) Request For Information (RFI) Response Analysis, December 2005.

24 John Battelle, *The Search: How Google and Its Rivals Rewrote the Rules of Business and Transformed Our Culture.* (New York: Portfolio, 2005).

25 One has to go to Appendix B of the OMB's response analysis report to get to the specifics on the OMB's conclusion.

26 GSA, Efficient and Effective Information Retrieval and Sharing Request for Information Response Analysis. December 2005, p. 12. GSA's response analysis can be read at http://tinyurl.com/9ljc6.

27 Report 107-174, op. cit.

28 http://www.whitehouse.gov/omb/memoranda/fy2006/m06-02.pdf.

29 These products are discussed in Circular A-130. http://www.whitehouse.gov/omb/circulars/a130/a130trans4.html.

30 http://www.whitehouse.gov/omb/fedreg/a130notice.html.

CHAPTER 3

THE REGULATORY SYSTEM FOR ACCOUNTABILITY:

THE FREEDOM OF INFORMATION ACT

In this chapter, I will review one of the most important laws governing citizen access to government information: the Freedom of Information Act (FOIA). This chapter will take a look at

- The history of the Act's development—including the resistance of some presidential administrations to full implementation of the FOIA;

- How amendments meant to extend the FOIA to the realm of government e-documents (E-FOIA) have been implemented—or not;

- How the failure to implement the FOIA's requirements continues to impede public access; and

- How post-September 11 laws and regulations, particularly the Critical Infrastructure Information Act (CII), have affected public access under the FOIA.

So far, I have mostly been discussing public access to government information in terms of our ability to find what we are looking for and the policies surrounding the dissemination of information: Is the information organized and accessible, are there lists and inventories that let us know what is available? And, has the government given us, the public, a chance to weigh in on the kinds of information we need and the ways that we need to access it? Are government records—including those created electronically—being preserved for future access and use? Under what circumstances can the government disseminate information? What constitutes dissemination? In that connection, previous chapters reviewed the Federal Records Act, the

Paperwork Reduction Act (with Circular A-130), and the E-Government Act of 2002.

I haven't yet discussed, though, one of the central laws governing public access: the Freedom of Information Act (FOIA). This law,[1] enacted in 1966, establishes the public's right to obtain information from federal government agencies. It not only creates that right, but it also establishes a procedure whereby we, as members of the public, are entitled to request and receive government information. This Act has been critically important, as you will see, to the public's knowledge of the activities of the federal government.

Some Background on FOIA

As Senator Daniel Patrick Moynihan once noted, laws and regulations can create a framework for accountability and public access—and, with the expansion of the government in the New Deal, "it became clear that public regulation needed to be made more accessible to the public."[2] All public regulations began to be published and made accessible with the first publication of the *Federal Register* in 1935. In 1946, the Administrative Procedures Act established procedures by which a citizen could question regulation. However, prior to the passage of the FOIA, public access to records of federal agencies was governed by § 3 of the Administrative Procedures Act, which had been interpreted as giving agencies unlimited discretion to withhold records. Efforts to amend this system began as early as 1955, but were not successful until 1966—with the passage of the FOIA.

Before enactment of the FOIA, the burden was on the individual to establish a right to examine records in the possession of agencies and departments of the executive branch of the U.S. government and to prove she or he had a need to know. There were no statutory guidelines or procedures to help a person seeking information or judicial remedies for those denied access.[3]

The FOIA, however, establishes a presumption that these records are accessible to the people, and shifted the burden of proof from the individual to the government. Those seeking information are no longer required to show a need for information. Instead, the "need to know" standard has been replaced by a "right to know" doctrine. The government now has to justify the need for secrecy.

Through the FOIA, every citizen of the United States, and anyone else in the world, gained the right to access and obtain reproductions of records created and maintained by federal government agencies. The Act was originally created to "ensure an informed citizenry, vital to the functioning of a democratic society, needed to check against corruption, and to hold the governors accountable to the governed."[4]

The statute requires federal agencies to provide the fullest possible disclosure of information to the public, although it does provide a limited set of exemptions for disclosure—for example, for national security information or confidential business information.[5] I will discuss those exemptions and some of the mechanics of the FOIA in more detail later in this chapter.

Who Has to Respond to a FOIA Request?

The FOIA, generally speaking, applies to the executive branch of the U.S. government: all 15 cabinet departments (such as Interior and Homeland Security), 73 other federal agencies (such as the EPA, the Federal Reserve System, and CIA), military departments, government corporations, government-controlled corporations, independent regulatory agencies such as the Securities and Exchange Commission (SEC), and other establishments in the executive branch.[6]

The Act does *not* apply to elected officials of the federal government, including the President, Vice President, and members of Congress (either chamber); to the federal Judiciary; or to parts of the Executive Office of the President that function solely to advise or assist the President (such as the National Security Advisor). The federal FOIA also does not apply to private companies or persons who receive federal contracts or grants,[7] or to state or local governments (all states have their own freedom of information statutes). Congress regularly exempts itself from the laws it passes regulating the executive branch, and the rules for each chamber of Congress are set by that body. The courts are pretty much a law until themselves on many matters (a separation-of-powers issue).

It's important to keep an eye on to whom the FOIA does and does not apply. For example, previous to the creation of the Department of Homeland Security (DHS) in 2002, the Secret Service was a component of the Department of Treasury. In January of 2007, the public learned[8] that the White House and the Secret Service had quietly signed an agreement in the previous spring (2006)—in the midst of the Jack Abramoff lobbying scandal—declaring that records identifying visitors to the White House complex belong to the White House as presidential records, rather than to the Secret Service as agency records. They were thus made not subject to public disclosure through the FOIA. Such records were previously "FOIAble."[9]

The FOIA: A History of Congressional-Executive Tension

Since 1966, Congress has amended the Freedom of Information Act six times: in 1974 (with minor amendments in 1976, 1978, and 1984); in 1986; and most recently in 1996. In each instance, the original Act has been broadened to include more information deemed necessary both to the public and to the oversight of the federal government.

Congress's first set of amendments, in 1974, was in reaction to the Nixon scandals. Congress's strengthening the FOIA allowed the courts to review classified documents to determine if they were being shielded for political purposes and order the release of documents even when the President said they shouldn't be released. The Ford Administration resisted these changes. President Ford's chief of staff at the time was Donald Rumsfeld. Rumsfeld's deputy was Dick Cheney. Rumsfeld and Cheney advised Ford to veto the legislation: President Ford vetoed the Freedom of Information Act amendments, telling Congress that the bill "would violate constitutional principles."[10] Fortunately, the veto was overridden.

This tension between the executive branch and Congress over the FOIA is an aspect of a more general contest over authority, including authority over information. In January 2002, Vice President Cheney told ABC, "In 34 years, I have repeatedly seen an erosion of the powers and the ability of the president of the United States to do his job. I feel an obligation ... to pass on our offices in better shape than we found them to our successors."[11] In a briefing with reporters in December 2005, he indicated that this White House was determined to take back some of the executive's control over information that had been "ceded to Congress" and had "eroded"[12] over the last 30 years. He said, "We've been able to restore the legitimate authority of the presidency," and that "an erosion of presidential power and authority" emerged during the Ford Administration/post-Watergate era (during which he was President Ford's chief of staff) but that the pendulum has now "swung back." He noted that "At the end of the Nixon administration, you had the nadir of the modern presidency in terms of authority and legitimacy. There have been a number of limitations that have been imposed in the aftermath of Vietnam and Watergate."

During the briefing, the Vice President said the Bush Administration has reversed that trend in a variety of ways, ranging from its successful fight to keep secret the deliberations of its energy task force to its muscular assertion of authority at home and abroad in the wake of the September 11 terror attacks.[13]

This belief in the power of the Chief Executive is not a new position for Cheney. As noted by the *Boston Globe*,[14] in July 1987, Cheney—then a U.S. Representative and the top Republican on the committee investigating the Iran-contra scandal—asserted that "President Reagan and his top aides were free to ignore a 1982 law[15] at the center of the scandal. When the committee issued a scathing, bipartisan report accusing White House officials of "disdain for the law," Cheney refused to sign it. Instead, he commissioned his own report declaring that the real lawbreakers were his fellow lawmakers, because the Constitution "does not permit Congress to pass a law usurping Presidential power."[16]

Plus ça change....

The Executive Branch Reaction

The Clinton Era

Particularly noteworthy in looking at the executive's attitude toward the FOIA are the memoranda from Attorneys General over the years setting out policy on FOIA requests. During the Clinton Administration, for example, Attorney General Janet Reno's memorandum[17] indicated that the Department of Justice (DOJ) would only defend an agency's refusal to disclose information when it could be argued that releasing the information would result in "foreseeable harm." The presumption was disclosure and agencies were encouraged (at least rhetorically) to release information.

The Bush Administration: The Ashcroft Memorandum (October 12, 2001)

In the Bush Administration, however, the Attorney General took a different approach. Attorney General Ashcroft's memorandum[18] encourages presumptive *non*disclosure. The memorandum changes the standard under which the DOJ will defend a challenged refusal of release. Under the new standard the DOJ will defend an agency as long as the decision rests on a "sound legal basis," a much lower standard than "foreseeable harm"—and one that the House Committee on Government Reform objected to as being an improper interpretation of the statute.[19] Although the memorandum acknowledges the importance of government accountability, it also actively encourages federal agencies to "fully consider" all potential reasons for nondisclosure and emphasizes national security considerations, effective law enforcement, and the protection of sensitive business information.

Speaking in 2006, Senator Patrick Leahy said of the Ashcroft memorandum (and the administration in general), "The Bush-Cheney Administration sent a powerful message government-wide with the Ashcroft FOIA policy in 2001. That shifted the upper hand in FOIA requests from the public to federal agencies. The new policy says, in effect, 'When in doubt, don't disclose, and the Justice Department will support your denials in court.' It undermines FOIA's purpose, which is to facilitate the public's right to know the facts, not the government's ability to hide them."[20]

The White House Memoranda on Sensitive Information (March 19, 2002)

The Ashcroft Memorandum was not the only announcement from the Bush Administration to effectively limit access to information, including through FOIA. On March 19, 2002, the White House issued joint Memoranda.[21] The first, from White House Chief of Staff Andrew Card, said that departments and agencies have an obligation to safeguard government records regarding weapons of mass destruction. The Card memorandum urged agencies to withhold information that is "sensitive" and related to homeland security, even if the information did not meet the criteria for classification and thus was not exempt from disclosure under the FOIA exemption for national security information. (See the box titled, "The FOIA Exemptions" near the end of this chapter.) All departments and agencies were directed to review their records management procedures in accordance with the attached guidance (which I discuss in the next paragraph). They had 90 days to report their review. Those reports have not been made public, which is not unusual or surprising.

The second, and more troubling, memorandum was guidance attached to the Card memo, from the Information Security Oversight Office and the DOJ Office of Information and Privacy. This second memorandum caused a wave of concern. It directed all federal departments and agencies to consider the need to safeguard information regarding weapons of mass destruction, *as well as other information that could be misused to harm the security of our nation or threaten public safety*. The need for safeguarding such information should be considered on *"an ongoing basis* and *also upon receipt of any request* for records containing such information that is made *under the Freedom of Information Act* (FOIA), 5 U.S.C. § 552 (2000)." (Emphasis added.)

This memorandum's broad sweep, affecting any information that could be thought to affect national security, was troubling. So was its policy for protecting that information. The memorandum noted that the information would be "safeguarded" according to the sensitivity of the information and whether it was classified, and noted three indicators of sensitivity:

- Classified Information;
- Previously Unclassified or Declassified Information; and
- Sensitive But Unclassified Information (SBU).

This last category struck those of us in the public access community as particularly troubling: The memorandum does not define this idea of "sensitive but unclassified" information, and the concept was viewed as potentially expansive, as indeed we later saw with a category of "Sensitive Homeland Security Information" (SHSI) in the Homeland Security Act. Moreover, as noted above, this second memorandum refers back to the attorney general's FOIA memorandum to give "full and careful consideration" to any reasons for withholding information—i.e., to the presumption of nondisclosure. It directs the "safeguarding" of "information that could be misused to harm the security of our nation or threaten public safety," and indicates that the need to safeguard such information should be considered on "an ongoing basis and also *upon request under the Freedom of Information Act.*" (Emphasis added.)

Our unease only grew after a 2003 meeting sponsored by the American Society of Access Professionals in Washington. At that meeting, Dan Metcalfe, then the Co-director of the DOJ's Office of Information and Privacy[22] and one of the co-authors of this second memo, emphasized that the DOJ sees a distinction between "safeguarding" information and decisions about "disclosure." *Safeguarding* has to do with identifying information for special attention and treating it procedurally in a proper manner. When considering *disclosure,* he referred to the attorney general's memo of October 12, 2001, and indicated—in an audience full of federal government FOIA officers—that agencies should apply existing law for possible nondisclosure, if they get a FOIA request. It was clear that disclosure was *not* encouraged, although not prohibited.

It is important to remember that Congress intended the general presumption to be mandatory *disclosure.* Congress intended the nine exemptions to the FOIA [5 U.S.C. § 552(b)(1)-(9)] to protect against disclosure of information that would substantially harm national defense or foreign policy, individual privacy interests, business proprietary interests, and the efficient operation of governmental functions. (For a list, see box titled "The FOIA Exemptions.") Thus, an agency has the authority to construe the exemptions as discretionary rather than mandatory when no harm would result from disclosure of the requested information.[23] Of course, the determination—or judgment—of harm is the crux of the matter. What Metcalfe was signaling agencies, then, was that although "sensitive" information falls under no exemption, they could surely find reasons (based on the Ashcroft memorandum) to withhold it—and the DOJ would defend them in any ensuing litigation.

Our impressions were confirmed later in 2003, when the DOJ issued guidance[24] based on court decisions that broadened the interpretation of the FOIA's disclosure exemptions. This guidance also discussed the new Exemption 3 provision of the Homeland Security Act of 2002 (Pub.L. 107-296) that protects "voluntarily-submitted critical infrastructure information." (The full story of this expansive exemption was created gives some important insight into how the erosion of FOIA has proceeded in recent years—I discuss it separately in Chapter 4).

The cumulative effect of these post-September 11 changes in the executive approach to the FOIA can be seen in the 2004 edition of the DOJ's more or less biennial *Freedom of Information Act Guide, 2004*. The 2004 *Guide* explained how an agency's ability to *restrict* the release of "sensitive" information via the FOIA would be broadened by the Ashcroft Memorandum of 2001, the White House Memoranda of 2002, and DOJ guidance.[25] Citing the September 11, 2001 attacks, the passage of the Homeland Security Act, and the creation of the Department of Homeland Security (DHS), the *Guide* urged careful consideration before the release of "sensitive" information:

> *Much greater emphasis is now placed on the protection of information that could expose the nation's critical infrastructure, military, government, and citizenry to an increased risk of attack. As a result of these changes, federal departments and agencies should carefully consider the sensitivity of any information the disclosure of which could reasonably be expected to cause national security harm.[26]*

The *Guide* reiterated,[27] however, that use of labels such as SBU, SHSI, and so forth does not "provide for any protection from disclosure under any [FOIA] exemption"—except for critical infrastructure information (CII), which is protected by statute (and for that discussion, see Chapter 4). Nevertheless, the *Guide* encouraged agencies to exempt from disclosure information labeled SHSI and other nonclassified information that is highly sensitive. Again, "sensitive" is not defined, leaving the door wide open for hiding information. Information that is sensitive enough to "cause national security harm" should be properly classified—not just hidden; the rest should be subject to review and disclosure when not covered by an exemption to FOIA.

Impact of the Ashcroft and the White House Memoranda

A 2002 report,[28]—sought from the General Accounting Office (GAO) by Senator Leahy (D-VT) and Representative Stephen Horn (R-CA)—asked for the views of FOIA officials and requesters about the impact of the post-September 11 environment on implementation of the FOIA. The GAO (which in 2004 was renamed as the Government Accountability Office) found that agency officials and FOIA requesters view the impacts differently. Agency officials characterized the effects on FOIA implementation as relatively minor, except for mail delays associated with the anthrax attacks[29] that plagued DC-area mail services in late September 2001. Members of the requester community, however, expressed general concern about information dissemination and access to government information in light of removal of information from government websites after September 11.[30] In addition, some requesters characterized post-September 11 DOJ policies as representing a shift from a "right to know" to a "need to know" that could discourage the public from making requests.

The 2002 GAO report drew no firm conclusions about the state of post-September 11 FOIA access, saying it was then too soon for the full effects of the post-September 11 regulations to be known. But as later developments showed, those who reported to the GAO that access had been significantly restricted were to be proved correct.

Increased Use of the FOIA Privacy Exemptions

According to a 2003 Reporters Committee for Freedom of the Press (RCFP) analysis,[31] those FOIA exemptions designed to protect individual privacy were invoked more than any other by federal agencies withholding information from release under the FOIA over the period 1998 to 2002. The use of privacy exemptions increased sixfold during that time: In 1998, the exemptions were invoked by the agencies about 55,000 times; in 2002, more than 380,000 times. However, invocation of the exemptions relating to national security did not increase significantly in 2002. The dramatic increase in 2002 most likely relates to the Administration's intent to keep its detentions of citizens and other activities related to its security initiatives out of the public eye. The names of detainees are not classified, but the Administration successfully claimed (for more than a year) they were protecting the privacy of these individuals—from attorneys, as well as the public.[32]

The privacy exemption also has been claimed by the government in its attempts[33] to block pictures of the coffins of American dead being returned from Afghanistan and Iraq.[34] It was also asserted[35] to try to prevent the release of the pictures from Abu Ghraib.

Expanded Use of the FOIA's Law Enforcement Exemption

As I discussed above, the first (and only) exemption to the FOIA that relates specifically to national security (see "The FOIA Exemptions box on page 80), Exemption 1, covers only records that are properly classified in the interest of national security or foreign policy. Nevertheless, following the Ashcroft Memorandum of 2001 and the White House Memoranda of 2002, the executive branch has pleaded—successfully—that "national security" interests excuse agencies from giving out records—even when they cannot use Exemption 1 to FOIA or the other far-reaching protection for national security information.[36] Instead, the executive branch has often successfully relied upon FOIA's Exemption 7, the "law enforcement" exemption. Before we look at the cases that have expanded the scope of this exemption, let's first remember what the exemption says about "national security" as written in the statute:

Records or information compiled for law enforcement purposes, but only to the extent that the production of such law enforcement records or information

> ... *(D)* could reasonably be expected to disclose the identity of a confidential source, *including a State, local, or foreign agency or authority or any private institution which furnished information on a confidential basis, and, in the case of a record or information compiled by a criminal law enforcement authority in the course of a criminal investigation* or by an agency conducting a lawful national security intelligence investigation, information furnished by a confidential source. (Emphasis added.)[37]

The courts have "recognized"[38] that "law enforcement" within the meaning of Exemption 7 extends beyond these traditional realms into the realms of national security and homeland security-related government activities as well. The DOJ notes, in its guidance about FOIA, that the decision in *Pratt v. Webster*[39] explained that "to pass the FOIA Exemption 7 threshold," agencies must establish that their activities are based on a concern that "federal laws have been or may be violated or *that national security may be breached*" (Emphasis added.) There is really nothing in Exemption 7 to support this "recognition." The DOJ also cites *Coastal Delivery Corp. v. United States Customs Service*,[40] which ruled that because terrorists could use certain information to avoid detection and to direct "merchandise to vulnerable ports," that information was exempted from FOIA disclosure under Exemption 7. The purported logic for this argument is Exemption 7(E), which exempts "records or information compiled for law enforcement purposes, but only to the extent that the production of such law enforcement records or information ... (E) would disclose techniques and procedures for law enforcement investigations or prosecutions, or would disclose guidelines for law enforcement investigations or prosecutions if such disclosure could reasonably be expected to risk circumvention of the law."

Two examples of how the second Bush Administration has employed the "law enforcement" exemption are the cases involving secret detentions after September 11 and the matter of Glen Canyon Dam.

Secret Detentions. *The Center for National Security Studies, an advocacy and research group in Washington, D.C., on behalf of 21 public interest and human rights groups, petitioned*[41] *the U.S. Supreme Court to hear arguments that the government should be required to release the names of hundreds of detainees jailed after September 11, 2001. In its request for review, the Center wrote the purpose was "to make clear that a national security crisis is no justification for courts allowing the Government to evade so easily its responsibilities under FOIA—and that courts cannot ignore the vital countervailing interests at stake such as the individual rights petitioners here seek to enforce." The Center urged the Supreme Court to reject the lower court opinion of Judge David Sentelle, who wrote in the June 2003 decision for the divided appeals panel (reversing a lower court) that the Justice Department is in a better position than the court to know what should be withheld in a terrorism investigation and, thus, the judiciary would defer to the government's expertise in a national security probe. Instead, the Center urged the views expressed in a lengthy and pointed dissent, by Judge David Tatel, which said the majority's approach "drastically diminishes, if not eliminates" the judiciary's role in FOIA cases involving national security. In January 2004, the U.S. Supreme Court denied the petition—thus letting the decision of the U.S. Court of Appeals for the District of Columbia stand.*[42]

Glen Canyon Dam. *In September 2001, a small environmental group filed a FOIA request for the federal government's projections as to where the waters would go if the dam burst. The Bureau of Reclamation, which creates the inundation maps projecting what might happen, denied the request. In March 2003, the federal district court in Salt Lake City upheld[43] the denial, ruling that the government could withhold the unclassified maps under an exemption to the FOIA for "law enforcement" records. One component of the law enforcement exemption protects against release of information that might help anyone circumvent the law—and the judge said that terrorists might make use of the information. The ruling included an oblique reference to "a dam failure as [seeking] a 'weapon of mass destruction.'"[44]*

Specific Agency Changes in Procedure

Although most federal agencies did not make significant changes to their procedures as a result of the Ashcroft and White House Memoranda,[45] there were a few, very important agencies that did change their procedures. Among the findings[46] of a 2003 study by the National Security Archive were that 5 of 33 federal departments or agencies surveyed (15 percent) indicated significant changes in regulations, guidance, and training materials and that the Ashcroft Memorandum was widely disseminated.

One of the more flamboyant agency responses: the Department of the Interior disseminated the Ashcroft Memorandum to all FOIA officers by an e-mail entitled "News Flash—Foreseeable Harm is Abolished." The departmental guidance implementing the memorandum required discretionary *releases* to be cleared by written approval of the Designated FOIA Attorney. The National Security Archive reported that other guidance within the Department indicated "[w]e wish to emphasize that the shift related to release of information under the FOIA has moved from a presumption of 'discretionary disclosure' of information to the need to safeguard institutional, commercial, and personal privacy interests."[47]

In a 2005 review of FOIA,[48] the Associated Press (AP) found that, in addition to increasing backlogs, many agencies decreased the amount of information they were willing to release in full. For example, it found a decline in FBI and CIA responsiveness. FBI authorities gave just 6 out of every 1,000 FOIA applicants everything they asked for, down from 50 out of every 1,000 in 1998, indicating an institution-wide inclination to avoid complying with the law. The CIA has seen a similar steady decline: just 11 percent of the FOIA requests processed at the CIA were granted in total in 2004, down from 44 percent in 1998.

The trend has continued; in a 2006 report[49] the AP noted that agencies involved with national security are clamping down on the amount of information they release to the public. The FBI, CIA, and Defense departments, all agencies that have considerable investigative branches, again reduced the percentage of requested information released in full in 2005, thus continuing a trend dating back at least seven years. The DOJ, however, showed a slight increase in the amount of information it released in full for the first time since the 2001 terror attacks.[50]

In a 2005 FOIA audit, the National Security Archive found "a rise in secrecy from 2003 to 2005." They note that the 2005 survey responses "suggest a greater tendency to withholding information from the public in 2005 than in 2003."[51]

The Hand of Congress and Exemption (b)(3)

Of course, the executive branch is not the only branch that sometimes wishes to limit access to information. Although, in the 110th Congress, legislation to reform the process of the FOIA has passed in the House and has moved out of Committee on the Senate side,[52] there has been a contravening impulse in the Congress for the last several years to prohibiting disclosure of specific information—not by open and debated exemptions to the FOIA, but by hiding the prohibitions in other legislation. These are Exemption 3 statutes, known colloquially as (b)(3)s (for their reference to the applicable FOIA section, 5 U.S.C. § 552(b)(3)). In the next chapter, I tell the story of one such exemption, the quite expansive Critical Infrastructure Information (CII) exemption, which succeeded only after a more than two-year struggle with the public access community.

As DOJ notes in its 2004 FOIA[53] Guide, while Exemption 3 statutes can "prohibit disclosure of specified information by a federal agency generally and universally," increasingly Congress has been enacting legislation specifically focused on prohibiting disclosure under the *FOIA only*. While we, of course, do not want to see universal prohibitions on disclosure information, it is the fact that such attempts usually are noticed and become highly controversial—and less likely of success. Hiding a prohibition to disclosure through FOIA in an unrelated bill is a much stealthier—and less transparent—way to achieve comparable ends. DOJ notes that Congress also has enacted legislation evidently aimed at achieving an "Exemption 3 effect" in an indirect fashion—i.e., by limiting the funds that an agency may expend in responding to a FOIA request.[54]

These exemptions are quite difficult to track, as they are buried in legislation and often refer only to the FOIA by its U.S. code moniker, 5 USC § 552. The E-FOIA Amendments of 1996 require agencies to list the Exemption 3 statutes upon which they rely in their annual FOIA reports[55] each year. The DOJ OIP reviews the agencies' reports, but has not since 2003 compiled any statistics from them.[56] The result is that this information is effectively buried, unless someone has the time to go through each of the 70 or so[57] agency reports. The most accurate count is one recently done by the Sunshine in Government Initiative; they found 140 such Exemption 3 statutes (a number that closely coincided with an unofficial count they were given by DOJ OIP).[58]

State of FOIA Process

How to File a FOIA Request

The procedure for filing a request for information involves writing a letter to the appropriate agency including the most precise detail possible about the information you are seeking. It is important to remember that the statute specifies that requests must be for existing *records*. Agencies are not required to collect new information, create new records, do new research, or analyze information.

There are many online sources with letter-writing guides, including each agency's FOIA Web site.[59] The House Committee on Government Reform's "Citizen's Guide on Using the Freedom of Information Act and the Privacy Act of 1974 to Request Government Records"[60] includes a sample FOIA request letter in the appendix. The Reporters Committee for Freedom of the Press has a user-friendly letter generator[61] on its Web site. It prompts you for all relevant information about your request and drafts the letter for you, then allows you to edit it before saving or printing. You must mail or e-mail it yourself—so that it comes from you personally.

As I indicated at the start of this chapter, the beauty of the Freedom of Information Act, and the reason it is such an important law, is that it enables anyone to ask the government agencies (and other government entities) to hand over their records. The scope of the term "record" is quite broad: records obtainable under the FOIA include all "agency records"—such as print documents, photographs, videos, maps, e-mail, and electronic records—that were created or obtained by a federal agency and are, at the time the request is filed, in that agency's possession and control.[62] Although the Act occasionally uses terms other than "record," including "information" and "matter," a requester may ask only for records, and an agency is required only to look for an *existing* record or document in response to a FOIA request. When a requestor asks for a set of documents, the Act indicates that the agency should release all documents, not just a subset or selection. Even if much of the information is redacted (blacked-out), the requestor has a right to know that the full record is released, not just those portions the agency want to get out. It also provides administrative and judicial remedies for those denied access to records.[63]

The Act sets standards for determining which records the government must disclose and which records it may withhold. If the agency wishes to withhold the requested records, it must make its case for withholding in terms of one of the Act's nine exemptions to disclosure. As noted earlier in this chapter, Congress intended the general presumption to be mandatory disclosure. Generally, Congress intended the nine exemptions to the FOIA (see "The FOIA Exemptions," box on the following pages) [5 U.S.C. § 552(b)(1)–(9)] to protect against disclosure of information that would substantially harm national defense or foreign policy, individual privacy interests, business proprietary interests, and the efficient operation of governmental functions. An agency has the authority to construe the exemptions as discretionary rather than mandatory when no harm would result from disclosure of the requested information.[64] Of course, the determination—or judgment—of harm is the crux of the matter. Unfortunately, in 2001 Attorney General John Ashcroft mandated that federal agencies abandon this "foreseeable harm" standard in favor of a "presumptive nondisclosure" standard, as described above. Although this is a misinterpretation of the law, for practical purposes "presumptive nondisclosure" is the existing standard.

E-FOIA: The 1996 Amendments

The FOIA was amended in 1996.[65] The congressional finding accompanying the 1996 amendments noted that the FOIA has "led to disclosure of waste, fraud, abuse and wrongdoing in the Federal Government," and has "led to identification of unsafe consumer products, harmful drugs, and serious health hazards." It also noted that, as of 1996, members of the public

The FOIA Exemptions

The FOIA has nine exemptions. I've listed each one here by the subsection of 5 USC § 552 that contains it, as you will often see them referred to in that way:[68] The following text that is set in italics is the exact wording found in the U.S. Code:

Exemption (b)(1)—National Security Information

(b)(1) This section does not apply to matters that are—

>*(A) specifically authorized under criteria established by an Executive order to be kept secret in the interest of national defense or foreign policy and*

>*(B) are in fact properly classified pursuant to such Executive order;*

Exemption (b)(2)—Internal Personnel Rules and Practices

– "High" (b)(2)—Substantial internal matters, disclosure would risk circumvention of a legal requirement

– "Low" (b)(2)—Internal matters that are essentially trivial in nature.

(2) related solely to the internal personnel rules and practices of an agency;

Exemption (b)(3)—Information exempt under other laws

(3) specifically exempted from disclosure by statute (other than section 552b of this title), provided that such statute

>*(A) requires that the matters be withheld from the public in such a manner as to leave no discretion on the issue, or*

>*(B) establishes particular criteria for withholding or refers to particular types of matters to be withheld;*

Exemption (b)(4)—Confidential business information

(4) trade secrets and commercial or financial information obtained from a person and privileged or confidential;

Exemption (b)(5)—Inter- or intra- agency communication that is subject to deliberative process, litigation, and other privileges

(5) inter-agency or intra-agency memorandums or letters which would not be available by law to a party other than an agency in litigation with the agency;

Exemption (b)(6)—Personal privacy

(6) personnel and medical files and similar files the disclosure of which would constitute a clearly unwarranted invasion of personal privacy;

The FOIA Exemptions (cont.)

Exemption (b)(7)—Law enforcement records that implicate one of six enumerated concerns

(7) *records or information compiled for law enforcement purposes, but only to the extent that the production of such law enforcement records or information*

    (A) *could reasonably be expected to interfere with enforcement proceedings,*

    (B) *would deprive a person of a right to a fair trial or an impartial adjudication,*

    (C) *could reasonably be expected to constitute an unwarranted invasion of personal privacy,*

    (D) *could reasonably be expected to disclose the identity of a confidential source, including a State, local, or foreign agency or authority or any private institution which furnished information on a confidential basis, and, in the case of a record or information compiled by criminal law enforcement authority in the course of a criminal investigation or by an agency conducting a lawful national security intelligence investigation, information furnished by a confidential source,*

    (E) *would disclose techniques and procedures for law enforcement investigations or prosecutions, or would disclose guidelines for law enforcement investigations or prosecutions if such disclosure could reasonably be expected to risk circumvention of the law, or*

    (F) *could reasonably be expected to endanger the life or physical safety of any individual;*

Exemption (b)(8)—Financial institutions

(8) *contained in or related to examination, operating, or condition reports prepared by, on behalf of, or for the use of an agency responsible for the regulation or supervision of financial institutions; or*

Exemption (b)(9)—Geological information

(9) *geological and geophysical information and data, including maps, concerning wells.*

Any reasonably segregable portion of a record shall be provided to any person requesting such record after deletion of the portions which are exempt under this subsection. The amount of information deleted shall be indicated on the released portion of the record, unless including that indication would harm an interest protected by the exemption in this subsection under which the deletion is made. If technically feasible, the amount of the information deleted shall be indicated at the place in the record where such deletion is made.

requested more than 600,000 records yearly from federal agencies, a volume that was seen as threatening to overwhelm some agencies.[66] Congress thus acted to allow for greater access to information—particularly electronic information.[67] Among other changes, the 1996 amendments provided that

- Electronic records were explicitly made subject to the FOIA;
- The deadline for responding to FOIA requests was expanded from 10 to 20 days;
- Agencies were required to provide FOIA reports to Congress; and
- In most cases, agencies were required to produce the record in the format sought by the requester, regardless of the form in which a record is maintained by the agency.[68]

Possibly the most important provisions of the 1996 amendments were those that created a new set of agency requirements to aid the public in finding and obtaining federal government records. By March 31, 1997, each agency was required to provide, in its reading room and through an electronic site,[69] reference material or a guide on how to request records from the agency. The guide must include

- an index of all major information systems of the agency; and
- a description of major information and record locator systems maintained by the agency.

The FOIA had also previously required agencies to make available[70] for public inspection and copying: copies of records released in response to FOIA requests that an agency determines have been or will likely be the subject of additional requests and a general index[71] of released records determined to have been or likely to be the subject of additional requests.[72] Under E-FOIA these materials must also be made available through "computer telecommunications."

In addition, the amendments reaffirmed that agencies are required to comply with other regulations, such as OMB Circular A-130. I have discussed A-130 in more detail on the opening pages of Chapter 2, but recall that it requires that agencies determine what records or information products are appropriate for an affirmative agency disclosure.[73]

The importance of these provisions is probably obvious to you, but let me give a more familiar example. If you are faced with finding information on a topic, one place you can go is a library catalog—where information is organized by creator, subject, and so forth. This cataloging information would roughly correspond to E-FOIA's requirement of a description of major information systems, the inventories, and indexes. These E-FOIA amendments were a long overdue response to the increasing volume of information, especially e-information, being held by the government. Or at least they would have been—if they had ever been fully implemented government-wide.

Implementation of FOIA and the E-FOIA Amendments—or Not

It isn't enough to have a FOIA *requirement* specifying that agencies must inventory and index their records. The questions are always: Is the law enforced? Do the agencies comply? Since 1995, in the Paperwork Reduction Act for example, federal agencies have been required to compile a complete inventory of their information resources but have not done so. Since 1996, the E-FOIA has required agencies to produce an index of their major information and record locator systems with instructions on how to obtain information.

Reliable inventories of the government's holdings would assist the government's own information management and planning. For example, it would allow agencies to find useful information that has already been collected and organized by their own and other government agencies. Inventories and indexes that truly allowed the public to identify information and policy-related databases and to understand how an agency organizes its records (records locators) would greatly enhance the ability of the public to use government publications, databases, and bulletins, or use the FOIA to conduct research. But as a government task force on access to government information observed in 1995, "[t]he public has no efficient and accurate way of learning what information the agency has," and no idea "how the files are arranged, how long they are kept, or where they are stored."[74]

The laws to accomplish these goals are not, however being enforced. On December 4, 1997, Public Citizen[75] filed a federal lawsuit[76] and a petition to enforce recent federal statutes designed to make it easier for the public to obtain access to the vast information resources of the federal government. According to the lawsuit, many agencies, including the OMB, had ignored these mandates and routinely violated federal laws requiring information to be provided to the public on matters ranging from military contracts to trade policies to law enforcement records.[77]

In April 2000, with a federal court ruling on the Public Citizen suit pending, OMB revised Circular A-130 to, among other things, say that agencies can decide what is a major information system. On December 11, 2000, a federal district court found,[78] among other things, that summary judgment should be entered against five of the defendant agencies on Public Citizen's claims because the undisputed facts showed that these agencies had misconstrued and misapplied the definition of "major information systems" in various respects.[79] OMB did not, however, go back and change its guidance on the term and its requirements.

The result: E-FOIA's provision in the law is essentially useless as a means for the public to understand what kinds of information systems—e.g., databases—the government has. If the public knew, or could easily find out, they might ask for them through a FOIA request. The horror!

In late 1997[80] (and again in 1999[81]), OMB Watch had conducted a study of agencies' implementation of some of the requirements of the E-FOIA amendments. (I testified on these studies in both June 1998[82] and 2000,[83] before the subcommittee on Government Management, Information and Technology of the House Committee on Government Reform and Oversight on the Implementation of the Electronic Freedom of Information Amendments of 1996.) OMB Watch found then that, while agencies were putting up all sorts of information, it was mostly not information required by the 1996 Amendments and that information was disorganized and hard to find. At that time, OMB Watch recommended that

- The goal of E-FOIA should be to make so much information publicly available online that FOIA requests become an avenue of last resort. In this same vein, the goal should be to provide the information directly online to as great an extent as feasible.

- Congress must allocate appropriate levels of funding for ongoing implementation of the E-FOIA amendments. It is difficult for agencies to make E-FOIA a priority when monies must be diverted from other important projects.

- Congress must search for new ways to ensure implementation of these amendments through an enforcement mechanism. Currently, agencies that are not in compliance are not penalized.

In March 2007, the National Security Archive reported in its government-wide audit, "File Not Found,"[84] that most federal agencies still do not follow the law. The audit systematically reviewed agency Web sites to cover all 91 federal agencies that have Chief FOIA Officers and the additional 58 agency components each of which handles more than 500 FOIA requests a year. Key findings included:

- Only 21 percent of agencies post on the Web all four categories of records that the law specifically requires;

- Only 36 percent of agencies provided required indexes and guides to agency records, and many of those are incomprehensible or unhelpful.

Here we are, 10 years out from the period by which the E-FOIA amendments were supposed to have been implemented, and the majority of agencies continue to ignore the law, abetted by bad guidance from OMB. DOJ, which ostensibly was intended by Congress to oversee agency compliance with the FOIA, has interpreted its responsibility to consist in guidance and training. As the National Security Archive notes in its review of the implementation of Executive Order 13392 (see below), "Although the Department of Justice's Office of Information and Privacy has been making valuable recommendations to agencies for years about managing their FOIA programs, the individual reports give the impression that many of those recommendations were ignored, only to now be considered years later."[85] So no one[86] is making agencies bring their practices in to accord with statute—to the public's loss.

The Impact of Not Enforcing E-FOIA

Why should anyone care if there is no inventory of an agency's information systems, of its databases? Well, for one thing, it makes it much harder for the public or reporters to find out what databases and other information systems an agency has. Drew Sullivan,[87] in a training for the American Society of Access Professionals, noted that reporters are information brokers who are paid to reformulate information. As paper records disappear in county, state, and federal offices, reporters need access to their electronic equivalents, such as databases. Sullivan pointed out that computer-assisted reporting (CAR) has become a very hot thing in journalism,[88] giving several examples of stories that won Pulitzer Prizes for their analysis of electronic data:

- The *Boston Globe* used a database of elevator inspections to show that elevators were not being inspected in Massachusetts, leading to unnecessary injuries and death.

- The *Atlanta Constitution* used Home Mortgage Disclosure Act data to show that banks in Atlanta were denying minorities loans at higher rates than whites.

- The *Miami Herald* analyzed wind speed data, Federal Emergency Management Agency (FEMA) data, and property records to show that the areas that had the greatest devastation during Hurricane Andrew were not the areas where the wind speeds were highest, but rather areas built after building codes were weakened by political pressure.[89]

More recently, the *Seattle Post-Intelligencer* used CAR in reporting[90] on a profound shift in the FBI's mission: due to a shift in focus to national security following 9/11, the FBI has failed to replace at least 2,400 agents transferred to counter-terrorism squads. The reporters built a database from the records the *Post-Intelligencer* collected for their investigation and "[the] newspaper was able for the first time to fully measure the dramatic decline in the number of cases and convictions resulting from the FBI moving resources to terrorism and walking away from areas of criminal enforcement." Using similar methods of database creation, the *Washington Post* reported in April 2007 that a majority of money from the U.S. Department of Agriculture's (USDA's) Rural Development program is ending up in urban areas.[91]

Despite the obvious importance of public access to agency databases, the fact is that this access is often quite difficult. While news organizations may have trained staff who are assigned to dig for and through government databases, the average person has no easy way to learn what information systems (databases) the government has that might be of interest and use—beyond those an agency decides it wants the public to know about or is required by law[92] to make publicly accessible. Prior to the current administration, many intermediary organizations (such as environmental groups) learned about obscure—but useful—government databases through contact with the civil servants who created and maintained them. As we will see in Chapter 8, that sort of awareness and access has been severely restricted.

Additionally, databases can be very complicated (as noted at the beginning of Part I), and agency FOIA officials are often not familiar enough with their own agency's databases to offer assistance—even assuming that they are inclined to do so. Of course, there is no way that agency FOIA officers are going to become familiar with the vast majority of their agency's electronic holdings because those holdings are, to this day, extremely unlikely (as noted above) to be compiled in a comprehensive inventory or index.

Executive Order 13392: A Cosmetic Reform

On December 14, 2005, President Bush issued Executive Order 13392, "Improving Agency Disclosure of Information."[93] The requirements of the executive order include the following

- The designation by the head of each agency (within 30 days of the date of the order) of a senior official of such agency (at the Assistant Secretary or equivalent level), to serve as the Chief FOIA Officer of that agency;

- The establishment of a FOIA Requester Service Center and FOIA Public Liaisons, in order to ensure appropriate communication with FOIA requesters and to serve as the first place a FOIA requester can contact to seek information concerning the status of the person's FOIA request and appropriate information about the agency's FOIA response;

- A review of the agency's FOIA operations;

- An agency-specific plan to ensure that the agency's administration of the FOIA is in accordance with applicable law and policies addressing the agency's implementation of the FOIA during fiscal years 2006 and 2007; and

- A report, no later than six months from the date of the order, to the Attorney General and the OMB Director that summarizes the results of the review and encloses a copy of the agency's plan.[94]

The directive does not modify the 2001 policy issued by then-Attorney General John Ashcroft in the Memorandum discussed earlier and will not address the other concerns with the FOIA and access looked at in this chapter.

In October 2006, the Attorney General issued the required report[95] to the President on the agency plans submitted in compliance with the executive order. It essentially lauds the executive order and provides an overview of the plans submitted by the agencies.[96]

This Executive Order has thus had little effect, and it is widely considered that its intended effect was to stave off FOIA reform legislation being promoted by Senator John Cornyn (R-TX) that would create process reforms to the Act. With the 110th Congress in Democratic hands, the legislation[97] has passed the House and at—literally—the 11th hour before the Senate recessed for the month of August, a compromise version of the Senate passed in the Senate. The final Senate bill contained compromises with the Department of Justice, channeled through Senator Jon Kyl (R-AZ). The House bill would repeal the Ashcroft Memorandum; the Senate version does not—in order to keep Senator Cornyn, a very loyal Bush ally in every respect except promotion of this piece of legislation (and immigration reform), as a co-sponsor. At this writing, Congress is on its summer vacation. The bills will either go to conference in September or the House will take up the Senate version. Either way, those of us who have worked on these bills are hopeful that the final outcome will improve the implementation of the FOIA and will solve a number of problems that have plagued FOIA requesters for years.

In Conclusion

FOIA requests to agencies continue to grow and, in many agencies, so do the backlogs of requests. Clearly, FOIA is a critical part of the regulatory system for accountability, but it is also clear that it is broken in many aspects. The process reform legislation is an important step toward addressing many of its chronic problems and the inhibitions agencies throw in the way of requestors. Nothing, though, will change and make FOIA the access enabler it is meant to be until we have both an Administration that is oriented toward openness and a Congress that engages in persistent oversight whatever the party in charge of the White House. Both of these require persistent public engagement. None of it is easy.

Notes

1 Codified at 5 U.S.C. Section § 552.

2 Daniel Patrick Moynihan, "Chairman's Foreword," Report of the Commission on Protecting and Reducing Government Secrecy. Government Printing Office, 1997 (GPO).

3 "A Citizen's Guide on Using the Freedom of Information Act and the Privacy Act of 1974 to Request Government Records." (Report 108-172). U.S. House Committee on Government Reform. Washington, DC:GPO, 1974, p. 9.

4 Citizen's Guide, op. cit., p. 10.

5 Citizen's Guide, op. cit., p. 11.

6 Citizen's Guide, op. cit., p. 12.

7 However, Pub. L. 105–277 states, "Provided further, That the Director of OMB amends Section 36 of OMB Circular A–110 to require Federal awarding agencies to ensure that all data produced under an award will be made available to the public through the procedures established under the Freedom of Information Act."

8 Citizens for Responsibility and Ethics in Washington (CREW), "White House visitor records closed." January 5, 2007. http://www.citizensforethics.org/node/20349.

9 http://www.treas.gov/usss/foia.shtml.

10 Congressional Record, "Freedom of Information Act—Veto Message from the President of the United States (H. Doc. No. 93-383)." November 18, 1974.

11 Cited in Charlie Savage, "Hail to the Chief—Dick Cheney's mission to expand—or 'restore'—the powers of the presidency." *Boston Globe,* November 26, 2006. http://www.boston.com/news/globe/ideas/articles/2006/11/26/hail_to_the_chief/.

12 Bill Sammon, "Cheney hails Bush restoration of executive power." *Washington Times,* December 21, 2005.

13 Id.

14 Savage, op cit.

15 The Boland Amendment, which banned U.S. assistance to anti-Marxist militants in Nicaragua.

16 Savage, op. cit.

17 http://www.usdoj.gov/04foia/011012.htm.

18 http://www.usdoj.gov/04foia/011012.htm.

19 Citizen's Guide, op. cit, p. 9.

20 Martha Mendoza, "AP review finds federal government missing deadlines and time limits." The Associated Press State and Local Wire, Thursday, March 9, 2006 Thursday 6:47 PM GMT. http://www.ap.org/FOI/foi_031306b.html

21 http://www.usdoj.gov:80/oip/foiapost/2002foiapost10.htm.

22 OIP manages the Department's responsibilities related to FOIA—which include coordinating and implementing policy development and compliance government-wide for FOIA, adjudicating all appeals from denials by any Department component under either FOIA or the Privacy Act, and handling the defense of certain FOIA and Privacy Act matters in litigation. http://www.usdoj.gov/oip/oip.html.

23 FOIAdvocates. http://www.foiadvocates.com/exemptions.html.

24 On June 25, 2003, officials from the DOJ's Office of Information and Privacy and from the National Security Council held a closed conference that was summarized on the DOJ Web site. U.S. Department of Justice, FOIA Officers Conference Held on Homeland Security" FOIA Post, July 3, 2003. http://www.usdoj.gov/oip/foiapost/2003foiapost25.htm.

25 FOIA Guide, 2004 Edition, Exemption One. http://www.usdoj.gov/oip/foi-act.htm.

26 Id.

27 Genevieve Knezo, "Open Access Publishing and Citation Archives: Background and Controversy," December 12, 2006, http://www.ncseonline.orgNLE/CRSreports/07Jan/RL33023.pdf.

28 General Accounting Office. "Update on Implementation of the 1996 Electronic Freedom of Information Act Amendments." GAO-02-493. August 30, 2002. http://www.gao.gov/new.items/d02493.pdf.

29 The attacks in Washington, D.C. occurred over the course of several weeks beginning on September 18, 2001 (a week after the September 11, 2001, attacks). Letters containing anthrax bacteria were mailed to several news media offices and two U.S. senators, killing 5 people and sickening 17 others.

30 For an early compilation of these removals, see OMB Watch, "Access to Government Information Post September 11th." http://www.ombwatch.org/article/articleview/213/1/1/.

31 Jennifer LaFleur, "Privacy tops reasons agencies withhold information" *The News Media & The Law,* Summer 2003, Vol. 27, No. 3, p. 27. http://www.rcfp.org/news/mag/27-3/foi-privacyt.html. The 25 agencies chosen for this study were the same examined by the General Accounting Office for a study it released in September 2002. Some data used in this study for 1999, 2000, and 2001 were obtained from the GAO. The GAO and the RFCP data come from the "self-reported information in the annual report that is required by Congress to be completed by each agency annually."

32 Dan Eggen, "Ashcroft Defends Not Listing Detainees—Privacy Rights At Issue, He Says" *Washington Post,* November 27, 2001, Page A04. http://foi.missouri.edu/secretcourts/ashcroft def.html.

33 In response to Freedom of Information Act requests and a lawsuit charging the Pentagon with failing to comply with the Act, in April 2005 the Pentagon released more than 700 hundred of the images.

34 Reporters Committee for Freedom of the Press, "Domestic coverage," Homefront Confidential. In March 2003, the Bush administration dusted off a 13-year-old policy that bans the photographing of coffins containing the remains of U.S. military personnel who died overseas. Set in place by President George H.W. Bush before the 1991 Gulf War, the policy has prevented journalists from showing the public how—and how often—flag-draped coffins arrive in the United States from abroad. http://www.rcfp.org/homefrontconfidential/domestic.html.

35 In March 2006, the U.S. Department of Defense withdrew its opposition to the release of images, dropping its appeal of a lower court ruling to the 2nd U.S. Circuit Court of Appeals in Manhattan. http://www.rcfp.org/news/releases/20060328-victoryina.html.

36 Such as a law that protects intelligence sources and methods. Rebecca Daugherty "'Securing' the Public with Secrets: Judicial deference to the government's widespread claims of national security is keeping unclassified records from public view." *The News Media and The Law,* Fall 2003, Vol. 27, No. 4, p. 34, Reporters Committee for Freedom of the Press. http://www.rcfp.org/news/mag/27-4/foi-securing.html.

37 http://www.usdoj.gov/oip/exemption7.htm.

38 US. Department of Justice, "Exemption 7," *Freedom of Information Act Guide,* May 2004. http://www.usdoj.gov/oip/exemption7.htm.

39 673 F.2d 408, 421 (D.C. Cir. 1982).

40 272 F. Supp. 2d 958, 964-65 (C.D. Cal. 2003).

41 Center for National Security Studies v. United States Department of Justice, Civil Action No. 01-2500 (D. D.C.); No. 02-5300 (D.C. Cir.); 331 F.3d 918 (D.C. Cir. 2003). http://www.usdoj.gov/oip/foiapost/2003foiapost24.htm.

42 http://www.gannett.com/go/newswatch/2004/january/nw0116-5.htm.

43 *Living Rivers, Inc. v. United States Bureau of Reclamation,* 272 F. Supp. 2d 1313 (D. Utah 2003). http://www.usdoj.gov/oip/foiapost/2003foiapost13.htm.

44 U.S. Department of Justice, "Exemption 7," op. cit.

45 The National Security Archive Freedom of Information Act Audit Phase One Presented March 14, 2003 *The Ashcroft Memo: "Drastic" Change or "More Thunder Than Lightning?"* http://www.gwu.edu/%7Ensarchiv/NSAEBB/NSAEBB84/findingsag.htm.

46 Ibid.

47 Ibid.

48 Martha Mendoza, "Four million FOIA requests in 2004 tops previous high." Associated Press, March 18, 2005. http://www.ap.org/FOI/foi_031805a_000.html.

49 Martha Mendoza, "AP review finds federal government missing deadlines and time limits." Associated Press, March 13, 2006. http://www.ap.org/FOI/foi_031306b.html.

50 Associated Press, "Agencies missing FOIA deadlines, AP finds." March 13, 2006. http://www.firstamendmentcenter.org/news.aspx?id=16627.

51 National Security Archive.,"A FOIA Request Celebrates Its 17th Birthday. A Report on Federal Agency FOIA Backlog." March 2006. http://www.gwu.edu/~nsarchiv/NSAEBB/NSAEBB182/index.htm.

52 As of April 2007.

53 U.S. Department of Justice, FOIA Guide, 2004. http://www.usdoj.gov/oip/exemption 3.htm#initial.

54 Id. For the latter form of exemption, the question of whether this type of legislation is properly treated as an Exemption 3 statute has not yet been entirely resolved by the courts, according to DOJ.

55 U.S. Department of Justice, Office of Information and Privacy, "Annual FOIA Reports, FY06." http://www.usdoj.gov/oip/fy06.html.

56 Up through the reports for 2003, they did provide compilations of statistics. The most recent was "FOIA Post (2004): Summary of Annual FOIA Reports for Fiscal Year 2003." http://www.usdoj.gov/oip/foiapost/2004foiapost22.htm. They do compile the "Annual FOIA Litigation and Compliance Report." It is actually two separate items: an "Annual FOIA Litigation and Compliance Report" and a "Description of Department of Justice Efforts to Encourage Agency Compliance With the Act." It does not document agency compliance.

57 The count varies, as agencies often meet the deadline for submitting the reports and some, like the Executive Office of the President, have components that also report.

58 Personal communications with Sunshine in Government Initiative Coordinator, Rick Blum.

59 For a comprehensive list, go to http://www.usdoj.gov/oip/other_age.htm.

60 An online version can be found at http://www.fas.org/sgp/foia/citizen.pdf, page 41 of 85.

61 http://www.rcfp.org/foi_letter/generate.php.

62 National Security Archive, op. cit.

63 Id.

64 FOIAdvocates. http://www.foiadvocates.com/exemptions.html.

65 In addition to the amendments noted earlier.

66 "Electronic Freedom of Information of 1996," Floor Debate, Congressional Record: September 17, 1996 H10451.

67 Electronic Freedom of Information Act Amendments of 1996, Pub. L. No. 104-231, § 1-12, 110 Stat. 3048 (codified as amended in 5 U.S.C. § 552) (1996).

68 The full wording of these exemptions may be found in 5 U.S.C. 552(b)(1)-(b)(9).

69 Citizen's Guide, op. cit, p. 14.

70 The statute says that the agency must make the reference material or guide "publicly available." The House Report says that "All guides should be available through electronic means, and should be linked to the annual reports." H.Rep. 795 at 30. Department of Justice guidance indicates that agencies are required to make the material available in both traditional and electronic reading rooms, as well as releasing it in response to requests. U.S. Department of Justice, Office of Information and Privacy. FOIA Update. Fall 1996, Vol. XVII, No. 4, p. 11.

71 The 1996 E-FOIA amendments require that these materials (created on or after November 1, 1996) must be made available by computer telecommunications and in hard copy.

72 The 1996 amendments to the FOIA require that this general index be made available by computer telecommunications. Since not all individuals have access to computer networks or are near agency public reading rooms, requesters would still be able to access previously released FOIA records through the normal FOIA process.

73 This is a significant change in the law. Unofficial Department of Justice guidance (FOIA and Privacy Act Seminar, July 1998) suggests that if agencies receive two requests for documents that are releasable and expect to receive a third, then the agency should place the document, or redacted documents, in its electronic reading room. For redacted (the blacking-out of material that is being withheld from release) documents released under the FOIA, the amount of deleted information must be indicated at the place where the record was redacted. The E-FOIA extends that requirement to electronic records if technically feasible. OIP *FOIA Update,* Winter 1998.

74 See, 59 Federal Register at 37920; OIP *FOIA Update,* Winter 1995.

75 Department of the Interior, Report of the National Performance Review Freedom of Information Act Reinvention Team, Gateway to Government Information at 11 (September 1995). Cited in *Public Citizen v. Raines,* No. 97-2891 SSH, United States District Court for the District of Columbia, April 27, 1998.

76 Public Citizen is a national, nonprofit consumer advocacy organization founded in 1971 to represent consumer interests in Congress, the executive branch, and the courts.

77 *Public Citizen v. Raines,* No. 97-2891 SSH, United States District Court for the District of Columbia, April 27, 1998 (originally *Public Citizen v. Lew*).

78 Public Citizen, "Federal Agencies Violating Freedom of Information Act, Lawsuit Alleges." Press Release, December 4, 1997. The lawsuit, filed in U.S. District Court for the District of Columbia, charged that seven major federal agencies—the OMB; the Office of Administration in the Executive Office of the President; the Office of the U.S. Trade Representative; the Department of Education; the Department of Energy; the Department of Justice; and the Department of State—had not complied with statutes requiring that they make available guides and indices to help the public obtain agency records. The Office of Management and Budget was supposed to take a leadership role in implementing these requirements.

79 Opinion of District Judge Stanley S. Harris in *Public Citizen v. Lew,* CA No. 97-2891. United States District Court for the District of Columbia, December 11, 2000.

80 The Court's ruling, however, did not constitute a final judgment because the Court concluded that the factual record was not adequate to determine whether the Office of Administration and the Department of Energy had made similar errors in determining which information systems should be included.

81 Jennifer Henderson with Patrice McDermott, "Arming the People...with the power knowledge gives: An OMB Watch Report on the Implementation of the 1996 'EFOIA' Amendments to the Freedom of Information Act." *Government Information Insider*, Special Issue, April 1998.

82 Patrice McDermott, "A People Armed? An OMB Watch Update Report on the Implementation of the 1996 'EFOIA' Amendments to the Freedom of Information Act." *Government Information Insider*, Special Issue, Spring-Summer 1999. http://www.ombwatch .org/info/efoia99/efoiareport.html.

83 U.S. House Government Reform and Oversight Committee, "Implementation of the Electronic Freedom of Information Amendments of 1996: Is Access to Government Information Improving?" June 9, 1998. Serial No. 105-197. http://www.access.gpo.gov/ congress/house/pdf/105hrg/98649.pdf.

84 http://www.ombwatch.org/article/articleview/499/1/233?TopicDI=3.

85 National Security Archive, "File Not Found: 10 Years After E-FOIA, Most Federal Agencies Are Delinquent." March 12, 2007. http://www.gwu.edu/~nsarchiv/NSAEBB/NSAEBB216/ index.htm0.

86 National Security Archive Letter to Senator Arlen Specter, Senator Patrick Leahy, Senator John Cornyn, Senate Committee on the Judiciary October 19, 2006 http://www.gwu.edu/ ~nsarchiv/news/20061019/Letter_to_Specter_Leahy_Cornyn.pdf.

87 Including Congress.

88 "Prior to August of 2000, Sullivan worked as the News Data Manager for the Associated Press (AP) in New York City doing computer-assisted reporting for the AP's Special Assignment Team and for AP bureaus worldwide. Sullivan also works with investigative reporters and editors and formerly served on the staff of the National Institute for Computer-Assisted Reporting. http://www.drewsullivan.com/journal.htm.

89 Drew Sullivan, "The Media, the FOIA, and Electronic Data." ASAP Training Series, June 15-17, 1998, Users' Panel "Focus on Electronic Access." http://www.drewsullivan.com/ training/asap.htm.

90 Id.

91 "FBI's terrorism mission leaves white-collar crime unpunished" *Seattle Post-Intelligencer*, April 13, 2007. http://www.ire.org/extraextra/archives/2007_04.html#001896.

92 "Data Show Rural Money's Urban Drift" *Washington Post*, April 6, 2007, P. A08. http://www.washingtonpost.com/wpdyn/content/article/2007/04/05/AR2007040501895.html.

93 Such as the Toxic Release Inventory.

94 Executive Order: Improving Agency Disclosure of Information. http://www.whitehouse .gov/news/releases/2005/12/20051214-4.html.

95 For reports on the agency reports, see "FOIA's 40th Anniversary: Agencies Respond to the President's Call for Improved Disclosure of Information," http://www.openthe government.org/otg/FOIAplans.pdf; and "Freedom of Information Act: Preliminary Analysis of Processing Trends Shows Importance of Improvement Plans," GAO-06-1022T, July 26, 2006. http://www.gao.gov/new.items/d061022t.pdf.

96 U.S. Department of Justice. "Attorney General's Report to the President Pursuant to Executive Order 13,392, entitled "Improving Agency Disclosure of Information" October 16, 2006. http://www.gwu.edu/~nsarchiv/news/20061019/AG_Report_to_President_EO13392.pdf.

97 National Security Archive. "Attorney General's Report Ignores Serious Problems in Agency FOIA Programs" October 19, 2006. http://www.gwu.edu/~nsarchiv/news/20061019/index.htm.

98 Versions in the House and Senate differ in a few key provisions.

CHAPTER 4

THE CRITICAL INFRASTRUCTURE INFORMATION ACT—

THE STORY OF A FOIA EXEMPTION

Although the post-September 11 actions by the executive branch have had a troubling impact on the state of access through FOIA, one of the biggest holes in the Act was created by Congress: the Critical Infrastructure Information Act. This Act, one of the pieces of legislation passed by Congress in the wake of September 11, is intended to protect critical U.S. infrastructure (such as bridges, power plants, and computer networks) by preventing information about risks and vulnerabilities from being easily accessed by potential terrorists. In reality, as this chapter will discuss, the Act's restrictions on information availability appear to have done little to strengthen and protect our critical infrastructures, and in fact could be a significant barrier to creating necessary protections.

Congress created this huge hole through what is informally known as the (b)(3) exemption to FOIA. As I discussed in Chapter 3, the Act contains a number of exemptions to its requirements that information be made available (see "The FOIA Exemptions," at the end of that chapter), but one of them—exemption (b)(3)—protects information exempted through other statutes. These (b)(3) statutes have proved to be problematic for a number of reasons, as I described in Chapter 3; one that was subject to extensive analysis and debate was the Critical Infrastructure Information Act.

The public access community fought this legislation excluding Critical Infrastructure Information (CII) from access under FOIA from 2000 to its final passage in 2002 (as part of the act creating the Department of Homeland Security). I think it might be helpful to take a detailed look at its history and our efforts as an example of a very open Exemption 3 fight and as an illustration of the complexity—and political nature—of many FOIA battles. It is also illustrative of what a difference events and elections can make in these issues. In particular, this chapter will focus on

- The (misplaced) origins of the Act in the year 2000 and cybersecurity legislation;

- The impact that corporations' desire to limit liability had on the drafting of the Act;

- The Act's negligible apparent effect on protecting CII; and

- The Act's potential to restrict the flow of information needed to protect CII.

It's Good to Share: Y2K and Disclosing Information

Remember Y2K—the threat that many of the systems on which we rely would shut down as the calendar rolled over from December 31, 1999, to January 1, 2000 because the programs running did not have a date field beyond 1999? Remember that the world did not actually come to an end at 12:01 on January 1, 2000? It was not just hype, but one of the reasons the problem did not become catastrophic might surprise you.

The reason the world didn't come to an end—or part of the reason, at any rate—was the "Year 2000 Information and Readiness Disclosure Act." The Act encouraged companies to share and *publicly disclose* information regarding Y2K vulnerabilities by providing a limited FOIA exemption for information given to the government, civil litigation protection for information shared with the government and others, and an antitrust exemption (so companies could share information among themselves, as well as with the government and the public).[1] It is critically important to note that this legislation required "Y2K readiness disclosures" to the public of software vulnerabilities. The main focus of the Y2K Act was protecting companies from the *liability* associated with the disclosure and exchange of Y2K readiness information. As the sponsors of the Y2K legislation explained, it made sense to limit the legal liability of companies "who in good faith *openly share information* about computer and technology processing problems and related matters in connection with the transition to the Year 2000.'[2] (Emphasis added.) Although there was a FOIA exemption, FOIA was a minor concern, and Y2K statements in any case were exempt under (b)(4) of the FOIA, the exemption for proprietary data.[3]

The Y2K legislation did become law and, in the opinion of many public access experts (including myself), its emphasis on disclosure and sharing information with the public was extremely beneficial and helped to prevent some of the disasters forecast for Y2K.

A Case History of Statutory Drafting Disaster: CII

What does Y2K legislation have to do with exemption of critical infrastructure information from the FOIA? What indeed. But as you will see, it played a critical role, and one that illustrates the need for a vigilant public access community.

CII's Cybersecurity Beginning

The first tug of the curtain being drawn over government accountability for the country's infrastructure came in legislation introduced by Representatives Tom Davis (R-VA) and Jim Moran (D-VA) in April 2000, the "Cyber Security Information Act of 2000." As the title indicates, cybersecurity concerns were the justification for this legislation and its restrictions to access on formerly public information. At its introduction, Representative Davis stressed the role of Y2K in highlighting these concerns:

> As we learned when planning for the challenges presented by the Year 2000 rollover, many of our computer systems and networks are now interconnected and communicate with many other systems.... A cyber threat could quickly shut down any one of our critical infrastructures and potentially cripple several sectors at one time....[4]

As examples of the risk, Representative Davis cited the year 2000 shutdowns of many popular sites, such as Yahoo, eBay, and Amazon.com, for several hours at a time over several days by a team of hackers. He stated that "it is not too difficult to imagine what would have occurred if the attacks had been focused on our utilities, or emergency services industries."[5] Representative Davis also pointed to the rise of hacker attacks and cybersecurity problems recorded by Carnegie-Mellon University's Computer Emergency Readiness Team Coordination Center (CERT). The Center had noted an increase in incidents from 1,334 in 1993 to 4,398 during the first two quarters of 1999.[6] What Representative Davis (and subsequently all the promoters of critical infrastructure information shielding) did *not* say was that, in a meeting at the White House, the companies that had been attacked in 2000 admitted *they knew of the vulnerability that allowed the denial-of-service attacks but had not bothered to fix it.*[7] Hmm. Nor did Mr. Davis mention that one of CERT's primary functions is to discourage just that kind of cybernegligence. CERT[8] alerts users to potential cybersecurity threats and vulnerabilities and provides information about how to avoid, minimize, or recover from the damage. Often CERT alerts users on a time-lagged basis, to give the producers an opportunity to fix the vulnerability. One of the most beneficial aspects of CERT is that this public notification does not allow the producer (or users of the software such as a bank, electric companies, government) to ignore the vulnerability and then pretend surprise when a hacker exploits the vulnerability and causes harm. Sounds like a good argument for notification and sharing of information, doesn't it?

The Davis-Moran cybersecurity bill, however, had four main components, none of which included required notification or information sharing with the public:

- an antitrust exemption (so that companies could share information among themselves);

- a FOIA exemption (so that if the companies did disclose any information to the government, that information would not be subject to public disclosure under FOIA);

- a disclosure and use limitation (to limit what government or other businesses could do with any shared information); and

- an exemption from the Federal Advisory Committee Act (FACA).[9]

The bill created a definition of "cyber security statements," and then exempted "any cyber security statements or other such information provided by a party in response to a special cyber security data gathering request" from disclosure under FOIA, its disclosure "to or by any third party," and *its use "by any Federal or State entity, agency, or authority or by any third party, directly or indirectly, in any civil action arising under any Federal or State law."* (Emphasis added.) As Jim Dempsey at the Center for Democracy and Technology noted, the FOIA and the disclosure/use issues were quite separate issues: "The disclosure/use limitations are limits on the government and on other businesses. They are very broad and, as drafted, could have many unforeseen consequences, including unintended negative effects on the very companies they are meant to protect."[10]

We had first learned about a draft of this legislation earlier in 2000 and the intent to "protect" voluntarily submitted information about "cyber security," i.e., "[the] vulnerability of any computing system, software program, or critical infrastructure to, or their ability to resist, intentional interference, compromise, or incapacitation through the misuse of, or by unauthorized means of, the Internet, public or private telecommunications systems, or other similar conduct that violates Federal, State, or international law, that harms interstate commerce of the United States, or that threatens public health or safety." Several members of the public access community (including myself) had one, testy and unfruitful, meeting with Representative Davis's staff. We were told that companies were telling Representative Davis that information about vulnerabilities in the nation's critical infrastructure (broadly defined), which they really wanted to be able to share with government, would not be held confidential by the government once it was in the government's hands.

We came out of that meeting with a number of very strong concerns—almost all of which, unfortunately, proved prescient in light of the final 2002 Homeland Security Act. It's worth noting here that in 2000, most of our discussions were focusing only on issues of cybersecurity and cyberinfrastructure, even though the definitions in the draft opened the door to the more expansive conception of infrastructure that would come later, after September 11. Our concerns included the following:

- *Definitions and scope.* What counts as "critical infrastructure" and as "vulnerabilities"—does critical infrastructure include physical infrastructure (bridges, highways, water systems)? Should the sought-after protection apply only to computer/telecommunications-related infrastructure (some of which is also physical)? And does potential political embarrassment count, as some suggested at the time? It was important that these definitions be narrowly drawn; any exemption statute should be easy to understand, clearly defined, and predictable.

- *Proportionality.* What level of restriction/prohibition—related to the asserted need to prevent information about unsafe practices engaged in by water systems, chemical plants, oil refineries, and so on, from providing objects of opportunity for would-be terrorists—is proportional with the public's right to know about (and protect themselves or demand that their government protect them from) these unsafe practices?

- *Process.* A specific process must be laid out for the designation of protected CII.

- *Oversight.* An oversight body—with significant opportunity for public participation—must be created for the appeal of the designation of protected CII to ensure its limited and proper use.

- *Duration.* The FOIA exemption and the disclosure/use limitations must have time limits (along the line of Y2K information protection, i.e., the understanding that the need for protections and restrictions can and do expire, just as the Y2K protections expired at 12:01 on January 1, 2000). The exemption per se should be revisited in a few years' time to assess the need and use of it.

- *Purpose.* The government should work to identify what kinds of CII businesses should be *required*[11] to share with the government in order to limit our nation's vulnerabilities while protecting the public's right to know.

We also asked whether industries could demonstrate the need for the expansive protections in the proposed bill by pointing to readily available examples of CII they had shared with government and which had then been released through FOIA—or were we being asked to trust the industries' word about this and to rely on the industries' judgment about what information needs to be protected? We never got a direct answer from either the industries or from the government (Congress or the executive branch); we were expected to trust with no possibility to verify.

Proportionality issues were especially significant because the proposals included liability immunity of unspecified duration for conduct of the parties submitting the information. Our concern was that, particularly where physical infrastructure is the consideration, there may be financial disincentives to fixing problems—but there are always great financial and legal incentives to shielding information about problems.

Unfortunately, as you will see, of these concerns only our recommendation concerning process made it into the final statute, two and a half years down the road.[12] None of our concerns were represented in the bill introduced by Representatives Davis and Moran.

Liability Limitation Raises Its Ugly Head

You will recall that the this Cybersecurity Information Act was based on an analogy with Y2K legislation. The analogy was a bad one—the Y2K Act was all about sharing and disclosing information, including *to the public*—whereas the Cybersecurity Information Act was about keeping information *from* the public—and government agencies and state governments. The reason this linkage was made by its sponsors can be found in one critical aspect of the Y2K Act, noted above: the main focus of the Y2K Act was protecting companies from the liability associated with the *disclosure and exchange* of Y2K readiness information.[13] Similarly, the companies with infrastructure information wanted the immunity from liability above all else[14] and they got it[15] (actually, the companies eventually obtained everything they could think to ask for).

The companies were also given another control that was critical to them: the limitation on the disclosure and use of the infrastructure information submitted by companies mentioned above. The "use" limitation included use of submitted information *"by any Federal or State entity, agency, or authority or by any third party, directly or indirectly, in any civil action arising under any Federal or State law"* (emphasis added), essentially giving the submitter of the information control over its use and disclosure.

There it was: this was not about keeping potentially damaging information out of the hands of the public and of competitors—or even of "terrorists." It was about keeping it out of the hands of government and private-sector lawyers who might sue these companies for their negligent failure to address and remedy those known risks and vulnerabilities. The analogy we used was that, if tires were critical infrastructure, no one would have been able to sue Firestone for those exploding tires—because Firestone had shared the information with the government.[16]

Hiding Behind FOIA

Businesses also argued that information about vulnerabilities in the nation's critical infrastructure, which businesses *said* they really wanted to be able to share with government, would not be held confidential by the government once it was in the government's hands.

FOIA experts repeatedly argued that court decisions would permit the government to successfully protect cybersecurity information against FOIA requests under the (b)(4) FOIA exemption for proprietary information.[17] In some cases, the FOIA exemptions for national security information (b)(1) and law enforcement information (b)(7) would also be available. But this was not enough to reassure legal counsel in the companies that really did—honest, we promise—want to share important information with the government.[18]

September 11 Gives Birth to CII Legislation

During the 107th Congress, both H.R. 4246 and its companion Senate bill (S. 1456) remained in committee. We were successful for 18 months in fending off this legislation, due in no small part to the Clinton Administration's indication to Congress in 2000 that it was neither needed nor wanted. Then came September 11, 2001.

On September 12, although most hearings were cancelled, the Senate Governmental Affairs Committee convened a hearing on America's critical information infrastructure. The hearing was originally scheduled to examine the security of the critical cyber infrastructure and to allow the Committee to hear the challenges that remain in *government's* efforts to secure the critical information infrastructure. Although the committee has jurisdiction over information infrastructure of government agencies only, the Senators—undoubtedly feeling the pressure of an attack on U.S. soil—addressed both government and private sector issues. Senator Lieberman, Chair of the Committee, said that the events of September 11 began a new era for American national security, and that future attacks will also target critical information infrastructure.

But should September 11 have made such a difference in our national approach to privately held critical infrastructure? Although this wasn't raised in the committee hearings, the U.S. Space Command, which monitors military networks, reported no rise in malicious or nuisance network activity on Tuesday (September 11) and Wednesday (September 12).[19] An alert sent by CERT said the organization "is not seeing any significant increases in incident activity on the internet."

Of course, despite the lack of any Internet-associated activity with the September 11 attacks, no one is arguing that U.S. information infrastructure has no vulnerabilities. As the primary committee witness, Joel Willemssen,[20] testified,[21] *federal* computer systems, in particular, continued to put critical operations and assets at risk. The *federal government* was lagging in protecting utilities, transportation, and financial service sectors. *Federal agencies* were inadequately implementing existing laws and directives. And a significant part of the government's vulnerability, according to another government witness, Roberta Gross,[22] is that

> *agencies were using private software "bought right off the shelf," and that much of that software has security holes in it because of private industry's "rush-to-market" mentality that relies on "patches" to fix problems only after the software has been installed and used.* (Emphases added.)

So it seems that the conclusion drawn should have been that our government needs to do a better job of enforcing its own risk reduction programs.

Unfortunately, the Senate went in the direction of restricting information access, drawing from the failed cybersecurity law discussed above. When witnesses at the committee hearings noted that private sector information could help prevent the spread of cyberattacks, but the private sector was often unwilling to share security information for fear of liability, Senator Fred Thompson (R-TN) suggested that the way to get the private sector to share information about cybersecurity with government is to give it the same sort of statutory protection that Congress gave in the Y2K Act.

Game and set. The match was finalized later. Over the course of that fall, the public interest community, including a wide coalition of organizations concerned with FOIA, environmentalists, good government groups, library organizations, and others, endeavored mightily to stop overly broad CII legislation. The Senate bill was the Critical Infrastructure Information Act (S. 1456), promoted by Senators Robert Bennett (R-UT) and Jon Kyl (R-AZ); the House bill was H.R. 2435, promoted by Representatives Tom Davis and Jim Moran.

Letters,[23] one in December 2001 signed by 27 public interest groups and another in May 2002 signed by 45, urged senators to oppose the Bennett/Kyl legislation. The organizations noted that, while the "intent of the Bennett/Kyl language is to encourage the sharing of information that would strengthen national security against terrorist attacks on and through computer systems, in practice, however, the legislation could have the following devastating effects" on the regulatory process and federal law enforcement:

- Bar the federal government from disclosing information regarding spills, fires, explosions, and other accidents without obtaining written consent from the company that had the accident;

- Give the manufacturing sector unprecedented immunity from the civil consequences of violating the nation's environmental, tax, fair trade, civil rights, labor, consumer protection, and health and safety laws; and

- Sweep aside record-keeping and disclosure requirements under federal laws other than the Securities and Exchange Act.

All to no avail.

Game, Set, and Match: CII Finds a Home in the Homeland Security Act

Although the President had initially resisted the creation of a Department of Homeland Security, by July 2002, legislation was making its way through Congress. President Bush's proposal for the creation of a new Homeland Security Department contained a single vague sentence describing a new FOIA exemption for information concerning "infrastructure" and "vulnerabilities" that was "voluntarily submitted." It took the proponents of CII-shielding no time to insert provisions that went much further. The proposal out of the House Select Committee reviewing the Homeland Security Act created a new blanket FOIA exemption—"not withstanding any other provision of law" (e.g., the FOIA)—which could be used to conceal even CII information *required* by the government (as opposed to voluntarily submitted).

That, however, was not enough. The proposal also tied the hands of government and other, third-party, lawyers by granting corporations unprecedented immunity (via the liability exemption) from the civil consequences of violating the nation's securities, tax, civil rights, environmental, labor, consumer protection, and health and safety laws.

Still not enough. The House proposals preempted all state and local open-records laws with regard to critical infrastructure information. State and local authorities would be barred from disclosing information *that is required to be public under state or local law* if it is withheld at the federal level. To gild the lily, the section contained a provision that would criminalize the release of this information with up to a year in jail.

These extreme proposals did meet with some brief resistance. In the Senate, the Government Affairs Committee, chaired by Senator Lieberman (D-CT), began by considering Sen. Lieberman's bill for establishing a Department of Homeland Security, the National Homeland Security and Combating Terrorism Act of 2002 (S. 2452), rather than legislation based on the administration's proposals. This bill did not include any restrictive information provision or FOIA exemptions. Several amendments addressing FOIA exemptions and information were filed, however, and, eventually, a compromise amendment emerged sponsored by Senators Levin (D-MI) and Bennett (R-UT). The compromise amendment—more moderate than the House version even if not as open as we hoped for—narrowly defined the information exempt from FOIA disclosure as being only those documents submitted to the new Department that addressed vulnerabilities *and* that no government agencies had the authority to request from companies. The legislation did not contain any liability immunity, preemption of state or local disclosure laws, or criminalization of disclosure.

According to Senator Bennett, the compromise language was endorsed both by the Bush Administration and, begrudgingly, by the business community. The Homeland Security Act was pushed into an additional session, though, held after the 2002 elections. When election results revealed that Republicans would take control of the Senate, House Republicans pushed hard with their more extreme version and met little opposition. The House version prevailed.

The law includes a provision (§ 204) that creates a broad exemption, indeed an exclusion,[24] from the FOIA: "Information provided voluntarily by non-Federal entities or individuals that relates to infrastructure vulnerabilities or other vulnerabilities to terrorism and is or has been in the possession of the Department shall not be subject to section 552 of title 5, United States Code" (the FOIA). As a result,

- Critical infrastructure information (CII) voluntarily submitted to the Department of Homeland Security that is designated as confidential by the submitter is exempt from disclosure under the FOIA unless the submitter gives prior written consent;

- Companies providing CII are given civil immunity—such information cannot be used in civil actions against the company by the government or anyone else;

- State sunshine laws are preempted if the CII is shared with state or local government agencies; and

- Criminal penalties of up to one-year imprisonment are imposed on government employees who disclosed the designated information.

The impact for the public is that the CII designation can prevent the public, other federal agencies, and state and local officials from being able to learn—and do something about—a wide range of information about vulnerabilities in "infrastructures," such as computer-related systems, physical plants, and emergency services. The federal government can receive the information, but it is under no obligation to use it to encourage companies to limit (or eliminate) the risks and vulnerabilities. And under the second Bush Administration, at least, we can be sure they will not use it to ascertain what information companies should be *required* to submit.

On November 22, 2002, Congress passed H.R. 5005, the Homeland Security Act of 2002 to create a Department of Homeland Security (DHS). It was signed into law (Public Law 107-296) by President Bush on November 25th.

Are We Safer with CII Behind Closed Doors?

So what has the government been able to learn from the vast amounts of information that surely flowed in from the protected industries and sectors that were so desirous of sharing it? What's that? Very little information has come in?! According to the GAO,[25] as of January 2006, the Program Office had received 289 submissions: 266 were validated as PCII (Protected CII); eight were in the process of being validated; 14 were rejected; and one was withdrawn.

GAO notes that, to increase submissions, the Program Office has initiated outreach efforts to publicize the PCII program to the public and private sectors. The office launched a public Web site in March 2004, presenting program facts and answers to frequently asked questions; prepared over 2,300 fact sheets and about 4,000 brochures that it distributed to public and private stakeholders; and activated e-mail and telephone help lines to respond to inquiries or comments. The office discussed the program in over 30 articles in trade publications, briefed infrastructure sector representatives and participated in industry conferences and seminars, and provided presentation kits that DHS analysts use to explain the program to potential submitters.

I guess the private sector was not all that keen to share, after all. It is not clear whether they still consider themselves unprotected from FOIA requestors (although it is hard to imagine how much more protected they could possibly be). Nor, it must be said, have they loaded up all the information on vulnerabilities, for which they might otherwise be liable, and shipped it off—as we expected. But that door remains open to them to avoid liability by packing information off to DHS when a company has advance warning of an impending liability risk or suit.

So why should we care—other than because of the hole that was carved out of the FOIA?

Well, for one thing, cybersecurity really is still a problem that the existing law seems to be doing nothing to solve. As noted above, the federal government can receive information about our cyber risks and vulnerabilities, but it is under no obligation to use it encourage companies to limit (or eliminate) them. Only recently (with the change of control) has Congress stepped up to the plate and begun to at least try to address some vulnerabilities in other parts of our critical infrastructure (although Representative Davis has kept a strong focus on the security of government information systems).

In September 2006, GAO reported[26] recent examples of attacks and threats that underscore the need to bolster the cybersecurity of our government's and our nation's computer systems and, more importantly, of the critical operations and infrastructures they support. These included the following

- *Our vulnerable electric grid.* In March 2005, security consultants within the electric industry reported that hackers were targeting the U.S. electric power grid and had gained access to U.S. utilities' electronic control systems. Computer security specialists reported that, in a few cases, these intrusions had "caused an impact." While officials stated that hackers had not caused serious damage to the systems that feed the nation's power grid, the constant threat of intrusion has heightened concerns that electric companies may not have adequately fortified their defenses against a potential catastrophic strike.

- *Threats to our financial system.* In June 2003, the U.S. government issued a warning concerning a virus that specifically targeted roughly 1,300 financial institutions, potentially allowing a hacker access to the banks' networks.

- *Continued hacking of known vulnerabilities.* In January 2003, the Slammer worm infected more than 90% of vulnerable computers worldwide within 10 minutes of its release on the Internet by exploiting a *known* vulnerability *for which a patch had been available for six months.* (Emphasis added.) Slammer caused network outages, canceled airline flights, and automated teller machine failures. In addition, the Nuclear Regulatory Commission confirmed that the Slammer worm had infected a private computer network at a nuclear power plant, disabling a safety monitoring system for nearly five hours and causing the plant's process computer to fail. The worm reportedly also affected communication on the control networks of at least five utilities by propagating so quickly that control system traffic was blocked. Cost estimates on the impact of the worm range from $1.05 billion to $1.25 billion.

- *Hacking of personal information.* There have also been multiple, repeated, instances—over a number of years—of hackers breaking into private sector databases, exposing credit card numbers, social security numbers, and other personally identifying information potentially compromising the identities and finances of tens of millions of persons.

Surely, though, the individual pieces of information that DHS *has* received must warrant all the protection given to it (and the companies providing it). The above examples provided by GAO[27] do not reassure us that the hole in FOIA was worth the information it is "protecting." All of the above examples of unfixed and unaddressed critical infrastructure vulnerabilities are based on information *not* submitted as PCII. If it were PCII, we would not be allowed to know about these vulnerabilities.

Nor should we be reassured by the examples provided by other government agencies that are, apparently, based on PCII.

- DHS's National Cyber Security Division (NCSD) reported that it received information that "was important to investigating a cyber-related incident," but that "would not have been provided by the infrastructure owners without CII Act protections."

- The Federal Emergency Management Agency (FEMA) learned one piece of information from *a state,* who "would not share the information unless it could be protected, that led to the development of *generic* best practices related to dam security that were presented at a workshop." (Emphasis added.)

- In February 2005, at the request of NCSD, the National Security Agency became the first non-DHS federal agency to receive PCII—"information used to assist in the research of a cyber-related incident which *did not result in any public alerts.*" (Emphasis added.)

- Officials from the Nuclear Regulatory Commission reported that they had *reviewed* one PCII report.[28]

And finally—in case you thought the government might take the lack of response and useful information in the few responses it has received as indication of a need to let the public know more about the risks and vulnerabilities to which it is exposed—in August 2004, the Federal Communications Commission (FCC), citing emergency response personnel's dependence on cell and satellite phones, told[29] wireless telecommunications companies that they would be required to provide detailed reports about service disruptions under a new FCC regulation. The wireless industry "was not thrilled with the decision and pushed hard for a voluntary reporting system." *Wired News* reported that the FCC countered that the voluntary system for CII already in place was not being widely used, and that reports lacked necessary details.[30] Nevertheless, the wireless companies and the Department of Homeland Security argued that the information could be used by terrorists to plot attacks on communications systems and persuaded the FCC to keep the reports secret and immune from FOIA.

After all of this effort, the FOIA exemption, the grant of liability immunity, the disclosure prohibition on state and local governments, what is the result? In June 2006,[31] GAO reported that the government was not yet adequately prepared to effectively coordinate public/private plans for recovering from a major Internet disruption. A private-sector organization[32] subsequently reported that our nation was unprepared to reconstitute the Internet after a massive disruption, noting that there were significant gaps in government response plans and that the responsibilities of the multiple organizations that would plan a role in recovery were unclear.

In Conclusion

Clearly, a reassessment of the protection provided to private sector Critical Infrastructure Information needs to occur. It is not clear what benefits it has provided to the security of country and the American public. That should be the measure of its utility.

Its impact on the ability of the federal, state, and local governments to do the work of government also needs study and analysis. Neither of these are likely to happen in the Bush Administration.

But there is hope. Senator Leahy (D-VT) introduced the Restore FOIA Act[33] in the 109th Congress. It would limit the scope of covered records provided by the private sector and ensure the release, pursuant to FOIA requests, of those portions of submitted records that are not covered by the CII exemption. It does not provide any civil liability immunity or preempt state or local sunshine laws, and it does not criminalize whistleblower activity. He is expected to introduce it in the 110th Congress.

The National Animal Identification System (NAIS)—An Illustrative Story

Sometimes you notice a government press release or an obscure (if you don't follow a particular agency) *Federal Register* notice catches your eye; sometimes a colleague brings something to your attention. Often this apparently singular notice sets off a little bell in your head and you store it away. Only later do the pieces start to fit together.

A good example is this story about tainted beef products and the creation of a National Animal Identification System (NAIS). You may recall that, in December 2003, a cow infected with mad cow disease was found in Washington State and that the infected meat entered the food supply, mixed with 37,000 pounds of meat from other cows. The tainted meat was sold in six western states. And because the USDA currently then (as now) did not have mandatory recall authority on tainted meat,[34] industry cooperation was essential in tracking down the bad beef.

March 2004: The USDA keeps business secrets

In March, I saw a colleague's commentary on a secrecy requirement that the USDA had imposed on states. According to *Consumer Reports*,[35] California was one of seven states that received a shipment of beef products subject to a USDA recall because it included meat and bones from a cow that tested positive for mad cow disease. Consumers in California—and seven other states—would not be privy to this information, however, because the USDA shares information about retailers that have received tainted beef and poultry only with states that sign an agreement, a memorandum of understanding (MOU),[36] with the USDA agreeing to keep secret the names of the retail outlets selling food subject to beef and poultry recalls. The MOU requiring secrecy covers all recalls of unsafe beef and poultry. Recalls of beef and poultry products tainted with other hazards, such as E. Coli, Listeria, and Salmonella, also would be covered by the secrecy agreement. According to *Consumer Reports'* analysis, USDA "maintains that secrecy is necessary in order to protect the proprietary interests of the beef and poultry industries."

Okay. This did not pass the openness (not to mention public health and safety) smell test. So, I stored it away in the "Suspicious" file in my brain. (Yes, my brain has a "Suspicious" file—doesn't yours?)

May 2005: The USDA develops an NAIS…in order to keep secrets?

Fast forward about 14 months and a Notice appears in the *Federal Register*[37] (May 6, 2005) about the development of a National Animal Identification System (NAIS). According to the Notice:

> *The National Animal Identification System (NAIS) is a national program intended to identify specific animals in the United States and record their movement over their lifespans. It is being developed by the U.S. Department of Agriculture (USDA) and State agencies—in cooperation with industry—to enable 48-hour traceback of the movements of any diseased or exposed animal. This will help to ensure rapid disease containment and maximum protection of America's animals….Animal heath officials must have immediate, reliable, and uninterrupted access to essential NAIS information for routine surveillance activities and in the event of a disease outbreak. Animal and Plant Health Inspection Service (APHIS) determined that this goal could best be achieved by having the data repositories managed by APHIS.*

Okay. But, then, the Notice went on to make this statement: "We are aware that many producers are concerned about the confidentiality of the information collected in the NAIS." And the Notice also asked this question: "Given the information identified in the draft documents, what specific information do you believe should be protected from disclosure and why?" And finally, the Notice made this statement: "Recently, however, an industry-led initiative suggested a privately managed database as an alternative for the management of data on animal tracking in the NAIS. The industry group stated that a private database would ensure that the needs of both government and industry would be fulfilled, and that the flow of information throughout the NAIS would be maintained in a secure and confidential manner." It almost sounded like the government was inviting industry to object to the NAIS, or at least to one that would give the public adequate access to any real information. Hmm.

July 2004: Isn't it nice that regulated and regulator agree

An article[38] in July 2004 quoted reasons the National Cattlemen's Beef Association gave for producers wanting a voluntary animal identification program: They were concerned about confidentiality, and feared that "animal activist groups or competitors could misuse information collected in the databases, including how many cows they have and where they have been— the data even could be used by a terrorist group to pinpoint when animals are moving through a collection point and to introduce a disease." Many producers wanted most of the information to be available exclusively to animal health inspectors—preferably at the state level only—and exempt from FOIA disclosure rules. The USDA coordinator for the NAIS agreed with the cattlemen's preference for a voluntary program, saying, "As long as the program is voluntary, it can be confidential and Homeland Security can declare it 'protected critical infrastructure information.' If it becomes mandatory, then Congress would have to pass legislation exempting the data from FOIA."

May 2005: The Consumers Union pushes back

I spotted an article in *Government Computer News*[39] reporting that the USDA had released a draft plan in the May 6 Federal Register for tracking animal movements and initiating an NAIS.

That same month, Consumers Union issued a release[40] to be published for public review. The rule was, however, withdrawn on April 29 for unknown reasons.

Remember at the beginning of this story, that a March 2004 *Consumer Reports*[41] had indicated that California was one of eight states that had signed a Memorandum of Understanding with the USDA, agreeing to keep secret the names of the retail outlets selling food subject to beef and poultry recalls? Well, by May 2005, that number of secrecy agreements (so the states could get some information out of USDA to protect the public without informing them of the risks they were exposed to) was up to 12 states; 38 had not complied, however, and something needed to be done.

September 2005: The USDA opts for a privately run tracking system

In a *Federal Register* notice[42] of a public meeting, the USDA APHIS concluded that "having multiple industry program databases 'feed' a centralized, *privately held* repository with all animal movement data can be achieved and can meet the needs of our animal health programs." (Emphasis added.)

November 2005: A private or public system? The struggle continues

A story on the Livestock Marketing Association (LMA) InfoLink site[43] reported that Senator Tom Harkin (D-IA) was seeking a federal probe of the proposed NAIS. They reported that in October he had asked USDA to justify its plan to turn the animal tracking database over to private entities. In November, Harkin sent a letter to the GAO asking for the probe, saying, "USDA has spent many hours and a lot of money developing an animal tracking database. Then, without seeking needed input from all sectors of the livestock and poultry industry, USDA scrapped the original plan and now wants the database privatized."

One might ask, what about the meat- and poultry-consuming public? But why would we want to know?

The December 1, 2005, *BEEF*,[44] quotes Attorney Kaleb Hennigh, an agriculture law specialist, that he is more concerned about producers' liability exposure in the event of a food-safety situation than about FOIA disclosure alone. This concern with the liability implications of FOIA disclosure is one we will encounter again, most particularly with critical infrastructure information. We should remember that FOIA has always included an exemption for confidential (including proprietary) business information.

So now we are up to 2006. In a January 10 LMA InfoLink story, we learn that USDA is considering a new approach to NAIS that would allow USDA to link to a network of private and state-operated animal tracking databases. This approach would let USDA tap into a "portal" of various animal identification and tracking systems run by commodity groups, breed organizations, other groups, and 20 existing state databases.

According to the report, Dr. John Clifford, USDA's chief veterinarian, speaking at the annual meeting of the American Farm Bureau Federation, in Nashville, Tennessee, said the agreement will define the legal responsibility of all parties involved concerning the system's specifications, which USDA has determined will be reliability, uninterrupted access for state health officials, and no user fees for states or federal entities accessing the system. Clifford said the federal and state governments would need access to the data at all times, but neither would pay for access to the system.

Clifford said the department would create and pay for a "metadata" system that would function like an Internet search engine to give the government access to any private animal ID systems, but producers and meat businesses will have to pay for the equipment to make their reports.

Producers had expected the government to pay the costs. According to Jerry Hagstrom, a *Congress Daily* reporter, writing in the *Grand Forks Herald*,[45] Dr. Clifford said the initial system would be voluntary, but the department can mandate the system under authority in a 2002 farm law. Mr. Hagstrom notes that other countries have made such systems mandatory in order to get information on 100 percent of their meat animals.

A January 12, 2006 LMA InfoLink story[46] reported that the U.S. Animal Identification Organization (USAIO), a new group, had announced it wants to manage the NAIS database. The group has submitted an MOU to USDA "to form a strategic partnership." The National Cattlemen's Beef Association (NCBA) also had indicated that it would submit a proposal to USDA to manage that database.

January 2006: The consumers almost win...sort of

LMA[47] reported that, after hearing strong opposition from the industry, USDA had abandoned its earlier decision to allow a single private entity to manage the livestock movement database. But that wasn't the only major announcement from the agency concerning NAIS: According to the NAIS coordinator, there would not be a mandatory ID program by 2009, as previously announced; and USDA attorneys were researching whether they have the legal authority to require producers to report livestock movement to a private entity.

March 2006: An industry-run tracking system is proposed

Michael Arnone reported in *Federal Computer Week*[48] that the private USAIO would oversee a national animal-tracking database "to protect public health and the economy." USAIO would run a Web-based system, the ViaHerd database system, which would also be a crisis-management tool. Users would be able to impose "specific, appropriate restrictions" and provide data to emergency management personnel. According to Arnone, industry groups, members of Congress, and Agriculture Secretary Mike Johanns had agreed they prefer an industry-run database to a government-run one, arguing that a private sector system would bypass the need for separate federal and state systems and protect data better.

Indeed.

February 2006: If you can't see a mad cow, is it really there?

Intervening in this happy narrative of protection of the industry is this story from the *Washington Post*:[49] "Agency Fought Retesting of Infected Cow." In it, Marc Kaufman reported that, according to the USDA's inspector general, department officials overruled field scientists' recommendation to retest an animal that was suspected of harboring mad cow disease last year because they feared a positive finding would undermine confidence in the agency's testing procedures. After protests from the inspector general, the specimen was sent to England for retesting and produced the nation's second confirmed case of mad cow disease.

The inspector general report also found that although there was no evidence that infected meat had made it into the human food chain, the USDA surveillance system did not collect the information needed to say whether slaughterhouses were following all mad cow-related regulations. In 9 of 12 facilities visited, inadequate record-keeping made it impossible to know whether proper procedures were being followed: "As a result, should serious animal disease be detected in the United States, USDA's ability to quickly determine and trace the source of infections to prevent the spread of disease could be impaired."

Indeed, according to David Thigpen writing in *Time*,[50] record-keeping was so poor that inspectors "could not immediately determine where the diseased animal was born or raised. Inspectors did not even know the animal's age and were forced to examine its teeth to make a guess (about 10 years old, the Food and Drug Administration (FDA) estimates). Investigators are also unsure where that cow, which was euthanized and buried after it fell sick, may have fed." Thigpen reports that, currently, "only about 10% of the herd is traceable through the USDA's tracking system." Moreover, "[the] United States tests 'about 1% of its cattle for mad cow disease, while Japan tests nearly 100% and the European Union tests all cattle over 30 months old."[51]

But any information that might, by happenstance, be collected will be fully protected from disclosure to the media and the public under the FOIA.

Hamburger or a nice juicy steak, anyone?

March 2006: About face—making recall information publicly available

In a surprising reversal, the Food Safety and Inspection Service (FSIS) of USDA published a notice of proposed rulemaking[52] on the "Availability of Lists of Retail Consignees During Meat or Poultry Product Recalls." According to the Notice, the agency will make available to the public "lists of the retail consignees of meat and poultry products that have been voluntarily recalled by a federally inspected meat or poultry products establishment if product has been distributed to the retail level." FSIS is also proposing to routinely post these retail consignee lists on its Web site "as they are developed by the Agency during its recall verification activities."

During the recall process, if the recall is to the retail level, the firm conducting the recall is supposed to provide FSIS with a list of the outlets to which the recalled meat or poultry products were distributed. FSIS also obtains lists from these outlets of all entities to which they further distributed the product and contacts those entities to ensure that they were notified, and so on to the retail level.

It is these distribution lists that FSIS had previously considered as confidential business information, and thus exempt from release under FOIA—where we began this story.

Nothing like a mad cow to bring some sense to our government.

Notes

1 Y2K Information and Readiness Disclosure Act, Pub. L. 105-271.

2 Id.

3 Jim Dempsey, Center for Democracy and Technology, "Davis-Moran Cyber Security Information Act—H.R. 4246." May 5, 2000. http://www.cdt.org/security/000504davismoran .shtml.

4 Hon. Thomas M. Davis, Introduction of the Cyber Security Information Act of 2000, Wednesday, April 12, 2000. http://www.fas.org/sgp/congress/2000/cybersec.html.

5 Id.

6 Davis, op. cit, citing an October 1999 report issued by the General Accounting Office (GAO).

7 Personal and confidential conversation with a well-placed insider in the Office of Management and Budget.

8 http://www.cert.org.

9 The Federal Advisory Committee Act (FACA)(Pub. L. 92-463, 5 U.S.C., App.) was enacted by Congress in 1972 to ensure that advice rendered to the executive branch by the various advisory committees, task forces, boards, and commissions formed over the years by Congress and the president, be both objective and accessible to the public. http://www.gsa.gov/Portal/ gsa/ep/channelView.do?pageTypeId=8203&channelPage=/ep/channel/gsaOverview.jsp&chann elId=-13170 ; http://www.redlodgeclearinghouse.org/legislation/faca2.html.

10 Dempsey, op. cit.

11 On this aspect, OMB Watch, for which I worked at the time, parted company with other organizations that did not believe that identifying information that should be *required* to be provided was a proper goal of our joint efforts. We agreed to disagree on this aspect.

12 Public Law 107-296.

13 Dempsey, op. cit.

14 Kevin Poulsen, "Cyberterror Bill Keeps Company Secrets." *SecurityFocus,* April 4, 2000. http://www.securityfocus.com/news/17.

15 Hon. Thomas M. Davis, Introduction of the Cyber Security Information Act of 2000, Wednesday, April 12, 2000. http://www.fas.org/sgp/congress/2000/cybersec.html.

16 While this was not a perfect analogy, it did help staff and the public understand the stakes. And we did not know it at the time, but the tire industry has, indeed, been trying to keep information it submits to the government secret. In a November 2006 story in the *Washington Post,* "The Secret Auto Files," by Cindy Skrzycki (Tuesday, November 21, 2006, (D01) http://www.washingtonpost.com/wp-dyn/content/article/2006/11/20/ AR2006112001338.html.

17 See *Critical Mass Energy Project v. Nuclear Regulatory Commn,* 975 F.2d 871, 880 (D.C. Cir. 1992 (en banc), cert denied, 507 U.S. 984 (1993) ("Exemption 4 protects any financial or commercial information provided to the government on a voluntary basis if it is of a kind that the provider would not customarily release to the public.").

18 Critical Mass was only decided in one Circuit (the District of Columbia Circuit), so they argued they just could not rely on it—even though the vast majority of FOIA litigation occurs in that circuit. The DOJ's FOIA Update at the time said the decision "stands as the Exemption 4 precedent most directly applicable to determinations made under that exemption. ...the impact of Critical Mass is heightened by the fact that the D.C. Circuit is the circuit of "universal venue" under the FOIA—which means that any FOIA lawsuit can be filed there and adjudicated under its case law. Most significantly, this is generally so as well for "reverse FOIA" lawsuits filed to enjoin agency disclosure of business information." http://www.usdoj.gov/oip/foia_updates/Vol_XIV_2/page1.htm.

19 Joshua Dean, " E-gov fails, succeeds in tragedy's wake." GovExec.com, September 13, 2001. http://www.govexec.com/dailyfed/0901/091301j2.htm. Another interesting tidbit from the story (which noted the shut-down of the Office of Personnel Management's Web site on the 11th): "The Federal Emergency Management Agency (FEMA) kept its site operating Tuesday and worked through the night to update it with the most current information. "We treat the site as a key communications tool," said FEMA spokesman Marc Wolfson. "We give it a lot of attention during emergencies. We know from our statistics that when disaster hits people tend to turn to our website for information."

20 Joel Willemssen, Managing Director of Information Technology Issues for the General Accounting Office (GAO), now called the Government Accountability Office.

21 The report on the hearing is drawn from accounts in *TechLaw Journal,* http://www.techlawjournal.com/alert/2001/09/13.asp; Maureen Sirhal, *National Journal's Technology Daily* http://www.govexec.com/dailyfed/0901/091201td1.htm; and Diane Frank, *Federal Computer Week,* http://www.fcw.com/fcw/articles/2001/0910/web-sec-09-13-01.asp.

22 Roberta Gross, National Aeronautics and Space Administration (NASA) Inspector General.

23 http://www.ombwatch.org/info/cii/cii.signonltr.htm; http://www.ombwatch.org/info/cii/5.7.02signonltr.pdf.

24 FOIA experts will question the use of this term, as it has a specific meaning in specific statutes. I choose to use it anyway because it more accurately reflects the reality of the restriction—the information is mandatorily not releasable with *no review (an essential component of the FOIA process)* and no time limit.

25 Government Accountability Office, "Information Sharing: DHS Should Take Steps to Encourage More Widespread Use of Its Program to Protect and Share Critical Infrastructure Information," April 2006. GAO-06-383. http://www.gao.gov/new.items/d06383.pdf.

26 Government Accountability Office, "Critical Infrastructure Protection: DHS Leadership Needed to Enhance Cybersecurity." Statement of David A. Powner, Director, Information Technology Management Issues, before the House Committee on Homeland Security, Subcommittee on Economic Security, Infrastructure Protection, and Cybersecurity, September 13, 2006. GAO-06-1087T. http://www.gao.gov/new.items/d061087t.pdf.

27 Id.

28 Id.

29 Ryan Singel, "FCC Pulls Blinds on Wireless Data." *Wired News,* August 11, 2004. http://www.wired.com/news/wireless/0,1382,64528,00.html.

30 Id.

31 Government Accountability Office, "Internet Infrastructure DHS Faces Challenges in Developing a Joint Public/Private Recovery Plan." June 2006, GA0-06-672. http://www.gao.gov/new.items/d06672.pdf.

32 Business Roundtable, "Essential Steps to Strengthen America's Cyber Terrorism Preparedness" Washington, D.C., June 2006. www.businessroundtable.org/pdf/20060622002CyberRecon Final6106.pdf.

33 S. 622, The Restoration of Freedom of Information Act of 2005. http://frwebgate.access .gpo.gov/cgi-bin/getdoc.cgi?dbname=109_cong_bills&docid=f:s622is.txt.pdf.

34 Rafael Ayuso for Consumers Union.org. http://www.consumersunion.org/pub/ campaignnotinmyfood/002224.html.

35 http://www.consumersunion.org/cgi-bin/db-mt/mt-view.cgi/1/entry/954/print_entry.

36 In April 2002, the Food Safety and Inspection Service (FSIS) promulgated regulations defining the circumstances and criteria under which it would share product distribution information and retail customer lists with States and other federal agencies. 67 Federal Register 20009, April 24, 2002.

37 http://a257.g.akamaitech.net/7/257/2422/01jan20051800/edocket.access.gpo.gov/2005/ 05-9113.htm.

38 http://www.govexec.com/features/0704-15/0704-15newsanalysis3.htm.

39 http://www.gen.com/vo11_no1/daily-updates/35751-1.html.

40 Raphael Ayuso for Consumers Union.org. http://www.consumersunion.org/poub/campaign notinmyfood/02224.html.

41 http://www.consumersunion.org/cgi-bin/db-mt/mt-view.cgi/1/entry/954/print_entry.

42 http://a257.g.akamaitech.net/7/257/2422/01jan20051800/edocket.access.gpo.gov/2005/ 05-18760.htm.

43 http://www.lmaweb.com/infonewspast.html#34.

44 http://beef-mag.com/mag/beef_nais_vs_foia/index.html.

45 Jerry Hagstrom. "Conflict Surrounds Animal ID System." *Grand Forks Herald,* January 16, 2006. Posted on http://www.mycattle.com/article_print.cfm?storyid=18150.

46 http://www.lmaweb.com/infonewspast.html#101.

47 http://www.lmaweb.com/infonewspast.html#115.

48 Michael Arnone, "Industry group announces new animal ID database." *Federal Computer Week,* March 1, 2006. http://www.fcw.com/article92471-03-01-06-Web.

49 Marc Kaufman. "Agency Fought Retesting of Infected Cow" *Washington Post,* February 3, 2006; A07. http://www.washingtonpost.com/wp-dyn/content/article/2006/02/02/AR2006020202240.html.

50 David Thigpen. "Mad Cow: Are We Still Unprepared? *Time Online Edition,* March 16, 2006. http://www.time.com/time/health/article/0,8599,1174011,00.html.

51 Id.

52 Federal Register, Proposed Rules, March 7, 2006, V. 71, No. 44, pp. 11326-11328. http://a257.g.akamaitech.net/7/257/2422/01jan20061800/edocket.access.gpo.gov/2006/06-2125.htm.

CHAPTER 5

ACCESS RESTRICTED—

THE BLACK HOLE OF "SENSITIVE BUT UNCLASSIFIED" INFORMATION

Of course it is the case that not all government information should be publicly disseminated. Who would want to see the detailed layout of a nuclear facility plastered all over the Internet? Sometimes information should be classified—although, as I discuss in the next chapter, our system of classifying information is often overused or misused. At least in theory, classification (and declassification) of information has a basis in an executive order or statute, and there is a presumption that only a limited amount of information will be classified information. Not so for information marked as *sensitive but unclassified* (SBU), which is rapidly becoming a black hole for public information, with no procedural mechanisms for the review and release of materials so marked. In this chapter I will review

- a brief history of how the SBU categorization of information developed;

- how efforts to rein in this proliferating category have largely failed; and

- why SBU is a serious problem for those committed to public availability of government information.

I will conclude with some concrete examples of abuse of the SBU categorization.

In the FOIA discussion in Chapter 3, I talked about the Card White House memorandum of 2002 and the attached guidance from Information Security Oversight Office (ISOO) and the Department of Justice (DOJ). That discussion introduced the concept of sensitive but unclassified (SBU) information that requires "safeguarding." The SBU category did not arise, as you might have expected, with the Bush Administration or after September 11th. As with much that would restrict access, it arose—in its broad understanding—in the Reagan Administration, specifically with John Poindexter.

So let me first take you through a little history of the concept and then bring us back up to the current situation.

At the outset, let me say that at least some uses of control markings (such as SBU) for nonclassified information are intended to address real concerns about the release of information in relation to the need to protect privacy and security. In our current era, for instance, there is a need to share information about security risks and threats with state and local officials, but there is a concern about wider dissemination. One solution would be to classify the information—but that brings with it a raft of problems, including the need to obtain security clearances for everyone who might conceivably need to have access to the information. (See the discussion of classified information in the next chapter.) A work-around for this problem would be "tear sheets" for declassifying and sharing information.[1] A tear sheet refers to a way of formatting an official record so that classified information is physically separated from the unclassified information in the record that can be disclosed. This formatting makes it possible, literally or figuratively, to "tear off" the classified portion and to release the rest, and contrasts with the more conventional approach in which classified information and unclassified information are intermingled throughout the record—complicating the declassification and disclosure process.[2] Another possibility is the preparation of versions of information for widespread public dissemination.

Each of these would, however, require work and attention. Far easier to just mark it the information as some version of "sensitive but unclassified," SBU. But that easy solution brings with it its own set of problems.

Origins of the SBU Concept: The Reagan Era

The concept of "sensitive, but unclassified" information—information to which access would be restricted, even though not classified as "secret"—had a limited origin in federal agencies in the 1970s.[3] The term, which has never been defined in statutory law,[4] was used by agencies mostly for scientific and technical information used in research and scientific publication.

Then came the Reagan era. In 1984, National Security Decision Directive (NSDD) 145 directed that "sensitive, but unclassified, *government or government-derived information,* the loss of which could adversely affect the national security interest..." should be "protected in proportion to the threat of exploitation and the associated potential damage to the national security." (Emphasis added.) NSDD-145 did not define the term "sensitive, but unclassified," but explained that even unclassified information in the aggregate (the "mosaic theory") can "reveal highly classified and other sensitive information..." harmful to the national security interest.[5] (See box later in this chapter for more information on the "mosaic theory.")

The access community criticized the Directive for its lack of a precise definition of "sensitive, but unclassified"; it was we who argued that the Directive could wind up restricting possibly innocuous information needed to make policy as well as national security-related information. The "mosaic theory" which lay dormant, post-Reagan, until the George W. Bush administration was strongly opposed on the same grounds. As a GAO witness testified in 1985, "...unclassified sensitive civil agency information affecting national security interests" could include information obviously valuable for other state or federal policymakers: "hazardous materials information held by the Department of Transportation, flight safety information held by the Federal Aviation Administration, and monetary policy information held by the Federal Reserve." The same witness recommended that the administration more clearly define the types of information that fall under the Directive.[6] (This will be yet another instance of *"plus ça change..."*)

The Reagan Administration did respond to some of the criticism...though not in a particularly helpful way. In 1985, the Office of Management and Budget issued a circular (Circular A-130, "Management of Federal Information Resources")[7] clarifying the definition of "sensitive" information to include information "whose improper use or disclosure could adversely affect the ability of an agency to accomplish its mission..." This "clarification" did not, of course, do anything to allay the concerns about the term's overbreadth.

Having once having introduced the vague category of *"sensitive but unclassified,"* the administration—unsurprisingly—expanded the rationale for its use. On October 29, 1986, President Reagan's National Security Advisor, John Poindexter,[8] issued the "National Policy on Protection of Sensitive, but Unclassified Information in Federal Government Telecommunications and Automated Information Systems," NTISSP No. 2.[9] This policy document widened the rationale for safeguarding "sensitive, but unclassified" information beyond reasons of national security (as in NSDD-145) to include also "other government interests." Specifically, it defined sensitive, but unclassified information as being "information the disclosure, loss, misuse, alteration, or destruction of which could adversely affect national security or other Federal Government interests. National security interests are those unclassified matters that relate to the national defense or the foreign relations of the U.S. Government. *Other government interests are those related, but not limited to the wide range of government or government-derived economic, human, financial, industrial, agricultural, technological, and law enforcement information, as well as the privacy or confidentiality of personal or commercial proprietary information provided to the U.S. Government by its citizens."* (Emphasis added.)

This policy was to be applicable to all federal executive departments and agencies, including their contractors, that electronically transferred, stored, processed, or communicated sensitive, but unclassified information—in other words, most agencies by the mid-80s.

The library and other access communities immediately criticized National Telecommunications and Information Systems Policy (NTISSP) No. 2. The criticism focused on both the scope of information to be restricted and the fact that the policy would hand over responsibility for civilian information activities to the intelligence community. Nor did criticisms come only from the public sector. An Office of Technology Assessment (OTA)[10] commentary (issued in 1995)[11] noted that the policy potentially could restrict access to information that previously was available to the public. As the Deputy Director of the National Bureau of Standards (which became the National Institute of Standards and Technology, or NIST) stated, during 1987 hearings on the Computer Security Act, the policy's definition of sensitive information was a 'totally inclusionary definition. . .[t]here is no data that anyone would spend money on that is not covered by that definition."[12]

In something of a victory for public access, these criticisms led to the withdrawal of both NTISSP No. 2 in 1987 (attendant to passage of the Computer Security Act of 1987) and the official use of this definition of *"sensitive, but unclassified."* Unfortunately, some agencies, notably the Department of Energy, still use this broad conceptualization of SBU.[13]

SBU Develops in the Computer Security Context

The withdrawal of NTISSP No. 2 and the passage of the Computer Security Act of 1987[14] were steps forward for both genuine security for the information on the government's computers and for access. The Computer Security Act established a federal government computer-security program to protect sensitive information in federal government computer systems and to develop standards and guidelines for unclassified federal computer systems to facilitate such protection.

The Act defines "sensitive information" as information that could affect the national interest, conduct of federal programs, or individual privacy. Specifically

> "...any information, the loss, misuse, or unauthorized access to or modification of which could adversely affect the national interest or the conduct of Federal programs, or the privacy to which individuals are entitled under section 552a of title 5, United States Code (the Privacy Act), but which has not been specifically authorized under criteria established by an Executive order or an Act of Congress to be kept secret in the interest of national defense or foreign policy."

While this is still quite broad, it is more limited than the Poindexter definition in NTISSP No. 2. It does not include NTISSP's coverage of information that could adversely affect "other government interests," with "other" interests as defined on the previous page. Additionally, the safeguarding is limited to information in agency-identified computer systems.

Significantly, the Act explicitly says that defining information as "sensitive" does not authorize withholding that information if sought under FOIA.[15] Indeed, the report accompanying the legislation specifically states, "The designation of information as sensitive under the Computer Security Act is not a determination that the information is not subject to public disclosure."[16]

Moreover, the Act does not use the term *sensitive but unclassified,* or specify how an agency should go about identifying or protecting the "sensitive" information referenced. However, guidance issued in 1992 by the National Institute of Standards and Technology (NIST) provides some guidance that agencies have been using to manage the ill-defined category of SBU. This guidance reiterated that interpretation of the Computer Security Act's definition of "sensitive" is, ultimately, an agency responsibility, and states that typically, protecting sensitive information means providing for one or more of the following:

- Confidentiality: disclosure of the information must be restricted to designated parties;

- Integrity: The information must be protected from errors or unauthorized modification; and

- Availability: The information must be available within some given time frame (i.e., protected against destruction).[17]

The emphasis on the responsibility of agencies to define "sensitive" information brings us down to our current predicament: in fulfillment of this responsibility, for example, "some individual agencies have created internal 'Limited Official Use' or 'For Official Use Only' designations for certain types of unclassified information having confidentiality requirements. In either case, however, the selection of specific security controls is usually left to the agency's or the individual user's discretion."[18]

Sensitive But Unclassified: After 9/11

As noted earlier, in March 2002, the White House memorandum (the Card Memorandum) and the attached guidance from the Information Security Oversight Office (ISOO) and the DOJ Office of Information and Privacy reinstated the broader Poindexter-era understanding of SBU by re-introducing the concept of *"sensitive but unclassified"* information to contexts beyond computer security.

In late September 2002, officials from the Office of Management and Budget (OMB) requested a meeting with representatives (including the author) of various public interest groups concerned with public access to government information. The purpose was to discuss OMB's upcoming efforts to define and develop policy guidance on *"sensitive but unclassified"* markings for government information, as requested by the White House Office of Homeland Security. We were told that the intended purpose of the SBU category was to preserve confidentiality without formal classification and to permit the sharing of such sensitive information with federal and local law enforcement or emergency response personnel who do not hold security clearances. At that meeting, Glenn Schlarman, then Chief of OMB's Information Policy and Technology Branch, endeavored to keep the government's focus on the protections (and limitations on scope) provided by the Computer Security Act of 1987 and to reassure the public interest community that would be the scope of the policy guidance. The Act had had such a limited impact on public accessibility of government information that many of the public interest participants at the meeting were largely unfamiliar with it. There was, however, palpable tension between the perspectives of the OMB officials and those of the White House representatives.

Nothing came out of OMB in the ensuing years. The agencies, however, took the permission given them by the Computer Security Act and proliferated new control markings. The "Secrecy Report Card" table below list federal agencies using SBU designations.

The Secrecy Report Card:
Sensitive but Unclassified Designations in Use at Selected Federal Agencies

#	Designation	Agency
1	Applied Technology *Department of Energy	(DOE)
2	Attorney-Client Privilege Department of Commerce (Commerce),	*DOE
3	Business Confidential	*DOE
4	Budgetary Information Environmental Protection Agency	(EPA)
5	Census Confidential	Commerce
6	Confidential Information Protection and Statistical Efficiency Act Information (CIPSEA)	(SSA)
7	Computer Security Act Sensitive Information (CSASI)	(HHS)
8	Confidential	Labor
9	Confidential Business Information (CBI)	Commerce, EPA
10	Contractor Access Restricted Information (CARI)	HHS
11	Copyrighted Information	*DOE
12	Critical Energy Infrastructure Information (CEII) Fed'l Energy Regulatory Comm'n	(FERC)
13	Critical Infrastructure Information Office of Personnel Management	(OPM)
14	DEA Sensitive Department of Justice	(DOJ)
15	DOD Unclassified Controlled Nuclear Information Department of Defense	(DOD)
16	Draft	EPA
17	Export Controlled Information	*DOE
18	For Official Use Only (FOUO)	Commerce, DOD, Department of Education, EPA, General Services Administration, HHS, DHS, Department of Housing and Urban Development (HUD), DOJ, Labor, OPM, SSA, and the Department of Transportation (DOT)
19	For Official Use Only Law Enforcement Sensitive	DOD
20	Freedom of Information Act (FOIA)	EPA
21	Government Confidential Commercial Information	*DOE
22	High-Temperature Superconductivity Pilot Center Information	*DOE
23	In Confidence	*DOE
24	Intellectual Property	*DOE
25	Law Enforcement Sensitive	Commerce, EPA, DHS, DOJ, HHS, Labor, OPM
26	Law Enforcement Sensitive/Sensitive	DOJ
27	Limited Distribution Information	DOD
28	Limited Official Use (LOU)	DHS, DOJ, Department of Treasury

29	Medical records	EPA
30	Non-Public Information	FERC
31	Not Available National Technical Information Service	Commerce
32	Official Use Only (OUO)	DOE,SSA, Treasury
33	Operations Security Protected Information (OSPI)	HHS
34	Patent Sensitive Information	*DOE
35	Predecisional Draft	*DOE
36	Privacy Act Information	*DOE, EPA
37	Privacy Act Protected Information (PAPI)	HHS
38	Proprietary Information	*DOE, DOJ
39	Protected Battery Information	*DOE
40	Protected Critical Infrastructure Information (PCII)	DHS
41	Safeguards Information Nuclear Regulatory Commission	NRC
42	Select Agent Sensitive Information (SASI)	HHS
43	Sensitive But Unclassified (SBU)	Commerce, HHS, NASA, National Science Foundation (NSF), Department of State, U.S. Agency for International Development (USAID)
44	Sensitive Drinking Water Related Information (SDWRI)	EPA
45	Sensitive Information DOD, U.S. Postal Service	USPS
46	Sensitive Instruction	SSA
47	Sensitive Internal Use	*DOE
48	Sensitive Unclassified Non-Safeguards Information	NRC
49	Sensitive Nuclear Technology	*DOE
50	Sensitive Security Information (SSI)	DHS, DOT, U.S. Department of Agriculture (USDA)
51	Sensitive Water Vulnerability Assessment Information	EPA
52	Small Business Innovative Research Information	*DOE
53	Technical Information	DOD
54	Trade Sensitive Information	Commerce
55	Unclassified Controlled Nuclear Information (UCNI)	DOE
56	Unclassified National Security-Related	*DOE

Source: GAO analysis of agency responses, March 2006: Information Sharing: The Federal Government Needs to Establish Policies and Processes for Sharing Terrorism-Related and Sensitive but Unclassified Information: GAO-06-385 http://www.gao.gov/new.items/d06385.pdf.

Note: The designations shown in the Secrecy Report Card table were reported to OpenTheGovernment.org by the 26 agencies in our survey as their sensitive but unclassified designations. Three of the agencies reported that they do not have sensitive but unclassified designations. The list may not be all-inclusive because of individual agency interpretations of what constitutes a designation. For example, agencies may use the designation "draft," but only one reported it as a designation. In addition, DOE has attempted to limit the number of designations it uses, but reported to us that some staff continue to use unofficial designations that they refer to as ad hoc designations. DOE's ad hoc designations have an asterisk symbol in front of them in the table.

The Information Sharing Environment (ISE) Attempts to Limit—or at Least Get a Handle on—SBU

In its September 2005 conference report (House Report 109-241) on the Department of Homeland Security Appropriations Act, 2006 (H.R. 2360),[19] congress had expressed concern about the proliferation of—and lack of control over—such SBU-type markings. In the report, Congress instructed the Department of Homeland Security (DHS) to clarify and tighten its procedures for generating *"sensitive security information"* (SSI) (another type of "sensitive but unclassified" information.) The report instructed the Department to reduce subjective factors in marking documents as SSI and to provide Congress with the titles of all documents that are so designated, noting that "because of insufficient management controls, information that should be in the public domain may be unnecessarily withheld from public scrutiny."[20] The congressional conferees directed DHS to "promulgate guidance that includes common but extensive examples of SSI" so as to "eliminate judgment ...in the application of the SSI marking."[21]

In December 2005, *Secrecy News* reported[22] that a U.S. Government official with subject matter expertise, speaking on condition of anonymity noted, "as is true with so many other subjects, they have done nothing with it." A government-wide policy on protecting a DHS control marking created by the Homeland Security Act—Sensitive Homeland Security Information (SHSI), "has been periodically discussed, pushed close to some action, and then sent back for further study. There are a dozen hard and fast deadlines that have been missed on this whole subject. I think it's fair to say it's dead. The concept is not dead but it's highly unlikely anything will come of it."

The same "U.S. Government official" also commented on a separate interagency initiative under way to define and regulate the category of "sensitive but unclassified" information. "That is far too big a task to come to fruition," the official predicted. Given that agencies were unable to reach consensus on the definition of terrorism-related SHSI, it will be "exponentially more difficult" to come to agreement on the vastly larger and more amorphous domain of "sensitive but unclassified" information, he said.[23]

This initiative was likely one created in June 2005, when the White House issued a memorandum to implement § 1016 of the Intelligence Reform and Terrorism Prevention Act of 2004, which created an Information Sharing Environment (ISE) to share terrorism information among federal, state, and local officials. This office was given the responsibility of developing the standard procedures. The law designates a program manager "responsible for information sharing across the federal government." The Program Manager, Thomas McNamara, was expected to make his recommendations in June 2006.

In the same month that the "government official" made the comments about the great difficulty of containing the proliferation of agency-initiated control marking, President Bush ordered that standards be created by the end of 2006 for designating, marking, and handling sensitive but unclassified (SBU) information. According to the Memorandum[24] issued on December 16, 2005, executive branch agencies are to develop standard procedures for handling of SBU information.

> *"To promote and enhance the effective and efficient acquisition, access, retention, production, use, management, and sharing of Sensitive But Unclassified (SBU) information, including homeland security information, law enforcement information, and terrorism information, procedures and standards for designating, marking, and handling SBU information must be standardized across the Federal Government."*[25]

There was no disagreement in many sectors that these standards were critically needed. As noted above, in September 2005 Congress had expressed concern about the proliferation—and lack of control over—SBU-type markings.

In March 2006, the Government Accountability Office, at the request of Senator Susan Collins and Representatives Tom Davis, Todd Platts, and Christopher Shays, reported[26] that agencies use 56 different "sensitive but unclassified" categories to restrict information—"16 of which belong to one agency." That includes such categories as "sensitive drinking water-related information," "not available national technical information service," and "protected battery information." This number is higher than the control markings that OpenTheGovernment.org had identified in its 2005 Secrecy Report Card. (See the box entitled, "Some SBU Designations," at the end of this chapter.)

In May 2006,[27] Thomas McNamara, who (as noted above) had just recently become program manager for the Information Sharing Environment (ISE), confirmed that there was a serious problem with the withholding of government information under SBU, SSI, and similar nonclassified control markings. He told the House Homeland Security Intelligence Subcommittee[28] that federal agencies do not have any legal justification for most information they withhold from the public: "There is, quite frankly, much that has no legal basis and doesn't deserve a legal basis. We should be getting that stuff out." McNamara also indicated that even GAO's number (above) was too low. He told the lawmakers that he had found that agencies use at least 65 different categories, and possibly 70.

And note that this number of SBU-type markings keeps rising. At a meeting with representatives of the public interest community (including the author) in late 2006, the ISE officers said there were about 16 statutes or regulations authorizing these markings—yielding 30 marking categories—plus another 70 that were just created by agencies without any clear authority.[29]

An additional problem, as many in the access community have noted, is that there are no procedural mechanisms for the review and release of materials thus marked "sensitive but unclassified" by government officials. SBU designations are especially problematic because there are no procedural mechanisms for the review and release of materials thus marked by government officials. This lack distinguishes them from the national security classification system and from the exemption system of FOIA. There are no limits on who can impose these markings or what they must do (if anything) to justify them. As there is no process for review and release, there is really no way to appeal the withholding of information. These control markings create a black hole into which information disappears: both that information which might be embarrassing or inconvenient and that information which may need protection for some time-delimited period.

Indeed, most of the 26 federal agencies surveyed by GAO reported they had no firm policies for such designations or individuals specifically authorized to impose them. State and local first responders told GAO investigators that the multiplicity of designations and lack of common federal standards "not only causes confusion but leads to an alternating feast or famine of information" that either left them in the dark or overwhelmed them with identical information from multiple federal sources.

McNamara has noted that his preliminary assessments show there are no government-wide definitions, procedures, or training for designating information. As the GAO found, "some of these marking and handling procedures are not only inconsistent, but are contradictory," and "many use the same terms, but with widely different definitions, or use different terminology or restrictive phrases for what is essentially the same information."[30] McNamara has indicated that one of his missions is to develop "a rational, limited set of categories"—as low as six—under which information is withheld. Most information that is now withheld or would be withheld could then be made public.

McNamara has continued to work on this problem, but as of the date of this book's publication, there has been no resolution. In his testimony[31] in April 2007, he reported that

> *"Among the twenty departments and agencies we have surveyed, there are at least 107 unique markings and more than 131 different label-ing and handling processes and procedures for SBU information. Even when SBU information carries the same label marking (e.g., For Official Use Only), storage and dissemination are inconsistent across Federal agencies and departments.... The result is an unmanageable collection of policies that leave both the producers and users of SBU information unable to know how a piece of information will be controlled as it moves through the Federal government...."*

McNamara noted that "[the] lack of a single, rationalized, standardized, and simplified SBU framework does contribute to improper handling or overclassification." At that hearing, he promised that the "Recommendations for Presidential Guideline 3 are coming to completion," but gave no date.[32]

SBU Finds Its Home in the Homeland Security Act

The new Homeland Security Act has consolidated many of the problems I've discussed above concerning the poorly defined and overbroad category of "sensitive but unclassified" information. The Act instructs the President to "identify and safeguard homeland security information that is sensitive but unclassified" (§ 892).[33] The Act created a new control marking, *Sensitive Homeland Security Information* (SHSI), to be used to restrict general access to government information relating to "terrorism," or that a "terrorist" or "terrorist organization" could use to carry out a "terrorist activity." None of these terror-related categories are defined in the Act, however. (The USA PATRIOT Act has some definitions of these categories; they are, unfortu-nately, circular—e.g., a terrorist is someone who commits a terrorist act.)

Like the DOJ/ISOO Memorandum, the Homeland Security Act fails to define the term "sensitive" when it restricts access to information, thus enabling its use to justify expansive new restrictions on the disclosure of unclassified information. Its inclusion in the Act is noteworthy in light of the Card and DOJ/ISOO memoranda discussed above, and the fact that *"while 'sensitive' information has been referenced in a number of laws such as the Computer Security Act of 1987, this is apparently the first time that the problematic category of 'sensitive but unclassified' information has appeared in a federal statute."[34]*

In May 2004, DHS issued a directive imposing extraordinary new access controls on unclassified information that it deems *"for official use only"* (FOUO), a subset of sensitive but unclassified information.[35] This directive requires that FOUO information be shared only with those who have been determined to have a "need to know." The DHS directive provides a form that allows any federal employee or contractor to restrict information as "official use only," simply by filling out the form and submitting it to DHS. The form generally follows the definition of "sensitive" information in the Computer Security Act of 1987; it defines as "sensitive" any information that could violate a person's privacy, or "adversely affect the national interest or the conduct of federal programs." It is not, however, limited to information contained in government information systems. Again, as noted earlier, this definition is a much lower barrier than "damaging national security," and it is one that could be so broadly interpreted as to include information important to oversight and accountability.

The directive also requires "DHS employees, contractors, consultants and others to whom access" is given to "execute a DHS Form 11000-6, Sensitive But Unclassified Information Non-Disclosure Agreement (NDA), upon initial assignment to DHS," and makes clear that "other individuals not assigned to or contractually obligated to DHS, but to whom access to information will be granted, may be requested to execute an NDA as determined by the program manager to which they will have access." Violation of the agreements could result in administrative, disciplinary, criminal and/or civil penalties.

The attitude embodied by this directive—that any information held by DHS (an agency with a vast field of authority) was presumptively unavailable to the public anyone without some undefined, but DHS-determined, "need to know"—was highlighted in December 2004, when it was reported[36] that DHS had asked *congressional aides* to sign nondisclosure agreements that would prohibit them from publicly disclosing information received from DHS even though the information was unclassified. It was not clear what the terms of the agreement were or which staffers were being asked to sign it. Congressional offices from both parties refused to sign the forms.

In early January 2005, the DHS rescinded the controversial policy.[37] The Department said that the "NDA's previously signed by DHS employees...will no longer be valid" and that "DHS will take reasonable steps to retrieve these documents and destroy them."

The nondisclosure agreements still apply to contractors, and other controversial caveats of the original directive remain intact, including the right of employees and contractors to mark something "For Official Use Only;" the vast definition (or, rather, lack of definition) of sensitive but unclassified information; and the possibility to cover up waste, fraud, and abuse by marking something "For Official Use Only."[38]

It is important to note, once again, that the information that DHS sought to control (and does control for contractors) is not limited to that needed to be secured in computers and information systems. It is information that an unknowable number of first, second, and third responders may need to know in the event of a catastrophic attack or disaster. Essentially, as with all the rest of government-declared "sensitive" information, the rationale is "because I say so."

As I said above, these control markings—what some call "pseudo-classifications"—constitute a black hole in the public's access to information. Some portions of marked information may need to be safeguarded and may need, temporarily, limited sharing. No process exists, though, for the public to even be aware of and request review of such information—as there is with both FOIA and classification. Moreover, even government officials face "an unmanageable collection of policies that leave both the producers and users of SBU information unable to know how a piece of information will be controlled as it moves through the Federal government.... "[39]

Here's Why SBU's "Need to Know" Is a Problem

So far, most of my discussion of "sensitive but unclassified" (SBU) information has been largely theoretical. But its impact on you, as a member of the public, is anything but. Think about it. Your government is asking: Do *you* have what it takes to be allowed to obtain information created or collected by the federal government in the course of its responsibilities for carrying out the laws? Can *you* be trusted to handle the truth? Increasingly, the culture of access, led by the expansion of the SBU concept, is moving from "right-to-know" to "legitimate need-to-know." This means, of course, that those controlling the information get to decide if you get to have it. They base that decision, variously, on who you are, what you plan to do with the information, and whether it could conceivably be used by a "terrorist." (I put this in quotation marks because terms such as "terror" and "terrorist" are often invoked, rarely defined, and usually intended to foreclose discussion, short-circuit review, and preclude appeal.) Appendix A at the end of this chapter provides a sampling of memoranda from the U.S. Embassy in Baghdad to the Secretary of State. The memoranda are all categorized as SBU.

What I have assembled below is an illustrative—not comprehensive—mosaic of restrictions on public access to government information. Compiled, they create an increasingly troubling picture of unaccountability mixed with some legitimate, but probably overstated, concerns with bits of information.

The Mosaic Theory

The mosaic theory posits that "[the] business of foreign intelligence gathering in this age of computer technology is more akin to the construction of a mosaic than it is to the management of a cloak-and-dagger affair. Thousands of bits and pieces of seemingly innocuous information can be analyzed and fitted into place to reveal with startling clarity how the unseen whole must operate." *Halkin v. Helms*, 598 F.2d 1, 8 (D.C. Cir. 1978). As discussed earlier in this chapter, this concept was promoted by John Poindexter in the 1980s, during the Reagan Administration. Access advocates find the mosaic theory as a reason for restricting access to information troubling because, while it is true (especially in the digital age), there is almost no useful government—or private sector—information that would not fall within its scope.

2006 CDC—Sensitive By Aggregation

In February, the Centers for Disease Control and Prevention (CDC) became the latest agency to articulate a policy on "Sensitive But Unclassified" (SBU) information that is to be withheld from disclosure, including "Sensitive by Aggregation": the mosaic theory redux.

The term "sensitive by aggregation" refers to the fact that information on one Web site may seem unimportant, but, when combined with information from other Web sites, it may form a larger and more complete picture than was intended or desired. Similarly, the compilation of a large amount of information together on one site may increase the sensitivity of that information and make it more likely that the Web site will be accessed by those seeking information that can be used against CDC.[40]

An earlier version of this document did not contain the designation "Sensitive by Aggregation."[41] The inclusion of the new category, as with all uses of the mosaic theory, makes any information on any Web site potentially SBU—an extraordinarily broad overreach.

2005 Names and Work Locations of Federal Civilian Workers

In December, the Transactional Records Access Clearinghouse (TRAC)[42] filed suit in the United States District Court, Northern District of New York. The suit claimed that the Office of Personnel Management (OPM) was withholding, without explanation, the names and work locations of about 900,000 of its civilian workers—over 40% of the federal civilian work-force—including information on employees in over 250 different agencies, such as the Environmental Protection Agency (EPA), the Occupational Safety and Health Administration (OSHA), and the Federal Emergency Management Agency (FEMA), and 650 different occupations. As TRAC argues, since 1816, the federal government has publicly named its employ-ees, their job category, salary, and workplace. The first entry in the 1816 register[43] was James Madison, identified as president of the United States in Washington at a salary of $25,000—and born in Virginia.

Since 1989, TRAC, using the FOIA, has obtained the data on compact discs every three months and has posted online a database with the name, work location, salary, and job category of all 2.7 million federal civilian workers (except those in some law enforcement agencies). The data are often used by reporters and government watchdog groups to monitor policies and detect waste or abuse. The last complete data set provided by OPM covered 2003. Since then, all records of civilian employees of the Department of Defense have been withheld, and name and duty locations have been with-held for an estimated 150,000 other civilian workers. (As of the date of publication, there have been no developments in this case.)

Is this an example of information being withheld because it is SBU? It is hard to say, because OPM has stonewalled TRAC and has not explained its reasons. But the Defense Department had previously stopped disseminating a telephone directory—of the *work* phone numbers and *office* locations of Pentagon employees—due, they say, to security concerns. Scott Armstrong, a senior investigator for the Senate Watergate committee and a former *Washington Post* reporter[44] tells of how, during the Iran-Contra scandals, reporters used the phone books to track the movements of certain players around from office to office and make surmises about relationships (and possible cover-ups).[45] That is, I guess, dangerous information now. It is also a way to control access to government officials so, as I discuss in Chapters 8 and 9, only the party line is given out and only approved phone calls get through.

2005 Public Access to Aeronautical Data To Be Blocked

In November, the National Geospatial-Intelligence Agency (NGA) announced its final decision to withdraw from public access, beginning in January 2006, extensive databases of aeronautical information that have long been publicly available.[46] NGA had initially given protecting the information from access by terrorists as the first of many reasons for withdrawing the maps. The final announcement revealed it was really about copyright concerns raised by foreign data sources. Industry experts said the information of concern could be redacted and the rest made available for public access.[47] Some companies will continue to have access, however, so the public can still *buy* the previously free information.

2005 Nuclear Plant Locations: Don't Fly Near Them— But Where They Are Is Secret

Ever since September 11, 2001, the federal government has advised airplane pilots not to fly near 100 nuclear power plants around the country unless they want to be forced down by fighter jets. But pilots said there was a hitch in the instructions: aviation security officials refuse to disclose the precise location of the plants because they consider that *"SSI"*—Sensitive Security Information.[48] So, the Aircraft Owners and Pilots Association sat down with a commercial mapping company, and plotted the exact geographical locations of the plants from data found on the Internet and in libraries. It made the information available to its 400,000 members on its Web site— until officials from the Transportation Security Administration asked them to take the information down. So—the government won't tell you where the plants are that you can't fly near, you are not allowed to share any information that you discover—and if you go near the plants, they will force you out of the air.

2005 You Can Get It, but Not Online: Non-Internet Public

In June, following a growing trend, FERC issued a rule on "Non-Internet Public (NIP) Designation" that endorsed the notion that some public information that is readily available in hard copy should not be disclosed in digital form: "Anyone wishing to obtain NIP may get it upon request from the Public Reference Room or from Commission staff; however it is not made available to the public through the Commission's Internet site."[49]

The government seems to believe that if you make the information difficult to obtain, no one who "should not have it" will be able to find and obtain it. The reality is that it is ordinary people—who want to protect their families, their property, and their communities—who will not have the time and resources to travel to reading rooms. And, in any event, the public should be able to have anonymous access to government information unless it is classified or they have requested it through FOIA (in which case their access is not, of course, anonymous). (And for related reasoning by the GAO, see "2004 Information about Judges' Conflicts of Interest," below.)

2005 Toxic Milk?

In May 2005, a scientific paper discussing the possibility of a terrorist attack on the U.S. milk supply was scheduled for publication in the prestigious *Proceedings of the National Academy of Sciences* (PNAS) until the Department of Health and Human Services (HHS) intervened, calling it a "road map for terrorists," and asked the journal to withdraw the paper.[50] The paper in question was a mathematical model of the possible consequences of the malicious insertion of botulinum toxin into the U.S. milk supply. In response to the HHS objections, PNAS agreed to delay publication for an indefinite period.

Despite the HHS concerns, one of the paper's authors, Stanford business professor Lawrence M. Wein, went on to make his case on the *New York Times* op-ed page on May 30, 2005 in a piece entitled "Got Toxic Milk?"[51] presenting the conclusions of his unpublished manuscript and explaining the concern in pretty substantial detail. But a subsequent review[52] of Dr. Wein's paper strongly disagreed. (Interestingly, the *Times* refused to publish this review, stating that as a policy matter it did not publish op-ed rebuttals.) The review found Wein's paper "flawed in its understanding of terrorist capabilities, his other assumptions in error, and the conclusion therefore both erroneous and inflammatory." The review's authors noted that there is "an extraordinary degree of uncertainty associated with Dr. Wein's estimates. The analysis of real and practical intelligence reveals a vastly different, more complicated, and much less frightening picture." The review's authors summarized:

> *"Thinking about the unthinkable has become a way of life in the war on terror. But too often, in our opinion, have the debates on securing the country against the threat of bioterrorism degenerated into worst case*

*scenarios which assume an easy and accomplished technical capability
for mass killing already or soon to be in the hands of terrorists.*"[53]

Sounds like a pretty useful public debate, doesn't it? PNAS agreed; it
published the paper in July 2005. In an explanatory editorial, PNAS argued
that "scientific free-for-all in the open literature leads to a refinement of the
original findings that will, over time, always make any analyses much more
reliable and better understood."[54]

2005 IRS Statistical Tables Harmful to Homeland Security

In April 14, TRAC filed a federal lawsuit against the Internal Revenue
Service (IRS) for illegally withholding information about its operations. The
IRS claimed, without substantiation, that some of the unclassified informa-
tion would compromise homeland security if released to the public.

The IRS has for almost 30 years (due to a consent decree from 1976
TRAC litigation) released statistical tables and other information that
enabled the public, Congress, tax lawyers, and others to make their own
judgments about how the agency is enforcing the tax laws. Starting in 2004,
however, the IRS refused to comply with the court order and failed to release
the data, asserting that it would have to be specially compiled since the
agency no longer keeps basic statistics about audits, appeals, and collection
activities that would provide details to support the agency's broad assertions
about IRS current practices. The IRS denied TRAC's three FOIA requests
for information about the IRS's database. In denying one request that sought
release of an IRS manual (that had in the past been available on the IRS's
public Web site) describing information systems used to compile statistical
information and numerical measures used to analyze the agency's operations,
the IRS cited "new federal security requirements."

In 2007, the IRS modified its recent closed-door policy and provided
TRAC with statistical data from an agency management system called Table
37. The agency's action was reluctant, taken in response to an April 4, 2006
ruling by Federal Judge Marsha J. Pechman of the Western District of
Washington. The ruling instructed the IRS to comply with a 1976 order
from the same court.[55]

TRAC reports, though, that the IRS is still dragging its feet on providing
both the prompt and complete monthly updates the court order requires, and
continues to sit on most of TRAC's requests—many pending now for two and
a half years. According to TRAC, "[the] trickle of official IRS FOIA responses
that TRAC is beginning to receive signal IRS's continuing intransigence and

unwillingness to provide public access to detailed statistics about many agency activities, along with a closed-door policy on releasing any meaningful results from taxpayer-financed studies on how our tax system is functioning."[56]

2005 Department of Transportation Expands SSI Authority

In January, in a Final Rule,[57] the Department of Transportation (DOT) expanded the authority of its senior officials to designate information related to transportation security as *"sensitive security information"* (SSI) to which public access is prohibited. The authority was extended to the administrators of all DOT agencies, the General Counsel, and the Director of Intelligence and Security. This expansion of authority—particularly as broadly as the administrators of *all* DOT agencies—is troubling, as it runs counter to efforts in the executive branch to bring the proliferation of these markings under control and puts unknown types and amounts of information into the black hole of sensitive but unclassified markings.

2004 Geospatial Information Shutdown Documented

A study in 2004 by the RAND Corporation found that the U.S. government has closed 36 Web sites and over 600 public databases (and that's just counting those with geospatial information) containing much information that was not critical for terrorists and that could have been obtained from other nongovernmental sources.[58]

2004 DHS and the National Environmental Policy Act

DHS proposed an ambiguous directive that can be read to provide that SBU categorization can serve as a basis for not releasing Environmental Impact Statements to the public as required by the National Environmental Policy Act (NEPA).[59] The final management directive[60] did indeed do so, declaring that sensitive security information (SSI) and protected critical infrastructure information CII, along with classified information will, where possible, be segregated into a nonpublic appendix. "If exempted material cannot be segregated, or if segregation would leave essentially meaningless material, the DHS component will withhold the entire NEPA analysis from the public. The protected NEPA analysis may be shared with appropriately cleared officials in CEQ [the Council on Environmental Quality, a White House body], EPA, and within DHS." In other words, *we regulators* will decide whether to comply with the law about access to Environmental

Impact Statements; in this, DHS is following the tone set by the second President Bush in his signing statements. (For more on signing statements, see Chapter 7.)

2004 Birth and Death Records

Buried within the Intelligence Reform and Terrorism Prevention Act of 2004 is a regulation that could lead to barring most public access to birth and death certificates for 70 to 100 years.[61] The law was passed in response to the 9/11 Commission's recommendation that "[the] federal government should set standards for the issuance of birth certificates, and sources of identification such as drivers' licenses." Prior to the passage of the Act, there were no national standards for the issuance of these vital records; rather, issuance was determined on a state-by-state basis.

Among other things, the Act requires that the Secretary of Health and Human Services "establish requirements for proof and verification of identity as a condition of issuance of a birth certificate, with additional security measures for the issuance of a birth certificate for a person who is not the applicant." However, it is up to the state to determine how nonofficial copies of birth certificates are issued.[62]

The National Center for Health Statistics (NCHS) is drafting minimum standards for vital records in response to a mandate in the Intelligence Reform and Terrorism Prevention Act of 2004 to be released in early 2007. The proposed regulations are expected to restrict access to state birth and death records. In anticipation of the NCHS standards, by early 2006 at least 12 states had sealed off or severely restricted access to birth records.[63]

The reason now given for the standards and restrictions on access to the records is to prevent identity theft. This is, however, a shift (to play into current public fears) from the reasons given at the time of passage—to prevent undocumented immigrants from obtaining driver's licenses and because a couple of the September 11th terrorists were able to obtain driver's licenses in Virginia.

As David Carlson, president of the Society of Professional Journalists, put it, though, "Birth and death records are among the most basic of public records. They are used by children trying to track their birth parents, by families researching their genealogy, by scientists tracking health trends, by journalists, and in a hundred more legitimate ways. Restricting access to them to solve identity theft is like closing up an entire library because a book was stolen."[64]

These records are not being marked in any manner, so they do not technically qualify as SBU, but the effect is likely to be the same. They will only be available to those with a government-sanctioned need to know.

2004 Results of Inspections of Nuclear Reactors Withheld From Public

In August, the Nuclear Regulatory Commission announced that while it will "continue to inspect and assess physical security of nuclear facilities, the results will no longer be made publicly available upon issuance" and "will no longer be updated on the agency's web site."[65]

2004 Wireless Communications Outages

In August 2004, *Wired News*[66] reported that "[the] telecoms [wireless telecommunications companies] and the Department of Homeland Security argued that information about wireless communications *outages* could be used by terrorists to plot attacks on communications systems and persuaded the Federal Communications Commission (FCC) to keep the reports secret and immune from the Freedom of Information Act." Michael Powell, then-Chairman of the FCC, said, "In order to prevent this information from falling into hostile hands, the commission has created appropriate protections for this data."

2004 Information about Judges' Conflicts of Interest (and other GAO restrictions)

In August, the *Washington Post* reported[67] that, "Nearly 600 times in recent years, a judicial committee acting in private has stripped information from reports intended to alert the public to conflicts of interest involving federal judges." Specialists in judicial ethics said they were startled at the breadth of the excisions—and particularly that the material cut included financial information that appeared to present little safety risk. The *Post* report was based on a Government Accountability Office (GAO) report, which is now itself unavailable on GAO's Web site. GAO said that, in response to requests from the judiciary and the Marshals Service, it is deviating from standard practice and making its study available only on specific request, because its findings are "sensitive." In a letter attached to the study, Marshals Service Director Benigno G. Reyna asked that it "not be made available to the general public via the Internet."[68]

GAO's new restriction policy isn't limited to the reports about judges, however. GAO has a restriction category—NI or non-Internet—for some of its reports.[69] According to staff on one of the congressional oversight committees, the criterion for its application appears to be simply that an agency requests this designation. You can still get the restricted reports faxed to you or request them in print—but you can't get them on the Internet. This is one of the silliest apparent applications of the mosaic theory—or, alternatively, a notion popular with the courts, "practical obscurity" (if it is hard to get, it is protected)—seen to date. It is, moreover, completely inappropriate for a congressional agency to impose it on no other—and more transparent—basis than an executive or as above, judicial branch agency request.

2004 Secret Public Testimony

When a top Federal Aviation Administration official testified in 2004 before the 9/11 commission, his remarks were broadcast live nationally. But when the administration included a transcript in a recent report on threats to commercial airliners, the testimony was heavily edited. "How do you redact something that is part of the public record?" asked Rep. Carolyn Maloney, (D-NY) at a recent hearing on the problems of government overclassification. Among the specific words blacked out were the seemingly innocuous phrase, "we are hearing this, this, this, this and this."

Government officials could not explain why the words were withheld, other than to note that they were designated SSI.[70]

2003 DoD to Withhold Information of "Questionable Value" to Public

In December, the Pentagon Office of the Inspector General (OIG) issued a new policy that lists five broadly defined categories of data that "will not be available to the general public via the OIG DoD Web site": "classified" and "for official use only" data, "information not specifically approved for public release," information "of questionable value to the general public," and information "for which worldwide dissemination poses an unacceptable risk to national security or threatens the safety and privacy of the men and women of the armed forces."[71] The most worrisome of these is the category of "questionable value to the general public." As Steve Aftergood notes, "In one sense, all of the Inspector General's publications are of 'questionable value to the general public.' Few members of the general public are likely to read the

145

OIG's detailed audit reports. But they are often of great value to the press and public interest organizations that specialize in defense policy."[72]

And for More Information? Good Luck!...

OMB Watch has the most comprehensive inventory (made in 2001–early 2002) of how agencies imposed restrictions on unclassified information, some even before the term "sensitive but unclassified" began to be used for other than computer security–related concerns in nearly twenty years, for the period of 2001 and early 2002.[73] Unfortunately, this inventory has not been updated since 2002.

In Conclusion

As discussed above, as this book goes to press there is a process in place to rein in the proliferation and use of control markings such as SBU. That process, though initiated by the White House, seems to lack the forceful leadership from the Executive Office of the President that is needed to move it to conclusion. The problem is not with the good intentions and efforts of the office of the Program Manager of the Information Sharing Environment.[74] The rumor around Washington is that the Program Manager is meeting with intransigence from the agencies that will have to give up some control—and power. The public access community has so far discouraged Congress from weighing in with legislation to impose control—because the problem is complex and one size probably will not fit all agencies, and the process in place should be allowed to run its course—but our patience and theirs is wearing thin. The markings seem to be spiraling even further out of control, and some order and discipline needs to be imposed. If the President won't lean on the agencies, then Congress may have to.

Some Sensitive but Unclassified Designations

1.	"Information [held by DHS] that could be sold for profit"	
2.	"Information that could pose a physical risk to personnel"	
3.	Chinese Space Program Equipment or Technology	
4.	Computer Security Act Sensitive Information	(CSASI)
5.	Confidential Business Information	(CBI)
6.	Contractor Access Restricted Information	(CARI)
7.	Controlled But Unclassified	(CBU)
8.	Controlled Unclassified Information	(CUI)

9.	Critical Energy Infrastructure Information	(CEII)
10.	Critical Infrastructure Information	(CII)
11.	DEA Sensitive	(DEA-S)
12.	Defense Information (Formerly Restricted Data)	(FRD)
13.	Department of Homeland Security Information Technology	(DHS IT)
14.	Export Administration Regulation Information	(EAR)
15.	Federal Information Security Management Act Information	(FISMA)
16.	For Official Use Only	(FOUO)
17.	General Services Admin. Sensitive But Unclassified Building Information	(GSA-SBU-BI)
18.	Grand Jury Information	
19.	International Traffic in Arms Regulation	(ITAR)
20.	Law Enforcement Sensitive	(LES)
21.	Limited Official Use Only	(LOU)
22.	Missile Technology Control Regime Annex	(MTCR)
23.	Missile Technology Control Regime U.S.-Nominated Agents	(MTCR)
24.	Nonpublic Information (Office of Government Ethics)	
25.	Nuclear Nonproliferation Act Information	(NNAI)
26.	Official Use Only	(OUO)
27.	Operations Security Protected	
28.	Secret Patents	
29.	Proprietary Information	(PROPIN)
30.	Safeguards Information (Nuclear Regulatory Commission)	(SGI)
31.	Select Agent Sensitive Information	(SASI)
32.	Sensitive But Unclassified (Department of Homeland Security)	(SBU DHS)
33.	Sensitive But Unclassified (Department of State)	(DOS-SBU)
34.	Sensitive But Unclassified Technical Information	(SBUTI)
35.	Sensitive Homeland Security Information	(SHSI)
36.	Sensitive Security Information	(SSI)
37.	Sensitive Unclassified	(SU)
38.	Special Nuclear Material	(SNM)
39.	Unclassified Controlled Nuclear Information	(UCNI)
40.	Unclassified Export-controlled Department of Defense Technical Data	
41.	United States Munitions List	(USML)
42.	Voluntarily-provided Information (Federal Aviation Administration)	

Appendix A

A Sample of SBU Memoranda from the American Embassy, Baghdad

```
R 121430Z JUN 06
FM AMEMBASSY BAGHDAD
TO SECSTATE WASHDC 5042
INFO IRAQ COLLECTIVE

UNCLAS BAGHDAD 001992

E.O. 12958: N/A

TAGS: PHUM, PREL, ASEC, AMGT, IZ
SUBJECT: Snapshots from the Office: Public
Affairs Staff Show Strains of Social Discord

SENSITIVE
```

(SBU) Beginning in March, and picking up in mid-May, Iraqi staff in the Public Affairs section have complained that Islamist and/or militia groups have been negatively affecting their daily routine. Harassment over proper dress and habits has been increasingly pervasive. They also report that power cuts and fuel prices have diminished their quality of life. Conditions vary by neighborhood, but even upscale neighborhoods such as Mansur have visibly deteriorated.

Women's Rights

(SBU) The Public Affairs Press Office has 9 local Iraqi employees. Two of our three female employees report stepped up harassment beginning in mid-May. One, a Shiite who favors Western Clothing, was advised by an unknown woman in her upscale Shiite/Christian Baghdad neighborhood to wear a veil and not to drive her own car. Indeed, she said, some groups are pushing women to cover even their face, a step not taken in Iran even at its most conservative.

(SBU) Another, a Sunni, said that people in her middle-class neighborhood are harassing women and telling them to cover up and stop using cell phones (suspected channel to licentious relationships with men). She said that the taxi driver who brings her every day to the green zone check-point has told her he cannot let her ride unless she wears a headcover. A female in the PAS cultural section is now wearing a full abaya after receiving direct threats in May. She says her neighborhood, Adhamiya, is no longer permissive if she is not clad so modestly.

(SBU) These women say they cannot identify the groups that are pressuring them; many times the cautions come from other women, sometimes from men who they say could be Sunni or Shiite, but appear conservative. They also tell us that some ministries, notably the Sadrist controlled Ministry of Transportation, have been forcing females to wear the hijab at work.

Dress Code for All?

(SBU) Staff members have reported that it is now danger-ous for men to wear shorts in public; they no longer allow their children to play outside in shorts. People who wear jeans in public have come under attack from what staff members describe as Wahabis and Sadrists.

Evictions

(SBU) One colleague beseeched us to weigh in to help a neighbor who was uprooted in May from her home of 30 years, on the pretense of application of some long-disused law that allows owners to evict tenants after 14 years. The woman, who is a Fayli Kurd, says she has nowhere to go, no other home, but the courts give them no recourse to this new assertion of power. Such uprootings may be a response by new Shiite government authorities to similar actions against Arabs by Kurds in other parts of Iraq. (NOTE: An Arab newspaper editor told us he is preparing an extensive survey of ethnic cleansing, which he said is taking place in almost every Iraqi province, as political parties and their militias are seemingly engaged in tit-for-tat reprisals all over Iraq. One editor told us that the KDP is now planning to set up tent cities in Irbil, to house Kurds being evicted from Baghdad.)

Power Cuts and Fuel Shortages a Drain on Society

Temperatures in Baghdad have already reached 115 degrees. Employees all confirm that by the last week of May, they were getting one hour of power for every six hours with-out. That was only about four hours of power a day for the city. By early June, the situation had improved slightly. In Hai al Shaab, power has recently improved from one in six to one in three hours. Other staff report similar variances. Central Baghdad neighborhood Bab al Mu'atham has had no city power for over a month. Areas near hospitals, political party headquarters, and the green zone have the best supply, in some cases reaching 24 hours. One staff member reported that a friend lives in a building that houses a new minister; within 245 hours of his appointment, her building had city power 24 hours a day.

8. (SBU) All employees supplement city power with service contracted with neighborhood generator hookups that they pay for monthly. One employee pays 7500 ID per ampere to get 10 amperes per month (75,000 TD = USD 50/month). For this, her family gets 6 hours of power per day, with service ending at 2 am. Another employee pays 9000 ID per ampere to get 10 amperes per month (90,000 = USD 60). For this, his family gets 8 hours per day, with services running until 5 am.

(SBU) Fuel lines have also taxed our staff. One employee told us May 29 that he had spent 12 hours on his day off (Saturday) waiting to get gas. Another staff member confirmed that shortages were so dire, prices on the black market in much of Baghdad were now about 1,000 Iraqi dinars per liter (the official, subsidized price is 250 ID).

Kidnappings, and Threats of Worse

(SBU) One employee informed us in March that his brother in law had been kidnapped. The man was eventually released, but this caused enormous emotional distress to the entire family. One employee, a Sunni Kurd, received an indirect threat on her life in April. She took extended leave, and by May, relocated abroad with her family.

Security Force Mistrusted

(SBU) In April, employees began reporting a change in demeanor of guards at the green zone checkpoints. They seemed to be more militia-like, in some cases seemingly taunting. One employee asked us to explore getting her press credentials because guards had held her embassy badge up and proclaimed loudly to nearby passers-by "Embassy" as she entered. Such information is a death sentence if overheard by the wrong people.

Supervising a Staff At High Risk
----

12. (SBU) Employees all share a common tale of their lives: of nine employees in March, only four had family members who knew they worked at the embassy. That makes it difficult for them, and for us. Iraqi colleagues called after hours often speak Arabic as an indication they cannot speak openly in English.

13. (SBU) We cannot call employees in on weekends or holidays without blowing their "cover." Likewise, they have been unavailable during multiple security closures imposed by the government since February. A Sunni Arab female employee tells us that family pressures and the inability to share details of her employment is very tough: she told her family she was in Jordan when we sent her on training to the U.S. in February. Mounting criticisms of the U.S. at home among family members also makes her life difficult. She told us in mid-June that most of her family believes the U.S.—which is widely perceived as fully controlling the country and tolerating the malaise—is punishing populations as Saddam did (but with Sunnis and very poor Shiites now at the bottom of the list). Otherwise, she says, the allocation of power and security would not be so arbitrary.

14. (SBU) Some of our staff do not take home their American cell phones, as this makes them a target. Planning for their own possible abduction, they use code names for friends and colleagues and contacts entered into Iraq cell phones. For at least six months, we have not been able to use any local staff members for translation at on-camera press events.

15. (SBU) More recently, we have begun shredding documents printed out that show local staff surnames. In March, a few staff members approached us to ask what provisions would we make for them if we evacuate.

Sectarian Tensions Within Families
----

16. Ethnic and sectarian faultlines are also becoming part of the daily media fare in the country. One Shiite employee told us in late May that she can no longer watch TV news with her mother, who is Sunni, because her mother blamed all government failings on the fact that Shiites are in charge. Many of the employee's immediate family members, including her father, one sister, and a brother, left Iraq years ago. This month, another sister is depart-

ing for Egypt, as she imagines the future here is too
bleak.

Frayed Nerves and Mistrust in the Office
----

17. (SBU) Against this backdrop of frayed social networks,
tension and moodiness have risen. One Shiite made
disparaging comments about the Sunni caliph Othman which
angered a Kurd. A Sunni Arab female apparently insulted a
Shiite female colleague by criticizing her overly liberal
dress. One colleague told us he feels "defeated" by
circumstances, citing the example of being unable to help
his two year old son who has asthma and cannot sleep in
stifling heat.

18. (SBU) Another employee tells us that life outside the
Green Zone has become "emotionally draining." He lives in
a mostly Shiite area and claims to attend a funeral "every
evening." He, like other local employees, is financially
responsible for his immediate and extended families. He
revealed that "the burden of responsibility; new stress
coming from social circles who increasingly disapprove of
the coalition presence, and everyday threats weigh very
heavily." This employee became extremely agitated in late
May at website reports of an abduction of an Iraqi working with MNFI, whose expired Embassy and MNFI badges were
posted on the website.

Staying Straight with Neighborhood Governments and the
"Alasa"
----

19. (SBU) Staff members say they daily assess how to move
safely in public. Often, if they must travel outside their
own neighborhoods, they adopt the clothing, language, and
traits of the area. In Jadriya, for example, one needs to
conform to the SCIRI/Badr ethic; in Yusufiya, a strict
Sunni conservative dress code has taken hold. Adhamiya and
Salihiya, controlled by the secular Ministry of Defense,
are not conservative. Moving inconspicuously in Sadr City
requires Shiite conservative dress and a particular lingo.
Once-upscale Mansur district, near the Green Zone, according to one employee, by early June was an "unrecognizable
ghost town."

20. (SBU) Since Samarra, Baghdadis have honed these
survival skills. Vocabulary has shifted to reflect new
behavior. Our staff—and our contacts—have become adept
in modifying behavior to avoid "Alasas," informants who
keep an eye out for "outsiders" in neighborhoods. The

Alasa mentality is becoming entrenched as Iraqi security forces fail to gain public confidence.

21. (SBU) Our staff report that security and services are being rerouted through "local providers" whose affiliations are vague. As noted above, those who are admonishing citizens on their dress are not known to the residents. Neighborhood power providers are not well known either, nor is it clear how they avoid robbery or targeting. Personal safety depends on good relations with the "neighborhood" governments, who barricade streets and ward off outsiders. The central government, our staff says, is not relevant; even local mukhtars have been displaced or coopted by militias. People no longer trust most neighbors.

22. (SBU) A resident of upscale Shiite/Christian Karrada district told us that "outsiders" have moved in and now control the local mukhtars, one of whom now has cows and goats grazing in the streets. When she expressed her concern at the dereliction, he told her to butt out.

Comment
----

23. (SBU) Although our staff retain a professional demeanor, strains are apparent. We see that their personal fears are reinforcing divisive sectarian or ethnic channels, despite talk of reconciliation by officials. Employees are apprehensive enough that we fear they may exaggerate developments or steer us towards news that comports with their own worldview. Objectivity, civility, and logic that make for a functional workplace may falter if social pressures outside the Green Zone don't abate.

KHALTZAD

NNNN

Notes

1 See, for example, National Academies on Science, Commission on Geosciences, Environment and Resources (CGER), "A Review of the Department of Energy Classification: Policy and Practice." 1995. OCR. p. 80. http://books.nap.edu/openbook.php?record_id=4967& page=67.

2 Thanks to Steven Aftergood for this succinct explanation.

3 Interview with Congressional Research Service specialist Harold Relyea, December 2005. Cited Genevieve Knezo, Specialist in Science and Technology Policy Resources, Science, and Industry Division, "'Sensitive But Unclassified' Information and Other Controls: Policy and Options for Scientific and Technical Information." February 15, 2006, Library of Congress. See also, Knezo, "'Sensitive But Unclassified' and Other Federal Security Controls on Scientific and Technical Information: History and Current Controversy." Updated February 20, 2004.

4 Although other control markings have been.

5 White House. National Security Decision Directive 145 (NSDD-145), National Policy on Telecommunications and Automated Information Systems Security (U) http://www.fas.org/irp/offdocs/nsdd145.htm.

6 "The Potential Impact of National Security Decision Directive (NSDD) 145 on Civil Agencies" Warren G. Reed, GAO, before the Subcommittee on Transportation, Aviation, and Materials, Committee on Science and Technology, June 17, 1985. Cited in Knezo, op. cit.

7 Revising and superseding Circular A-71.

8 Those who are not old enough to remember him (ever so fondly) from the 1980s will recognize him (equally fondly) as the instigator and former head of the Defense Advanced Research Projects Agency's Total Information Awareness research program.

9 NTISSP No. 2, "National Policy on Protection of Sensitive, but Unclassified Information in Federal Government Telecommunications and Automated Information Systems." October 29, 1986. Issued by John Poindexter. In U.S. Congress, Office of Technology Assessment, *Defending Secrets, Sharing Data: New Locks and Keys for Electronic Information*, OTA-CIT-31O (Washington, D.C.: U.S. Government Printing Office (GPO), October 1987), Appendix B. http://www.wws.princeton.edu/ota/ns20/alpha_f.html). Cited in Knezo (2006), op. cit.

10 A congressional agency killed after the 1994 "Gingrich Revolution." As noted before, elections matter.

11 U.S. Congress, Office of Technology Assessment, Issue Update on Information Security and Privacy in Network Environments, OTA-BP- ITC-147 (Washington, D.C.:U.S. Government Printing Office, June 1995). http://ftp.cerias.purdue.edu/pub/doc/privacy/infosec_update/11appb.txt.

12 Raymond Kammer, Deputy Director, National Bureau of Standards, testimony, "Computer Security Act of 1987: Hearings on H.R. 145 Before the Subcommittee on Legislation and National Security of the House Committee on Government Operations." 100th Cong., 1st Sess., Feb. 26, 1987. See also House Report. 100-153, Part I, footnote 12, p. 18.) Cited in Office of Technology Assessment (1995), op. cit.

155

13 Genevieve Knezo, "'Sensitive But Unclassified' Information and Other Controls: Policy and Options for Scientific and Technical Information," CRS, February 15, 2006.

14 http://www4.law.cornell.edu/usc-cgi/get_external.cgi?type=pubL&target=100-235.

15 Computer Security Act, Sec. 8. Rules of Construction of Act. "...nothing in this Act shall be construed to: (1) constitute authority to withhold information sought under the Freedom of Information Act; or (2) authorize any Federal agency to limit, restrict, regulate, or control the collection, maintenance, disclosure, use, transfer, or sale of any information that is privately-owned information, information disclosable under the Freedom of Information Act or other law requiring or authorizing the public disclosure of information, or information in the public domain."

16 *House Report* 100-153, Part I, June 11, 1987.

17 National Institute of Standards and Technology, Computer Systems Laboratory *CSL Bulletin,* "Advising Users on Computer System Technology," Nov. 1992. http://csrc.nist.gov/publications/nistbul/csl92-11.txt.

18 Id.

19 Conference Report on H.R. 2360, Department of Homeland Security Appropriations Act, 2006. House of Representatives, September 29, 2005.

20 http://thomas.loc.gov/cgi-bin/query/F?r109:1:./temp/~r109BbryhI:e111888.

21 http://thomas.loc.gov/cgi-bin/query/F?r109:1:./temp/~r109BbryhI:e63917.

22 *Secrecy News* "The Demise of Sensitive Homeland Security Info (SHSI)", December 12, 2005. http://www.fas.org/sgp/news/secrecy/2005/12/121205.html.

23 Id.

24 "Guidelines and Requirements in Support of the Information Sharing Environment," including Guideline 3 on Standard Procedures for SBU. Not available on the White House site. http://www.fas.org/sgp/news/2005/12/wh121605-memo.html.

25 Id.

26 Government Accountability Office, "Information Sharing—The Federal Government Needs to Establish Policies and Processes for Sharing Terrorism-Related and Sensitive but Unclassified Information." March 2006, GAO-06-385.

27 Chris Strohm, "Official Says More 'Sensitive' Information Should Be Public." Congressional Daily AM, Thursday, May 11, 2006. http://nationaljournal.com/pubs/congressdaily/am060511.htm#9.

28 http://www.fas.org/irp/congress/2006_hr/051006mcnamara.pdf.

29 Statement by Thomas McNamara at meeting with public interest representatives, October 2006.

30 GAO (March 2006), op. cit.

31 Thomas McNamara, "Statement for the Record," House Committee on Homeland Security, Subcommittee on Intelligence, Information Sharing, and Terrorism Risk Assessment, April 26, 2007. http://www.ise.gov/docs/HHSC-20070426-%20McNamara%20Testimony.pdf and http://www.gpoaccess.gov/serialset/creports/911.html.

32 Id.

33. Pub. L 107-206. Sec. 892. Facilitating Homeland Security Information Sharing Procedures. http://www.fas.org/sgp/congress/2002/hr5710-111302.html#his.

34 *Secrecy News.* http://www.fas.org/sgp/news/secrecy/2002/11/112702.html.

35 Department of Homeland Security Management Directive System, "MD Number: 11042. Safeguarding Sensitive but Unclassified (For Official Use Only) Information. Issue Date: May 11, 2004. http://www.fas.org/sgp/othergov/dhs-sbu.html. I defy you, if you are not a DHS official, to find this directive (or its rescission below) on the DHS site.

36 Spencer S. Hsu, "Homeland Security Employees Required to Sign Secrecy Pledge—Gag Order Raises Concern on Hill" *Washington Post.* Tuesday, November 16, 2004, P. A23. http://www.washingtonpost.com/wp-dyn/articles/A52977-2004Nov15.html?nav=hcmodule.

37 Department of Homeland Security, Management Directive 11042.1 "Safeguarding Sensitive But Unclassified (For Official Use Only) Information." 1.6.2005. http://www.fas.org/sgp/othergov/dhs-sbu-rev.pdf.

38 Eileen Sullivan, "Homeland modifies secrecy policy." *Federal Times,* January 11, 2005. http://federaltimes.com/index.php?S=594837.

39 McNamara, "Statement for the Record," op. cit.

40 Office of Security and Emergency Preparedness Manual Guide, Information Security CDC-02, Sensitive but Unclassified Information. Posted on the CDC intranet in February 2006. www.fas.org/sgp/othergov/cdc-sbu.pdf.

41 Office of Security and Emergency Preparedness Manual Guide, Information Security CDC-02, Sensitive but Unclassified Information, Date of Issue: July 22, 2005. http://www.fas.org/sgp/othergov/cdc-sbu.pdf.

42 Transactional Records Access Clearinghouse, "Federal Government Withholds Information About Nearly One Million Workers—Close to Half the Total Civilian Workforce," December 6, 2005. http://trac.syr.edu/foia/opm/20051206/. Other documents related to the case: http://trac.syr.edu/foia/opm/20051206/complaint.pdf;http://trac.syr.edu/foia/opm/20051206/opm_letter_20050202.pdf.

43 http://trac.syr.edu/foia/opm/20051206/1816_register.pdf.

44 For more information on Mr. Armstrong, go to http://www.mediagiraffe.org/profiles/index.php?action=profile&id=41.

45 Conversation with Scott Armstrong.

46 *Secrecy News,* "Public Access to Aeronautical Data Will Be Blocked." FAS Project on Government Secrecy, November 30, 2005, Vol. No. 109. http://www.fas.org/sgp/news/secrecy/2005/11/113005.html.

47 http://naco.faa.gov/content/naco/SpecialNotices/FLIP-Distribution.pdf; http://www.fas
.org/sgp/news/2005/11/nga112905.pdf.

48 Bruce Schneier, "The Silliness of Secrecy." Schneier on Security, March 24, 2005.
http://www.schneier.com/blog/archives/2005/03/the_silliness_o.html, quoting from Robert
Block, "Information Incognito: In War on Terror, U.S. Tries to Make Public Data Secret; The
Almanac Under Wraps?" *The Wall Street Journal* online, March 22, 2005. http://online.wsj.com/
article/SB111145546123985866.html.

49 http://www.fas.org/sgp/news/secrecy/2005/07/070605.html.

50 *Secrecy News* June 14, 2005. http://www.fas.org/sgp/news/secrecy/2005/06/061405.html.
See also, Malcolm Dando, "The bioterrorist cookbook," *Bulletin of the Atomic Scientists,*
November/December 2005, Vol. 61, No. 06. pp. 34–39. http://www.thebulletin.org/article
.php?art_ofn=nd05dando.

51 Lawrence M. Wein, "Got Toxic Milk?" Op-Ed *New York Times,* May 30, 2005.
http://www.nytimes.com/2005/05/30/opinion/30wein.html?ex=1143003600&en=4d987576e2
31dae1&ei=5070.

52 Milton Leitenberg and George Smith, "Terrorists and Toxic Milk—A Rebuttal," National
Security Notes, June 18, 2005. http://www.globalsecurity.org/org/nsn/nsn-050618.htm.

53 Id.

54 Bruce Alberts, "Modeling Attacks on the Food Supply," PNAS, July 12, 2005.

55 On April 4, 2006, Judge Marsha Pechman of the U.S. District Court for the Western District
of Washington ordered the IRS to turn over statistical data to Susan B. Long, a professor at
Syracuse University and co-director of the non-profit research organization Transactional
Records Access Clearinghouse. http://trac.syr.edu/foia/irs/20060404/ruling.pdf.

56 TRAC, "DOJ Denies IRS Request to Appeal Court Order to Turn Over Audit Statistics;
Request for a Stay Also Denied." December 12, 2006. http://trac.syr.edu/foia/.

57 *Federal Register,* January 18, 2005 Volume 70, Number 11.

58 Baker, John, et al., "Mapping the Risks: Assessing the Homeland Security Implications of
Publicly Available Geospatial Information" (RAND Corporation, 2004).

59 http://www.dhs.gov/xabout/laws/editorial_0468.shtm. 69 *Federal Register* 33043, 33063
(June 14, 2004), § 6.2. See also American Bar Association, Section of Administrative Law and
Regulatory Practice, Report to the House of Delegates, February 2006. http://www.abanet.org/
adminlaw/midyear/2006/112%5B1%5D.pdf.

60 http://a257.g.akamaitech.net/7/257/2422/01jan20061800/edocket.access.gpo.gov/
2006/06-3078.htm.

61 Meghan E. Murphy, "Governments may restrict access to birth records," Society of
Professional Journalists. *SPJ News,* July 19, 2006. http://www.spj.org/news.asp?ref=597.

62 Charles N. Davis, "Public Access to Vital Records Threatened by Terrorism Prevention
Act," Society of Professional Journalists, *SPJ News,* March 8, 2006. http://www.spj.org/news
.asp?ref=552.

63 Id.

64 Meghan Murphy, op. cit.

65 See http://www.nrc.gov/reading-rm/doc-collections/news/2004/04-111.html.

66 Ryan Singel, "FCC Pulls Blinds on Wireless Data." *Wired News,* August 11, 2004. http://www.wired.com/news/wireless/0,1382,64528,00.html.

67 Joe Stephens, "U.S. Judges Getting Disclosure Data Deleted: GAO Cites 661 Requests to Withhold Information From Ethics Act Reports." *Washington Post,* Thursday, August 5, 2004, p.A04. http://www.washingtonpost.com/wp-dyn/articles/A40982-2004Aug4.html.

68 Id.

69 See also, Aliya Sternstein," GAO policy reflects security concerns" *Federal Computer Week,* October 4, 2004. http://www.fcw.com/fcw/articles/2004/1004/pol gaosec-10-04-04.asp.

70 Bruce Schneier, op. sit.

71 John M. Donnelly, "Pentagon IG Sets New Policy On Web Information" *Defense Week Daily Update,* December 18, 2003. http://www.fas.org/sgp/news/2003/12/dw121803.html.

72 Steven Aftergood, "DOD Inspector General to Curtail Web-based Info" Secrecy News, December 19, 2003 Vol. 2003, No. 110 Federation of American Scientists Government Secrecy Project. http://www.fas.org/sgp/news/secrecy/2003/12/121903.html.

73 OMB Watch "Access to Government Information Post September 11th." http://www.ombwatch.org/article/articleview/213/1/1/.

74 http://www.ise.gov/.

CHAPTER 6

CLASSIFIED INFORMATION—

RECLASSIFIED, OVERCLASSIFIED, AND MISUSED

"Those who control the present control the past, and those who control the past control the future."—George Orwell, 1984

"It is important to understand that there is no rigorous, consensual definition of what constitutes classified information. Instead, in a practical sense, classified information is whatever the executive branch says it is."—Steven Aftergood[1], February 26, 2006

Not all government information can be publicly available; there will always be a need for some small amount of information to be classified as secret. But the power to so classify information is a dangerous one and is subject to abuse—especially when information that is already legitimately in the public domain is reclassified or retroactively classified.

In this chapter, I will discuss

- A brief history of the power to classify information, its concentration in the executive branch, and the occasional contest of that power by Congress;

- The re-expansion of the classification system under the second Bush Administration, in an apparent effort to control—or attempt to regain control over—information that is embarrassing or ideologically inconvenient;

- Some disturbing examples of public information's being taken out of the public arena and returned to the classified domain.

On March 25, 2003, the Bush administration issued Executive Order (E.O.) 13292,[2] which made a few—but significant—changes to the 1995 Clinton order, E.O. 12958.[3] As I will detail below, the Bush order is, in many ways, a return to the Reagan era of expansive official secrecy in national security information. While it "amends" the Clinton Order, it severely undercuts the more limited and more controlled scope of classifiable (and particularly re-classifiable) information. In this way, it is in keeping with the Bush Administration's general trend toward greater secrecy and constrained accountability.

A Brief History of Classified Information

Although the history of securing and safeguarding information related to the security of the country goes back to the very founding, until World War II Congress had the primary role in limiting access to information, and the government's concern with protecting information was confined to a relatively small amount of information closely related to military and diplomatic matters. That World War II had a profound effect, not least of which was shifting control of security classification clearly into the office of the President.

The Espionage Act of 1917: Still Limiting the Spread of Information

Prior to World War II, Congress had the primary role in limiting access to information. Of all the statutes that Congress created, the one that continues to have serious repercussions to this day is the Espionage Act of 1917.

The Espionage Act of 1917 was passed at the urging of President Woodrow Wilson, who feared any widespread dissent in time of war constituted a real threat to an American victory. The Act made it unlawful to disseminate information relating to the "national defense" or "public defense." The main objective of this and the Defense Act of 1911 was to punish spies, but the Espionage Act made it a crime to help wartime enemies of the United States.

A section of the Espionage Act allowed the Postmaster General to declare all letters, circulars, newspapers, pamphlet books, and other materials that violated the Act to be un-mailable. As a result, about 75 newspapers either lost their mailing privileges or were pressured to print nothing more about World War I between June 1917 and May 1918.

The Sedition Act of 1918 was an amendment to the Espionage Act of 1917. It forbade an American to use "disloyal, profane, scurrilous, or abusive language" about the United States government, flag, or armed forces during war. The act also allowed the Postmaster General to deny mail delivery to dissenters of government policy during wartime. In practice, the Espionage Act, as amended by the Sedition Act, was used to persecute individuals or groups who disagreed with presidential or congressional policy.

The Sedition Act was repealed in 1921. Major portions of the Espionage Act remain part of United States law (18 USC §§ 793, 794). This WWI enactment is still having an inhibitory effect. The government has charged Steven J. Rosen and Keith Weissman, former lobbyists for the American Israel Public Affairs Committee (AIPAC), with conspiring to obtain national defense information from U.S. officials and pass it on to the media and Israeli officials. They are the first U.S. citizens—not employed by the government—to be charged under the 89-year-old Espionage Act for allegedly receiving and orally transmitting information that was in classified documents, related to public defense.[4]

Not that Congress has been completely absent from the field of classification regulation; in the years since World War II, Congress has passed a handful of pieces of legislation that provide the statutory basis of our modern system for secrecy and the security systems used to protect secrets, most of which were designed to give specific officials authority to control information. For example, the National Security Act of 1947 made the Director of Central Intelligence responsible for protecting intelligence sources and methods. Others, like the Atomic Energy Act of 1954 and the Intelligence Identities Act of 1982, were designed to protect specific kinds of information—usually after a controversy in which the information had been compromised.[5]

Although Congress has, on occasion, considered statutorily establishing security classification policy, it has not actively pursued the matter.[6] Various congressional committees have investigated ways to bring some continuity to the classification system[7] and to limit the President's broad powers to shield information from public examination—but the bottom line is that Congress has left the area to executive control. This is a critical point to any understanding of our system of classifying information: that it is a system not only maintained, but established, for the greatest part, by the executive branch. Congress' tensions with the Executive Branch in this regard are discussed more below.

Without a statutory standard for determining what is proper, courts have therefore been left with standards based on the Executive Orders issued by the President. And the Supreme Court has honored Congress's deference to executive branch determinations in this area, *EPA v. Mink,* 410 U.S. 73 (1973).[8]

Growth of the Power of the Executive

In 1940, President Franklin Roosevelt issued the first Executive Order on national security classification[9] authorizing government officials to protect national security. Harold Relyea notes that this development was "probably prompted somewhat by desires to clarify the authority of civilian personnel in the national defense community to classify information, to establish a broader basis for protecting military information in view of growing global hostilities, and to better manage a discretionary power seemingly of increasing importance to the entire executive branch."[10] Prior to the New Deal, classification decisions were largely left to military regulation.[11]

Presidents since have followed this precedent, with one important difference: President Roosevelt cited specific statutory authority for his action; later presidents have cited general statutory and Constitutional authority.[12] E.O. 10290, issued in September 1951 by President Truman, indicated that he was relying on "[the] authority vested in me by the Constitution and statutes, and as President of the United States." Mr. Relyea notes that "this formulation appeared to strengthen the President's authority to make official secrecy policy; it intertwined his responsibility as Commander in Chief with the constitutional obligation to "take care that the laws be faithfully executed."[13]

As will be shown in the examples of classification abuses later in this chapter, there is an inherent tension between the authority of Congress to make law and the claims of the Chief Executive in relation to national security. Proponents of expansive presidential power claim that classified national security information "belongs" to the executive branch and is shared with Congress only as a matter of grace. The Congress has objected to this view on numerous occasions.[14] In the Freedom of Information Act (Exemption 1) Congress added a requirement that information withheld under that exemption be "properly classified pursuant to an executive order."

Eisenhower to Reagan

There was widespread criticism of President Truman's executive order owing to its assertion of constitutional authority, and so President Eisenhower, shortly after his election, directed his Attorney General to review the order. The Attorney General's recommendation was a new directive, E.O. 10501. From the issuance of E.O. 10501 in 1953,[15] and for most of the next 30 years, presidential classification directives narrowed the bases and discretion for assigning official secrecy to executive branch documents and materials.

The trend toward more limited secrecy was reversed with E.O. 12356, issued by President Ronald Reagan in April 1982. This order expanded the categories of classifiable information, mandated that information falling within these categories be classified, authorized the reclassification of previously declassified documents, admonished classifiers to err on the side of classification, and eliminated automatic declassification arrangements.

The Clinton Era

In 1995, the Clinton Administration issued Executive Order 12958, starting a new trend toward more limited secrecy and toward more active declassification. E.O. 12958 set limits for the duration of classification, prohibited the reclassification of properly declassified records, authorized government employees to challenge the classification status of records, re-established the balancing test of E.O. 12065 weighing the need to protect information vis-a-vis the public interest in its disclosure, and created two review panels—one on classification and declassification, and one to advise on policy and procedure.[16]

As the government's Information Security Oversight Office (ISOO)[17] has noted, the 1995 order was a paradigm shift in the nation's declassification policies and, in effect, reversed the resource burden.[18] In previous years, agencies had to expend resources to justify *de*classifying older information; information, once classified, remained so indefinitely and very often did not become available to the general public, researchers, or historians without persistent and continuous effort. Under the Clinton-era order,[19] however, agencies had to expend the resources to demonstrate why information needed to *remain* classified. All agencies that originated classified information were required to systematically review[20] that information for potential declassification. An additional step in the Order toward more declassification was automatic declassification of information (with a few narrow exemptions) more than 25 years old and appraised as having permanent historical value. (Information older than 25 years that is not considered of permanent value might well be eligible for destruction.)

Return to Expanded Official Secrecy: The Bush Era

The 2003 Bush Executive Order 13292, in effect, brought this era to an end. It's worthwhile taking a look at some of the changes made to the Clinton order, as a demonstration of how even small changes in wording can have a big impact.

- *Reclassification of Properly Released Material.* As originally issued, Clinton's E.O. 12958 prohibited the reclassification of information after it had been released to the public under proper authority (e.g., not "leaked"). Bush's E.O. 13292 restores the ability, under the predecessor E.O. 12356, to reclassify such information, but only under "[the] personal authority of the agency head or deputy agency head" and only if the material may be "reasonably recovered."(§ 1.7(c)).

- *Classifying Documents After Request Under the FOIA.* The original language of E.O. 12958 required special procedures for classifying or reclassifying documents after they had been requested under the FOIA, and prohibited it entirely for documents more than 25 years old. The language prohibiting the classification or reclassification of 25-year-old information has been dropped, though the special procedures remain (§ 1.7 (d)).

- *Categories of Classifiable Information Clarified.* Additional categories of information, specifically defense against transnational terrorism, infra-structures, and protection services, were explicitly spelled out as included in those that were eligible for classification. "Weapons of mass destruction" was added as a separate category. Arguably, all such information was already covered by the existing order (§ 1.4 (e) (g) and (h)).[21]

It is also interesting to note one category that did not significantly change: compilations of unclassified information.

> *Compilations of items of information that are individually unclassified may be classified if the compiled information reveals an additional association or relationship that: (1) meets the standards for classification under this order; and (2) is not otherwise revealed in the individual items of information. As used in* this order, "compilation" means an aggregation of pre-existing unclassified *items of information (Sec.§ 1.7(e)).*[22] (Emphasis added.)

Congressional-Executive Tension

The return by the Bush Administration to an era of expanded secrecy raises the question: Why did Congress not object? There is nothing new about tension between Congress' authority to make law and the President's claims of power in relation to national security. Although proponents of expansive presidential power claim that classified national security information "belongs" to the executive branch and is shared with Congress only as a matter of grace, Congress has objected to this view on numerous occasions.[23]

It is true, however, that Congress has generally been reluctant to exercise its authority. For example, when Congress was concerned that the Executive Branch may have declared some documents to be "national security information" that were not vital to national security, it added a requirement in the FOIA (Exemption 1) that such information be "properly classified pursuant to an executive order."[24] That meant only, however, that the executive branch must comply with its own regulations.

Nevertheless, Congress, however reluctant it may be to exercise it, does have the authority: it codified its right to receive classified information in the Intelligence Oversight Act of 1980, which explicitly requires that the president keep congressional intelligence committees fully and currently informed of all intelligence activities, including significant anticipated intelligence activities.[25] As Kate Martin notes, "The Oversight Act incorporates Congress' understanding that it has equal right to classified national security information because the Constitution vests shared responsibilities in the Congress and the president for making decisions about national security and foreign policy matters."[26] Moreover, the rules of the Congress[27] expressly recognize *Congress's concurrent constitutional authority to declassify* information; they specify a procedure for Congress to publicly disclose classified information when it determines that it is in the public interest to do so, even over the objection of the president, after giving due consideration to that objection.[28] (Emphasis added.)

But that only returns us to the question, especially in regard to some of the examples below of congressional objections; why did they not exercise this authority? A fair question, for which I do not have a good answer— other than loyalty to George Bush in a Republican-controlled Congress. As I noted above, an inherent tension exists—and sometimes bare knuckles are required by Congress to assert its (and ultimately our) rights and its authority in decisions on access to government information.

Where We Are Now

While we have not gone all the way back to the Reagan order, we have seen in the Bush Administration a strong use of classification (and re- and declassification powers) to control—or attempt to regain control over—information that is not harmful to the national defense or security (and thus cannot be seen as primarily a response to the events of September 11), but is embarrassing or ideologically inconvenient.[29] In many ways, E.O. 13292 should be read together with Bush's E.O. on presidential records to get a full sense of

167

the control asserted over executive branch, and particularly presidential, information.

The other issue assertion of power in regard to classification has been the assertion by the Vice President that he can declassify materials that his office did not originally classify. The Bush E.O on national security classification does not grant this authority to the Vice President, although he seems to think he has it—and may have exercised it.[30]

In late June 2007, it was revealed that for three years, Vice President Cheney's office refused to divulge its classification statistics to ISOO. Prior to 2002, such information had routinely been transmitted and reported in ISOO's annual reports to the President.

The disclosure requirement, ISOO Directive 1 (at §2001.80), appears explicit: "Each agency that creates or handles classified information shall report annually to the Director of ISOO statistics related to its security classification program." President Bush wrote in Executive Order 13292 (section 5.1) that such ISOO directives "shall be binding upon the agencies." Significantly, an "agency" here means not only a statutorily defined executive branch agency (which would not include the Office of the Vice President), but also refers to "any other entity within the executive branch that comes into the possession of classified information" (which would include the Office of the Vice President).[31] Vice President Cheney had refused onsite inspections by ISOO (to ensure the proper handling of classified documents, as the Office of the Vice President had not submitted the reports required by the executive order) and, after ISOO took the issue to the Attorney General, the Vice President recommended that the executive order be amended to abolish the ISOO.[32]

The Vice President proclaimed in June 2007 that his office was not "an entity within the executive branch" (because he has minimal duties as the President of the Senate, e.g., to cast a tie-breaking vote) and, thus, is not bound by the Executive Order. The President's press people backed him up. The proclamation led to great and widespread derision. In an example of the "bare knuckles" struggle between Congress and the White House, Representative Rahm Emanuel (D-IL) introduced legislation to[33] strike all $4.4 million of the Vice President's budget needed annually to run Vice President Cheney's office and home.[34] The vote, on an amendment to a 2008 spending bill for the Treasury Department and executive-branch agencies, was defeated, 217 to 209 on June 28th.[35]

Using Classification Authority To Take Material Out of the Public Domain

As noted above, the Clinton E.O. prohibited the reclassification of information after it had been released to the public under proper authority. The Bush E.O.—unfortunately—restored that ability, subject to a few limitations. Reclassification is almost never good public policy, or even a realistic way of protecting secrets. It is therefore important that if the information is to be reclassified, after once being declassified under proper authority (and herein lie some big constitutional questions about the authority of Congress and, indeed, of the Vice President to declassify information not created by the Congress or the Vice President, respectively), then that reclassification must not happen summarily—and especially not secretly. Such reclassification undermines trust in the workings of the government and raises questions of the motive of the reclassifier.

Retroactive classification is always suspect and should be prohibited.

Fifty-five Thousand Pages of Information Reclassified at NARA

In 2006, we discovered from the National Security Archive at George Washington University that, since 1999, at least six government agencies— including the Central Intelligence Agency (CIA), the Defense Intelligence Agency (DIA), the Defense Department, the military services, and the Department of Justice—have been secretly, and continuously, engaged in a wide-ranging historical document reclassification program at the National Archives and Records Administration (NARA) research facility at College Park, Maryland and at the Presidential Libraries run by NARA.[36] In that time, some 9,500 formerly declassified and publicly available documents— totaling more than 55,500 pages—have been withdrawn from the open shelves at College Park and reclassified. The documents, all at least 25 years old,[37] included some already published by the State Department and others photocopied years ago by private historians.

According to the government agencies, the documents had been improperly and/or inadvertently released. The actual issue, however, was that one agency had properly released the documents, but the agencies involved in this reclassification effort disagreed with the release—after the fact.[38] The reclassification program was itself shrouded in secrecy, governed by a classified memorandum that prohibited the National Archives even from saying which agencies were involved.

In early 2006, at the request of the National Security Archive and others,[39] ISOO conducted an audit of the reclassification effort. ISOO Director Bill Leonard authorized the audit after sampling some of the 55 documents provided: "If those sample records were removed because somebody thought they were classified, I'm shocked and disappointed. It just boggles the mind."[40]

In March 2006, the Archivist of the United States, Allen Weinstein, announced a moratorium on the reclassification efforts, to give the ISOO time to complete the audit of the removed material.

In April, ISOO issued its report,[41] finding "a total of ten unrelated efforts to identify such records, which resulted in the withdrawal of at least 25,315 publicly available records." ISOO said that materials that had been created in unclassified form or correctly declassified were reclassified, and unclassified material was classified in order to cover up the reclassification program. This truly "boggles the mind."

The report notes the "most significant deficiency" identified by this audit was the "absence of standards, including requisite levels of transparency, governing agency re-review activity at NARA." Absent these standards, NARA along with the CIA and USAF resorted to ad hoc agreements[42] that, in retrospect, "all recognize should never have been classified in the first place."

More specifically, 24 percent of sampled records were clearly inappropriate for continued classification. An additional 12 percent were "questionable classification decisions"—but were withdrawn from public access nonetheless. Approximately 40 percent of the records were withdrawn because the reviewing agency purported that its classified information had been declassified without its permission, and about 60 percent were identified by the reviewing agency for referral to another agency for declassification or other public disclosure review.[43] Such referrals are also potentially endless deferrals of public release.

The problem of "equities"—the interests of various and varying agencies in the status of classified materials in government records—bedevils declassification efforts and reviews, whether for the automatic declassification[44] of most documents older than 25 years, or for release under FOIA when a mandatory declassification review[45] is requested.

The issue of equities among agencies with conflicting interests is one that needs serious Congressional attention. It creates extensive delays in the processing of FOIA requests and it has almost certainly slowed the progress of current efforts to finish reviewing the backlog of classified records more than 25 years old, estimated at 400-million pages,[46] by the end of 2006, as required by both the Clinton E.O. and the Bush E.O. This problem is brought home by testimony given by ISOO Director Leonard during an August 24, 2004, hearing by the House Government Reform Committee's Subcommittee on National Security. Leonard noted that federal law divides the authority for writing the rules that govern secrets. The CIA director has authority to protect intelligence sources and methods, the Energy Department has power to write regulations to shield nuclear secrets, the Pentagon has control over classifying NATO data, and the National Security Agency can define eavesdropping communications secrets.[47] This is a recipe for crosscutting interests and conflicts, with public access the victim.

Reclassification, particularly on this scale, is a serious problem. As I noted above (but it bears repeating), the reclassified documents included some already published or already in the hands of historians. One concern—felt particularly by these historians[48]—is that anyone who may possess one or more of these 55,000 documents might, under current law, be in technical violation of the Espionage Act for receipt of classified (or, in this case, re-classified) information.[49]

These secret "Spy agency vs. Spy agency"[50] reclassifications would also create great peril for anyone who conveyed (orally or in print) what they might believe to be declassified information if legislation were to pass that has been introduced three[51] times in Congress (most recently in 2006)—and passed once and was vetoed, at the last minute, by President Clinton. This legislation would make it a felony to "knowingly and willfully" disclose, or attempt to disclose, any classified information to a person known to be not lawfully authorized to receive it. What is most disturbing, is the definition of "classified information" as

> "information or material properly classified and clearly marked or represented, or *that the person knows* or has reason to believe *has been properly classified by appropriate authorities, pursuant to the provisions of a statute or Executive Order, as requiring protection against unauthorized disclosure for reasons of national security."*
> (Emphasis added.)

Recovery of Leaked Information—Jack Anderson's Papers

Jack Anderson, a well-known political reporter and muckraker for 40 years—including reporting on the CIA's scheme to assassinate Fidel Castro, the Mafia's crime network, corruption among congressmen, and American involvement in the Indo-Pakistan War[52]—bequeathed his papers to George Washington University after his death in December 2005. In 2006, agents from FBI told officials at George Washington University and members of Jack Anderson's family that they wanted to go through the archive of his papers.[53]

According to Mark Feldstein, the director of the journalism program at George Washington University, who had been reading 25-year-old documents as part of his research for a book he was writing about Anderson and whom the FBI visited in March 2006, the reason given by the FBI was "Violations of the Espionage Act." The agents said they were investigating espionage involving two indicted lobbyists for the pro-Israel lobbying group AIPAC, the American Israel Public Affairs Committee, and they wanted Feldstein to tell them the names of former Jack Anderson reporters who were pro-Israel in their views or who had pro-Israeli sources. Feldstein reports that one of the agents "helpfully" noted, "Just because the documents aren't marked 'classified' doesn't mean they're not."[54]

Kevin Anderson, Jack Anderson's son, said the FBI had originally approached his mother earlier in 2006. He told the *New York Times*,[55] "They talked about the AIPAC case[56] and that they thought Dad had some classified documents and they wanted to take fingerprints from them. But they said they wanted to look at all 200 boxes and if they found anything classified they'd be duty-bound to take them."[57]

On the one hand, the Anderson family as represented by Kevin: "It's my father's legacy. The government has always and continues to this day to abuse the secrecy stamp. My father's view was that the public is the employer of these government employees and has the right to know what they're up to." On the other, Bill Carter, an FBI spokesman: "It's been determined that among the papers there are a number of classified U.S. government documents. Under the law, no private person may possess classified documents that were illegally provided to them. These documents remain the property of the government."[58]

There are multiple implications of this FBI effort. As we have seen in the NARA case discussed above, government agencies are not necessarily to be trusted in their decisions about what is classified and properly declassified—and the statement by the FBI agent quoted by Mr. Feldstein above does nothing to reassure me that I overstate the case. Turning government officials lose in the files of a reporter is an invitation to an obscurement of history and fact for the foreseeable future. Moreover, as Mr. Feldstein, a former investigative reporter himself, notes: "Whistle-blowing sources would be scared off from confiding in reporters about abuses of power if they had reason to fear that the government would find out about it by rifling through journalistic files even past the grave. And the public justifiably won't trust the press if it's turned into an arm of law enforcement."[59]

Recovering Papers in Open Archives

In February 2005, five federal government officials, three from the CIA and one each from the Department of Energy and the Department of Defense, removed[60] several documents from the archival papers of the late Senator Henry M. "Scoop" Jackson housed at the University of Washington Suzzallo-Allen library. A self-identified CIA "civilian employee" initially found a document stamped "classified" among the papers in 2004.

The CIA came back, uninvited, in February with the five-person team. This could have turned into a wholesale removal of documents—classified (and never properly released), previously declassified, and other (as in the NARA situation). The ISOO, though, also sent a representative to ensure that no "wholesale withholding" went on and that documents did not go "into a black hole."[61] The team combed through 1,200 boxes of material using a five-binder index to find the targeted papers. The officials blacked out sections of 20 papers and pulled a further eight documents out altogether, pending declassification.[62]

Retroactively Classified Open Congressional Briefings

In June 2004, the Project On Government Oversight (POGO) sued[63] then-Attorney General John Ashcroft and the U.S. Justice Department (DOJ) for retroactively classifying information related to whistleblower Sibel Edmonds' allegations of wrongdoing in an FBI translation unit post-September 11th.[64] Attorney General Ashcroft and the DOJ had retroactively classified this information (about the specifics of Mr. Edmonds' complaint), even though the FBI had already presented that information to the Senate Judiciary Committee during two unclassified briefings in 2002. And not only had the FBI already presented the information to the Senate, but two U.S. senators—Patrick Leahy (D-VT) and Charles Grassley (R-IA)—had referenced that information in letters they had written to DOJ officials. They had then posted those letters on their Senate websites. The letters were removed from the senators' websites after the FBI notified the Senate in May 2004 that the information had been retroactively classified.[65]

Attorney General Ashcroft defended the retroactive classification during a June 2004 Senate Judiciary Committee hearing, claiming that the further dissemination of the information about Mr. Edmonds' complaint could seriously impair the national security interests of the United States[66]—even though for more than two years the information had been widely available to the public. As noted in POGO's suit, though, under the standards of the Bush E.O., the information, which was posted on the internet and remains available on numerous Web sites, was not "reasonably recoverable,"[67] and thus was ineligible for reclassification (much less retroactive classification—as the information was not classified at the time of its release by the government).

In February 2005, the DOJ gave up,[68] just before a hearing scheduled before U.S. District Judge John D. Bates, and admitted that the information it had retroactively classified was "releasable in full" to the public "pursuant to the Freedom of Information Act."[69]

The DOJ's efforts at retroactively classifying what can only be called public information should disturb you. As noted earlier, the Clinton E.O. 12958 prohibited the reclassification of information after it had been released to the public under proper authority. Although the Bush E.O. 13292 restores the ability, under the predecessor Reagan E.O. 12356, to reclassify such information, it does so but only under "[the] personal authority of the agency head or deputy agency head" and only if the material may be "reasonably recovered." (§ 1.7(c)).

In this case, the government was not even seeking to *re*-classify information. The information was openly and publicly released in the first instance. "Retroactive classification" is an absurd concept for material that is in the public domain in the first instance. It is what, in the Reagan era, we called "born-again classified."[70]

Overclassification: If we told you...

In late October 2005, the Senate Judiciary Committee was told[71] that the "National Strategy for Transportation Security," which Congress had ordered as part of a 2004 intelligence bill, did in fact exist—even though the Department of Homeland Security had refused even to acknowledge its existence to most members of Congress. Former Senator and 9-11 Commission member Slade Gordon told the Committee that the agency had already turned the plan over to certain cleared members of Congress,[72] but refused to let anyone without a security clearance—including state and local emergency-response officials—see it. Apparently, even the 9-11 Commission has not seen anything but an early version. The December 2005 Final Report on 9/11 Commission Recommendations says, "DHS has transmitted its National Strategy for Transportation Security to the Congress. While the strategy reportedly outlines broad objectives, this first version lacks the necessary detail to make it an effective management tool."[73]

So, should we be concerned about this egregious overclassification? Yes. According to news reports,[74] some lawmakers who have seen the transportation security plan said it evaluates highways, bridges, tunnels, pipelines, commuter rail, and other infrastructure nationwide that must be protected from terrorist attack. The plan also was said to have set standards and risk-based priorities that agencies should use to draw up security requirements, as well as the relationships between various agencies. According to others, it could also include evacuation plans and logistics of emergency responses, such as outlining who would be in charge to ensure the availability of food, fuel, medicine, and other supplies in the event of an attack. At a minimum, this information needs to be shared with federal, state, and local emergency-response officials. Of course, some of it may also be protected as critical infrastructure information (CII)—in which case they might not be able to get or use it even if it were declassified or given to them in a partially declassified format.

Lest you think that the National Strategy for Transportation Security is an isolated example, consider these additional examples.

The 9-11 Commission. The Commission criticized excessive government secrecy. It concluded that Washington stamps "classified" on too many documents, keeping vital information hidden from Congress and the public, and undermining efforts to thwart terrorism. Commission Co-Chairman Thomas Kean, noted that "three-quarters of what I read that was classified shouldn't have been."[75] The commission report found, "Secrecy stifles oversight, accountability, and information sharing. Unfortunately, all the current organizational incentives encourage overclassification."[76]

Santa Claus and Cocktail Napkins. Nor were these conclusions of the 9-11 Commission news to federal government officials. During an August 24, 2004, hearing by the House Government Reform Committee's Subcommittee on National Security[77] into the Commission's conclusion that secrecy is undermining efforts to thwart terrorism, Carol A. Haave, deputy undersecretary of defense for counterintelligence and security, acknowledged[78] that probably half of all government classified documents may be unnecessarily or improperly classified. According to Haave, the problem is that "we overclassify information...[but] not for the purpose of wanting to hide anything. But I will tell you that with respect to military operations, people have a tendency to err on the side of caution."[79] At that same hearing, however, participants learned that the items "cautiously" classified include the cocktail napkin of Augusto Pinochet, and a "terrorist plot" to hijack Santa Claus made up by a CIA employee and inserted into classified traffic as a holiday joke.[80]

Invisible Ink and National Security. In 2002, Judge Thomas Penfield Jackson of the U.S. District Court for the District of Columbia ruled[81] that the National Archives and Records Administration, acting at the behest of the CIA, can withhold the six oldest U.S. classified documents currently in NARA's custody, which date between 1917 and 1930. Although the documents are nearly 100 years old, the CIA argued that the antiquated formulas and techniques for preparing and using invisible ink were "(1) currently viable for use by CIA agents; (2) building blocks for the CIA's more modern and sophisticated methods of using or detecting secret writing; (3) used to test current CIA secret writing systems for vulnerabilities; and (4) used to develop new formulas and techniques for secret writing." Judge Jackson ruled that release of the secret World War I formula—because it remains viable for use by the CIA—could compromise national security.

Misusing Classification

If overclassification poses a threat to our national security, arguably misuse of classification of information poses an even greater one. By "misuse" I mean classification that is aimed at something other than preventing demonstrable harm to our national security. For some recent examples, read on.

Identities of Members of Congress

You may recall that in December 2005, the *New York Times* revealed that, in 2002, the President issued an executive order authorizing the National Security Agency to wiretap phone and e-mail communications involving U.S. persons within the United States, without obtaining a warrant or court order as required by the Foreign Intelligence Surveillance Act of 1978 (FISA), which prohibits unauthorized electronic surveillance.[82] When a firestorm of criticism ensued, the White House claimed that members of Congress had been briefed—in classified meetings—about which members, therefore, could not speak. In May 2006,[83] then-House Minority Leader Nancy Pelosi asked President Bush's national security advisor, Stephen

Hadley, to review the administration"s decision to classify the dates and the names of the Congress members who were briefed on the Administration's warrantless surveillance program.[84] This followed her request, in December 2005, for "[the] dates and locations of, as well as the names of members of the Senate and House of Representatives who attended briefings on the National Security Agency surveillance program discussed by the President in his December 17, 2005 radio address."[85] The National Security Agency responded to that request by informing her the information she sought had been sent to the House Intelligence Committee for secure storage because it was "classified and compartmented."[86] After that, President Bush and his top advisers said repeatedly that dozens of briefings were held for congressional leaders and repeatedly described the National Security Agency's program publicly, sometimes providing operational details.[87]

This sequence of events raises the question why the Administration would have wanted to classify precisely who had attended these briefings—while at the same time loudly trumpeting that the briefings had taken place. In her May 2006 letter,[88] Ms. Pelosi noted, "To hold that the information covered by those statements was not classified, but that the identities of those briefed and when those briefings took place is, encourages the belief that the administration makes classification decisions solely for political purposes."

The July 2004 Senate Select Committee on Intelligence Report

Another concrete example of apparent misuse of classification—rather more disturbing than Santa Claus' security status—involved the July 2004 report, issued by the Senate Select Committee on Intelligence, documenting intelligence failures in the lead up to the war in Iraq. For weeks, there had been a heated back-and-forth on what needed to stay secret in that 500-plus page report. When it came back from review by intelligence officials, massively blacked out, Senator Trent Lott, a senior committee member, called that "absolutely an insult…they redacted half of what we had," including many portions "that revealed nothing" and were "everyday, unclassified words."[89] For example, the CIA deleted the amount Iraqi agents paid for aluminum tubes[90] from the Senate report. The CIA was quoted as concluding "their willingness to pay such costs suggests the tubes are intended for a special project of national interest." But as the *Washington Post* reported, that cost was revealed elsewhere in the same document—the same security reviewers let it be made public that the Iraqis paid as much as $17.50 for each tube, and perhaps as little as $10 each.[91] It is hard to know what to make of this;

perhaps some of the reviewers were more sensitive to the potential impact on the Administration's claims about the use of such tubes than were others—who saw the irrelevance of classifying such information.

2003 Congressional Investigation Report

The White House forced a joint congressional committee investigating the 9/11 attacks to black out an entire portion of its report said to deal with Saudi Arabia, saying that senior intelligence and law enforcement officials recommended keeping the 28 pages classified.[92] Then on May 1, Senator Bob Graham (D-FL) and Representative Porter Goss (R-FL)[93] had sent a letter to then-CIA Director George Tenet, asking the agency to accelerate the declassification of the 800-page inquiry's main findings.[94] In July, Senators Graham and Richard Shelby (R-AL) accused the administration of refusing to declassify information about possible Saudi Arabian financial links to U.S.-based terrorists because the material would be embarrassing and would heighten political tensions with the desert kingdom. Former Senate Intelligence Committee Chairman Shelby commented that he had carefully reviewed those sections "and my judgment is that 90 to 95 percent could be released and not compromise our intelligence in any way."[95]

On July 30, President Bush refused, despite requests from Saudi officials, to declassify the chapter, saying disclosure of the deleted section, which centers on accusations about Saudi Arabia's role in financing the hijackings, "'would help the enemy'" and compromise the administration's campaign against terror.[96]

Invoking § 8 of Senate Resolution 400 (discussed earlier in this chapter), Senator Graham asked the chairman of the Intelligence Committee, Senator Pat Roberts (R-KS), and the ranking member on the committee, Senator John D. Rockefeller IV (D-WV), to start a process that permits the declassification of information if the Senate voted to release it—even over the objections of the administration.[97] That section of the Report, "Part Four—Findings, Discussion and Narrative Regarding Certain Sensitive National Security Matters," is almost totally blanked out still.[98]

CIA's Continuing Refusal to Release FOIA-Requested Material Regarding 9/11

In May 2007, a bipartisan group of legislators (Senator Ron Wyden, D-OR, and two other intelligence committee leaders—chairman Jay Rockefeller, D-WV, and the senior Republican in the group, Kit Bond, R-MO) decided to push legislation that would force the CIA to declassify the executive summary of an inspector general's report on the terrorist attacks of September 11, 2001, within one month and submit a report to Congress explaining why any material was withheld. The CIA is the only federal office involved in counterterrorism operations that has not made at least a version of its internal 9/11 investigation public and, as of May, had spent more than 20 months weighing requests under the FOIA for its internal investigation of the attacks, but it has yet to release any portion of it.[99]

In Conclusion

It has been often stated, but bears repeating, that the misuse and abuse of the classification authority makes it harder to protect those pieces of information that do truly need to remain secret. This book does not address in more than passing reference the issues of those who leak classified information and those who are whistleblowers (in either the national security arena or elsewhere in the government), but committed public servants may come to believe that the only way to expose abuse of authority is to expose classified information. It is a difficult problem for our polity, but one that is made worse by excessive secrecy. It is up to Congress to curb the excesses and the Administration to restore the balancing test of the Clinton era's E.O. 12065 and E.O. 12958, weighing the need to protect information vis-à-vis the public interest in its disclosure. It looks like the latter will have to wait for a new administration more committed to openness.

Notes

1 Steven Aftergood, "What's Classified and What's Not," *Secrecy News,* February 20, 2006. Federation of American Scientists Project on Government Secrecy. http://www.fas.org/blog/secrecy/2006/02/whats_classified_and_whats_not_1.html. Aftergood notes that "A minority of classified information, such as nuclear weapons design information, is specified and protected by statute. The remainder, the large majority, is classified by executive order." A commenter on Aftergood's blog noted, "There's a helpful if slightly informal and not entirely complete (e.g., 18 USC 798 isn't mentioned) survey of such matters at http://www.rbs2.com/OFAC2.pdf, that being 'U.S. Government Restrictions on Scientific Publications: Statutes and Federal Regulations' by Ronald B. Standler, 13 July 2004."

2 George W. Bush, "Executive Order Further Amendment to Executive Order 12958, as Amended, Classified National Security Information," The White House. March 25, 2003. http://www.whitehouse.gov/news/releases/2003/03/20030325-11.html. A version of Executive Order 13292 that indicates the changes made to the Clinton-era order 12958 can be found on the Federation of American Scientists Project on Government Secrecy site, http://www.fas.org/sgp/bush/eo13292inout.html. A synopsis of what the Information Security Oversight Office (ISOO) considers the most significant changes to the executive order can be found on its site, at Information Security Oversight Office, "An Assessment of Declassification in the Executive Branch." http://www.archives.gov/isoo/reports/2005-declassification-report.html; http://www.archives.gov/isoo/reports/2004-declassification-report.html.

3 William J. Clinton, "Executive Order 12958 Classified National Security Information," The White House April 17, 1995. http://www.fas.org/sgp/clinton/eo12958.html.

4 Walter Pincus, "Justice Dept. Given 2 Weeks to Weigh Use of Classified Data in Espionage Case" *Washington Post,* Friday, April 20, 2007, p. A16. http://www.washingtonpost.com/wp-dyn/content/article/2007/04/19/AR2007041902295.html.

5 Bruce Berkowitz, a research fellow at the Hoover Institution, "Secrecy and National Security" *Hoover Digest* 2004, No. 3, Hoover Institution. http://www.hooverdigest.org/043/berkowitz.html.

6 Harold C. Relyea, a specialist in American National Government with the Congressional Research Service (CRS) of the Library of Congress, cites U.S. Congress, House Permanent Select Committee on Intelligence, A Statutory Basis for Classifying Information, hearing, 103rd Cong., 2nd Sess., March 16, 1994 (Washington, (GPO), 1995); U.S. Commission on Protecting and Reducing Government Secrecy, Secrecy (Washington: GPO, 1997); U.S. Congress, Senate Committee on Governmental Affairs, S. 712—Government Secrecy Act of 1997, hearing, 105th Cong., 2nd sess., Mar. 25, 1998 (Washington, D.C.: GPO, 1998).

7 See, e.g., Availability of Information from Federal Departments and Agencies: Hearings Before the House Committee on Government Operations, 85th Cong., 1st Sess. (1955).

8 CRS Report RL31245, Protection of National Security Information: The Classified Information Protection Act of 2001, by Jennifer Elsea, see also Note, *Keeping Secrets: Congress, the Courts, and National Security Information* 103 Harv. L. Rev. 906 (1990).

9 Executive Order No. 8381 (1940).

10 Harold C. Relyea, 2005, Statement Before House Government Reform Subcommittee on National Security, Emerging Threats, and International Relations, "Emerging Threats: Overclassification and Pseudo-classification," March 2, 2005. http://reform.house.gov/UploadedFiles/Relyea%20Emerging%20threats.pdf.

11 Elsea, op. cit.

12 Nathan Brooks, Legislative Attorney, American Law Division, "The Protection of Classified Information: The Legal Framework." RS21900 Updated August 5, 2004. CRS, Library of Congress. p. 6. http://www.fas.org/sgp/crs/RS21900.pdf.

13 Relyea (2005), op. cit. He also notes that, with this E.O., "information was now classified in the interest of 'national security,' a somewhat new, but nebulous, concept, which, in the view of some, conveyed more latitude for the creation of official secrets."

14 Kate Martin, "Congressional Access to National Security Information." Center for American Progress, Center for National Security Studies, and OpenTheGovernment.org, March 2007. http://www.openthegovernment.org/documents/congressional_paper.pdf.

15 Relyea (2005), op. cit.

16 Relyea (2005), op. cit.

17 ISOO is responsible to the President for policy and oversight of the Government-wide security classification system and the National Industrial Security Program. It receives its authority from Executive Order 12958.

18 ISOO. 2004 Report to the President. http://www.archives.gov/isoo/reports/2004-annual-report.html.

19 E.O. 12958, Sec. 3.3. "Automatic Declassification. ...All classified records that (1) are more than 25 years old and (2) have been determined to have permanent historical value under title 44, United States Code, shall be automatically declassified whether or not the records have been reviewed. Subsequently, all classified records shall be automatically declassified on December 31 of the year that is 25 years from the date of its original classification, except as provided in paragraphs (b)-(e) of this section."

20 "Systematic Review for Declassification," which began in 1972, is the program under which classified permanently valuable records are reviewed for the purpose of declassification after the records reach a specific age. Under E.O. 12356, the predecessor Order, the National Archives and Records Administration (NARA) was the only agency required to conduct a systematic review of its classified holdings. ISOO, op.cit.

21 http://www.archives.gov/isoo/speeches-and-articles/article-revised-eo12958.html.

22 http://www.fas.org/sgp/bush/eo13292inout.html.

23 Kate Martin, op. cit.

24 5 U.S.C. § 552(b)(1).

25 See National Security Act of 1947, Title V. Martin, op. cit., notes that "The Oversight Act also specifically requires the director of National Intelligence to provide any information requested by the committees; in the case of covert actions, the President is required to inform members of the committees." (Covert actions do not include classic espionage; rather, they are secret operations designed to influence events overseas without the role of the United States becoming known.)

26 Martin, op. cit.

27 Senate Resolution 400, section 8, agreed to May 19, 1976 (94th Congress, 2nd Session); Rules of the 109th Congress, U.S. House of Representatives, Rule X, section 11. Available at http://www.rules.house.gov/ruleprec/RX.htm.

28 Martin, op. cit.

29 Overviews of developments in classification and declassification can be found in the ISOO reports to the President assessing declassification in the executive branch, and its annual report to the President in which they present their analysis of statistical data regarding each agency's security classification program and other relevant information. http://www.archives.gov/isoo/reports/. Statistical summaries can be found in the Secrecy Report Cards issued by OpenTheGovernment.org. "Secrecy Report Card: Quantitative Indicators of Secrecy in the Federal Government," http://www.openthegovernment.org/otg/secrecy_reportcard.pdf; "Secrecy Report Card: An Update," http://www.openthegovernment.org/otg/OTG_RC_update .pdf; "Secrecy Report Card 2005," http://www.openthegovernment.org/otg/SRC2005.pdf; "Secrecy Report Card 2006," http://www.openthegovernment.org/article/subarchive/14.

30 Fox News Interview, February 15, 2006. http://www.thewashingtonnote.com/archives/001252.php.

31 Steve Aftergood, "ISOO Asks Attorney General to Rule on Cheney's Role" *Secrecy News,* February 6, 2007. http://www.fas.org/blog/secrecy/2007/02/isoo_asks_attorney_general _to.html.

32 Deb Riechmann "Waxman Decries Cheney Security Exemption" Associated Press, June 22, 2007. http://www.washingtonpost.com/wp-dyn/content/article/2007/06/21/AR200706210 1663.html.

33 Elana Schor and Mike Soraghan, "Secrecy may cost Cheney, Dems warn" *The Hill,* June 26, 2007. http://thehill.com/leading-the-news/secrecy-may-cost-cheney-dems-warn-2007-06-26.html.

34 Leora Falk, "Emanuel seeks to cut funding for Cheney's office, home," Chicago Tribune, June 26, 2007. http://www.chicagotribune.com/news/nationworld/chi-cheney_wedjun26,1,6424091 .story?coll=chi-news-hed&ctrack=1&cset=true.

35 Jim Abrams, "Cheney budget survives House vote decried as stunt," Associated Press, June 29, 2007. http://www.philly.com/inquirer/world_us/20070629_Cheney_budget_survives _House_vote_decried_as_stunt.html.

36 Matthew M. Aid, "Declassification in Reverse: The U.S. Intelligence Community's Secret Historical Document Reclassification Program," The National Security Archive, February 12, 2006. http://www.gwu.edu/%7Ensarchiv/NSAEBB/NSAEBB179/#report. NARA provides background—and a mea culpa—at National Archives and Records Administration, "Background on NARA Classified MOUs." Undated. http://www.archives.gov/declassification/background.html.

37 In an interesting look at the issue from the perspective of the move of the government to almost entirely digital record-creation and -keeping, Aliya Sternstein noted that the declassified documents in question are at least 25 years old, meaning they are mostly paper records. Little thought, she notes, has been given to how such removals might be discovered in the future when everything is electronic. Aliya Sternstein, "Feds secretly reclassify data. Thousands of documents have been taken off the shelves but left on the Internet," *Federal Computer Week,* February 27, 2006. http://www.fcw.com/article92436-02-27-06-Print.

38 For an enlightening article on this issue, see Alasdair Roberts, "ORCON creep. Information sharing and the threat to government accountability." *Government Information Quarterly* Vol. 21, pp. 249-267, 2004. ORCON is "ORiginator CONtrol"—allowing originating agencies (or governments) to retain control over declassification or release of information to non-government parties.

39 http://www.historians.org/perspectives/issues/2006/0604/0604nch1.cfm.

40 Scott Shane, "U.S. Reclassifies Many Documents in Secret Review," *New York Times,* February 21, 2006. http://select.nytimes.com/search/restricted/article?res=F30C16F93A5A0 C728EDDAB0894DE404482#. As Shane notes, if Mr. Leonard finds that documents are being wrongly reclassified, his office could not unilaterally release them. But as the chief adviser to the White House on classification, he could urge a reversal or a revision of the reclassification program.

41 National Archives and Records Administration, Information Security Oversight Office, "Audit of the Withdrawal of Records from Public Access at the National Archives and Records Administration for Classification Purposes," April 26, 2006. http://www.archives.gov/isoo/reports/2006-audit-report.html.

42 Memorandum of Understanding (MOU) between NARA and the CIA. http://www.archives.gov/declassification/mou-nara-cia.pdf; MOU between NARA and the United States Air Force. http://www.archives.gov/declassification/mou-nara-usaf.pdf.

43 ISOO Audit, op. cit.

44 Long delayed, but now in process in most instances.

45 Information Security Oversight Office. http://www.archives.gov/isoo/speeches-and-articles/keys-for-declassification.html.

46 ISOO, "Revisions to Executive Order 12958 on Classified National Security Information." http://www.archives.gov/isoo/speeches-and-articles/article-revised-eo12958.html.

47 http://www.fas.org/sgp/congress/2004/082404leonard.html. and Michael J. Sniffen, "'Secrets' Perplex Panel. Classified Data Growing to Include 'Comically Irrelevant,'" Washington Post, September 3, 2004. http://www.washingtonpost.com/wp-dyn/articles/A57823-2004Sep2.html.

48 http://www.historians.org/perspectives/issues/2006/0604/0604nch1.cfm.

49 See Espionage Act. For more on why this is a potentially legitimate concern, see Walter Pincus, "First Amendment Issues Raised About Espionage Act," *Washington Post*, Friday, March 31, 2006, P. A06. http://www.washingtonpost.com/wp-dyn/content/article/2006/03/30/AR2006033001777.html.

50 A lighthearted reference to the long-running *Mad* magazine cartoon series—Spy vs. Spy.

51 Most recently, by Senator Bond in August 2006 (apparently at the behest of the White House, as neither he nor his primary co-sponsor, Senator John Cornyn, seemed to know much about its implications when openness lobbyists spoke with their offices). Personal conversation with confidential source.

52 Scott Carlson, "George Washington U. to Receive Jack Anderson's Papers—but FBI Wants to See Them First," *Chronicle of Higher Education*, April 18, 2006. http://chronicle.com/free/2006/04/2006041801n.htm.

53 Id.

54 Mark Feldstein, "A Chilling FBI Fishing Expedition," *Washington Post*, Saturday, April 29, 2006, P. A17. http://www.washingtonpost.com/wp-dyn/content/article/2006/04/28/AR2006042801854.html.

55 Scott Shane, "F.B.I. Is Seeking to Search Papers of Dead Reporter," *New York Times*, April 19, 2006. http://www.nytimes.com/2006/04/19/washington/19anderson.html?ex=1303099200&en=01a0e29c2d12f334&ei=5088&partner=rssnyt&emc=rss.

56 Use of the Espionage Act against lobbyists for AIPAC.

57 Shane, op. cit.

58 Shane, op. cit.

59 Feldstein, op. cit.

60 Lara Bain, "CIA seizes Sen. Jackson papers," Herald.net, Tuesday, February 15, 2005. http://www.heraldnet.com/stories/05/02/15/100loc_jackson001.cfm.

61 J. William Leonard on Martin Kaste, "CIA's Seizure of Files Raises Questions" National Public Radio, *Morning Edition*, March 15, 2005. http://www.npr.org/templates/story/story.php?storyId=4535175.

62 Personal conversation with Bill Leonard.

63 POGO was represented in the case by lawyers from the Public Citizen Litigation Group and the Institute for Public Representation at Georgetown University Law Center. http://www.pogo.org/m/gp/a/Complaint.pdf.

64 POGO, "Justice Department Caves In: Allows Publication of Retroactively Classified Information—Lawsuit Challenged Classification of Public Information" February 22, 2005. http://www.pogo.org/p/government/ga-050202-classification.html.

65 http://www.pogo.org/m/gp/gp-EdmondsRetroClassification.pdf.

66 POGO, "Justice Department... ," op. cit.

67 As required by Executive Order 12958, as amended by Executive Order 13292.

68 Public Citizen, "Justice Department Caves In: Allows Publication of Retroactively Classified Information" February 22, 2005. http://www.citizen.org/pressroom/release.cfm?ID=1882; and "Attorney General's Reclassification of Information Critical of FBI Is Illegal" June 23, 2004. http://www.citizen.org/pressroom/release.cfm?ID=1731.

69 http://www.pogo.org/m/gp/gp-02182005-JusticeDeptLetter.pdf.

70 Playing on the claim made at the time that some information is "born classified."

71 Lisa Friedman, "National Strategy for Transportation Security plan off-limits" *Pasadena Star News,* October 27, 2005. http://www.populistamerica.com/national_strategy_for_transportation_security_plan_off_limits.

72 In September 2005, the Department of Homeland Security (DHS) delivered a classified report to Congress on a "National Strategy for Transportation Security." David Randall Peterman, Coordinator, Resources, Science, and Industry Division, "Transportation Security: Issues for the 109th Congress." Updated June 23, 2006. CRS, Library of Congress. http://fpc.state.gov/documents/organization/68824.pdf.

73 Final Report on 9/11 Commission Recommendations, December 5, 2005. http://www.9-11pdp.org/press/2005-12-05_report.pdf.

74 Friedman, op. cit.

75 "Lawmakers Frustrated by Delays in Declassifying Documents," Cox News Service, July 21, 2004.

76 National Commission on Terrorist Attacks Upon the United States, "Final Report, Executive Summary." July 22, 2004. http://www.9-11commission.gov/report/911Report_Exec.htm.

77 http://www.fas.org/sgp/congress/2004/082404transcript.html.

78 http://www.fas.org/sgp/congress/2004/082404haave.html.

79 http://www.fas.org/sgp/congress/2004/082404transcript.html.

80 Id.

81 *The James Madison Project v. National Archives and Records Administration,* Civil Action No. 98-2737 (D.D.C.), February 14, 2002. http://www.jamesmadisonproject.org/ocd3.htm.

82 James Risen and Eric Lichtblau, "Bush Lets U.S. Spy on Callers Without Courts" *New York Times,* December 16, 2005.

83 Letter from Nancy Pelosi to National Security Advisor, Stephen Hadley, "This is not national security information by any definition, and I therefore find the decision to classify it to be inconsistent with classification standards and completely without merit." Pelosi: ID Members Briefed on NSA Program, Associated Press, May 3, 2006.

84 http://www.house.gov/pelosi/press/releases/Jan06/declassified.html.

85 http://www.house.gov/pelosi/press/releases/Dec05/classified.html.

86 Of possible related interest, L. Britt Snider, "Sharing Secrets With Lawmakers—Congress as a User of Intelligence" *Studies in Intelligence,* Spring 1998. https://www.cia.gov/csi/studies/spring98/Congress.html.

87 "Pelosi Requests Review of Decision to Classify Information on NSA Surveillance Program" May 2, 2006. http://democraticleader.house.gov/press/releases.cfm?pressReleaseID=1539.

88 Pelosi. Op. Cit.

89 "Lawmakers Frustrated...," op. cit.

90 The White House claimed attempts by Iraq to acquire the tubes pointed to a clandestine program to make enriched uranium for nuclear bombs—one of the asserted reasons for attacking Iraq.

91 Michael J. Sniffen, "'Secrets' Perplex Panel. Classified Data Growing to Include 'Comically Irrelevant'" *Washington Post,* September 3, 2004. http://www.washingtonpost.com/wp-dyn/articles/A57823-2004Sep2.html.

92 Associated Press, "U.S. Wants to Probe Saudi Linked to 9/11 Hijackers; Bush Won't Release Congress 9/11 Report Pages," July 29, 2003. http://web.archive.org/web/20030811230409/http://abcnews.go.com/wire/Politics/ap20030729_2136.html.

93 A former CIA officer and chair of the House Select Intelligence Committee—who went on to become the Director of Central Intelligence.

94 Helen Fessenden, "Graham, Goss Accuse CIA of Blocking Release of Classified Sections of Sept. 11 Report" *CQ TODAY,* May 9, 2003. Fessenden notes that "Since then, however, Goss tempered his criticism. On May 9, he said negotiations with Tenet on declassification have made 'great progress.'"

95 Associated Press, "U.S. Wants... ," op. cit.

96 David Johnston and Douglas Jehl, "After the War: Intelligence Findings; Bush Refuses to Declassify Saudi Section of Report" *New York Times,* July 30, 2003. http://select.nytimes.com/search/restricted/article?res=FB0617FD3C5A0C738FDDAE0894DB404482.

97 Id.

98 Congressional Reports: Joint Inquiry into Intelligence Community Activities Before and After the Terrorist Attacks of September 11, 2001. GPO, http://www.gpoaccess.gov/serialset/creports/911.html.

99 Katherine Shrader, "Senators Want CIA to Release 9/11 Report" Associated Press, May 17, 2007. http://www.sfgate.com/cgi-bin/article.cgi?f=/n/a/2007/05/17/national/w131436D49.DTL.

PART I CONCLUSION

The preceding chapters have, I hope, made it clear that we are not lacking in policy to create a regulatory scheme to sustain a culture of openness and to, at a minimum, contain the culture of secrecy about which Senator Moynihan wrote ten years ago. These chapters have looked at the important laws on the books that were passed to make government more open and more accountable to the public.

We have also examined the implementation of the laws. Sometimes that implementation has gone reasonably well; take, for example, the revisions to OMB Circular A-130 in 1994. Guidance from OMB, or the Department of Justice in the case of the FOIA (when that guidance has been aimed at openness, unlike the Ashcroft Memorandum), does not necessarily translate, however, into practices that allow and promote openness and truthfulness at the agency level. The problem here does not lie, in the vast majority of cases, with the civil servants of this country, many of whom dedicate their careers to providing what is determined to be appropriate access to government information—and some of whom sacrifice those careers to do so. The problems lie with the political appointees and our elected officials.

Part II will look at them and the state of secrecy they have created.

Part II

Approach to Openness and Accountability

There are more instances of the abridgment of the freedom of the people by gradual and silent encroachments of those in power than by violent and sudden usurpations.

—James Madison, speech to the Virginia
Ratifying Convention, June 16, 1788

INTRODUCTION

In the preceding chapters, we have reviewed the state of public access in those aspects that do have statutes and regulations what I am calling our regulatory system for accountability and public access.

In Part II, I plan to illustrate the importance of the White House's approach toward openness and accountability. This importance stems in part from inherent features of our three-branch system of government, in which the executive, legislative, and judicial branches regularly test and contest the distribution and exercise of power. The person we elect to the presidency has a tremendous influence on the openness and accessibility of our government's information and our ability to use that information to hold our government accountable. The willingness of our Congress to contest the executive's assertions of its power is also critical.

The White House's approach to openness is most important where there is no clear regulatory system (as discussed in the previous chapters). As Senator Daniel Patrick Moynihan insightfully noted in the 1997 Report of the Commission on Protecting and Reducing Government Secrecy,[1] a system and culture of openness is necessary to countervail an otherwise prevalent and expansive culture of secrecy. Mr. Moynihan was referring to a culture surrounding national security. The second Bush administration has certainly made that culture more pervasive. This part of the book also looks at other facets of a culture of secrecy: the resistance to accountability—to the Congress and to the public—through assertions and exercise of executive power; the second Bush Administration's propagandistic use of information to shape both domestic and foreign opinion; and its politicization of science and expansive controls on access to informed government officials.

As in Part I, the work of journalists in unearthing, documenting, and telling important stories about access is critical to my work here and in my work as an advocate. As always, the research and advocacy of others in the public interest community informs this section of the book.

Notes

1 Daniel Patrick Moynihan. "Chairman's Foreword," Report of the Commission on Protecting and Reducing Government Secrecy. Washington, D.C., Government Printing Office 1997, p. xxxvi. http://www.fas.org/sgp/library/moynihan/index.html.

CHAPTER 7

THE EXECUTIVE'S POWER OVER
INFORMATION ACCESS

An informed public is the most potent of all restraints upon misgovernment. They alone can here protect the values of democratic government.

Today, the Executive Branch seeks to take this safeguard away from the public by placing its actions beyond public scrutiny....The Executive Branch seeks to uproot people's lives, outside the public eye, and behind a closed door. Democracies die behind closed doors. When the government begins closing doors, it selectively controls information rightfully belonging to the people.

—Circuit Judge Damon Keith[1],
U.S. Court of Appeals, 6th Circuit, August 26, 2002

Where there's no functioning regulatory system for openness and accountability—or where what does exist is totally ignored, dismantled, or dismissed—what happens is pretty much whatever the White House and the agencies want. In an administration committed, however rhetorically, to openness, such a lack may not be a problem. To some extent, this was the case in the Clinton Administration. But the following Bush Administration was another story, as you will see.

I will therefore focus primarily on the second Bush Administration (with some discussion of the Clinton Administration) and, in particular, how the Bush Administration used claims of executive power to

- interpret (and misinterpret) the law through an expanded use of statements made before signing a bill into law;

- resist accountability to Congress;

- resist disclosure of Presidential records; and

- impede investigation of events surrounding September 11.

Congress's Glass House

This book focuses primarily on the Executive Branch, as it's the President and the executive agencies that play the greatest role in the government's creation of and control over information. But it is important to note that Congress has exempted itself from every regulatory system for accountability and public access. These include the FOIA and the E-Government Act.

One example of Congress' unwillingness to provide access to its publications is the way that research by the Congressional Research Service is handled. American taxpayers spend nearly $100 million a year to fund the Congressional Research Service, a "think tank" that provides reports to members of Congress on a variety of topics relevant to current political events. Yet these reports are not made available to the public in any systematic way. For a while, an index and some of the reports were available through a few congressional offices, but that practice was summarily ended when the experiment sunsetted in late 2003 and Bob Ney, chair of the House Administration Committee, refused to reinstate the database.[2] According to Associated Press, Mr. Ney said, "Why give your opposition free research?"[3] Access to these valuable reports has not been determined by statute, but by the rules of the respective chambers. The reports do somehow get disseminated to individuals, organizations, and companies, but through nonsystematic and often nontransparent means.

Then take something as basic as information on how members of Congress vote. Commercial services provide information on how members vote on particular bills, as does (currently) the *Washington Post* (at http://projects.washingtonpost.com/congress/). But your government does not—and it is difficult to find out from any source how a member votes on a particular issue (as opposed to a particular bill), or across time. Unless you are one of the lobbyists involved (or know and have good relations with the relevant congressional staff people), it is nearly impossible to get hold of earmarks or amendments to legislation until they are voted on. In the 109th Congress, it was almost as difficult for members of the minority party to get this information as it was for outsiders. So much for accountability.

Although attempts have been made to include Congress in accountability and openness statutes, it is Congress that passes the legislation. In the 110th Congress, legislation has passed in one chamber or the other to improve disclosure of congressional financial information—and earmarks. The proof of the pudding will, of course, be in the eating.

Let a Thousand—Well, Five Hundred—Flowers Bloom: The Clinton Years

The Clinton Administration, whose beginning coincided with widespread adoption of the internet in agencies across the government, is an example of both accountability and openness. This era seemed to many a golden age of dissemination of information, a "Let a thousand flowers bloom" for government on the internet. Clinton's Office of Management and Budget (OMB) became *more* open and accountable. He encouraged, in two presidential memoranda,[4] agencies to put more information online that is "identified and organized in a way that makes it easier for the public to find the information it seeks." The memoranda contained directives for improving public access to government information, including organizing information by the ways people may seek it rather than along bureaucratic lines. Agencies were singled out to perform specific tasks; for example, the Environmental Protection Agency was tasked to develop a "national strategy" for using information technology and public access to information to drive environmental cleanup and pollution prevention efforts. So, the rhetoric—and in many cases, the practice—was great.

On the other hand, not everyone was swept away. James Love, a longtime access advocate, argued[5] in late 1994 that, while the administration had, indeed, given agencies a green light to undertake new dissemination projects—leading to an explosion of new information products and services, many available for free through the Internet—it also had taken initiatives such as putting its own press releases online and providing ready electronic access to hot reports such as the Vice President's National Performance Review, or the text of the General Agreement on Tariffs and Trade (GATT) or North American Free Trade Agreement (NAFTA) agreements. Love noted that the administration had not, however, done much "about the bread and butter details of dissemination policy," including such issues as

- Privatization of government information (shutting down the DOJ's JURIS electronic legal research system, effectively ceding the ground to commercial companies);

- Failure to give concrete support to EDGAR (a successful and popular National Science Foundation (NSF)-funded demonstration project at New York University to provide free access to the Securities and Exchange Commission (SEC's) EDGAR database of corporate disclosure filings—which eventually became available on the SEC site;[6] and

- Inconsistency in access and dissemination practices across the government (some agencies, like the Bureau of Labor Statistics, provided catalogs of databases and documentation, while other agencies, such as the Food and Drug Administration (FDA), made little or no effort to provide the public with any idea of what types of databases the agency maintains).

And the third item is still true today—*plus ça change*!

Love also noted the Clinton Administration provided no mechanisms for systematic assessment of the type of products and services that are needed, and opposed proposals that would force federal agencies to regularly solicit public comments on the types of information products and services that citizens want. Love remarked that "many observers believe that the White House is largely focused on using the technology to provide propaganda functions. . . over the more mundane but important systems that would provide systematic access to complete collections of records."[7]

A lot of this sounds depressingly familiar, but the point is that even an administration that appears favorably disposed to public access will not go out of its way to promote the public's access to what we want to know as opposed to what they want us to know.

The big difference, however, is whether the government acknowledges (even if it does not always honor) a public right to know, or requires proof that the public has a "legitimate" need to know. Although I spent much of the late 1990s locking horns with the Clinton OMB, only sometimes successfully, I think it is fair to characterize the Clinton Administration, whatever its real failings, as "right-to-know." The same cannot be said about the George W. Bush Administration.

Where Have All the Flowers Gone? The Bush Era

Back in late 2002–early 2003, it was pretty clear—at least to those of us who were paying reasonably close attention—that whatever openness in government we had secured during previous administrations was disappearing rapidly. At that time I wrote

> *"The current Bush Administration has frequently been characterized as the most secretive in recent history. They are undoubtedly very focused on controlling the message and they clearly appreciate that "information is power." This Administration appears to understand even more clearly, moreover, that lack of information leads to lack of*

> *power. I argue that these tendencies do not all fit neatly under the usual attribution of "secrecy" but, rather, that there are four different threads to the Bush Administration's approach to public access to government information. These are* secrecy; *a* resistance to accountability *to the public and, even more pointedly, to Congress; a belief in a* need-to-know *approach to information, i.e., that access should depend on who you are and whether the government considers that you are fit to receive the information; and, finally, what I characterize as* ideological purity."[8]

I think now I would characterize the last thread as control and politicizing of science, and I would add propaganda to the list.

When the Executive Resists Accountability

The George W. Bush Administration has provided a case study in what happens when the White House has a pervasive resistance to accountability. This resistance can be seen not only in the changes set out in Attorney General Ashcroft's October 12, 2001, memorandum, which encouraged agencies to take an attitude of presumptively *not* disclosing information (see Chapter 3), but also in a number of specific attempts to stiff-arm the public and, especially, Congress. Bush and Cheney came into the White House with a belief that executive power had been ceded—or, in the case of President Clinton, squandered—over the past 30-plus years. They were determined to take it back, and given a complacent Congress (prior to the 2006 elections) and a judiciary that strongly tends to defer to the executive branch, they have (as of mid-2007) been largely successful. Louis Fisher, a noted scholar on the separation of powers in our constitutional system, has noted that maintaining the balance of powers in our government requires bare-knuckles struggles between the executive and legislative branches.[9] Until November 2006, the knuckles were applied from only one side.

Ignoring the Question

In November 2003, for example, the White House sent an e-mail message, titled "congressional questions," to the staff of the House and Senate Appropriations Committees indicating that it would no longer entertain direct questions from opposition lawmakers, i.e., Democrats. (The trigger for this e-mail was apparently that House Committee Democrats—then the minority party in both chambers of Congress—had asked for information about how much the White House spent making and installing the "Mission

Accomplished" banner used by the President on his notorious visit to the *USS Abraham Lincoln* in May 2003.) According to the *Washington Post*,[10] the e-mail message read:

> *Given the increase in the number and types of requests we are beginning to receive from the House and Senate, and in deference to the various committee chairmen and our desire to better coordinate these requests, I am asking that all requests for information and materials be coordinated through the committee chairmen and be put in writing from the committee.*

No requests from Democrats unless the Republican committee chairs approved them. In other words, no requests from Democrats, period.

Signing Statements

Resisting accountability by simply refusing to entertain requests was one "bare-knuckles" approach. Others have been based on constitutional arguments and issues surrounding relations between the legislative and executive branches. These other separation-of-power approaches include claims of "executive privilege," presidential signing statements, and the related concept of the "unitary executive."

As of August 2006, President Bush had used the separation-of-powers doctrine at least 132 times when signing legislation into law, issuing an executive order, or responding to a congressional resolution.[11] The President announced in these signings[12] that he would construe provisions in a manner consistent with his "constitutional authority to supervise the unitary executive branch." (See *Secrecy Report Card: Sensitive but Unclassified Designations in Use at Selected Federal Agencies*, Chapter 5.)

In the least expansive version, the unitary executive doctrine is only a claim that the President has the power to appoint, control, and remove executive officers, as well as the duty to interpret the law as it applies to his office.

The doctrine is being used extensively by the Bush Administration, however, to claim the authority to decide what is and what is not the law through the medium of the presidential signing statement—that is, the statement that the President makes when signing a bill passed by Congress into law.[13] Although signing statements are not new, the tactic used by the Bush Administration—to announce an interpretation of the law to assert the superceding authority of the President regardless of Congress's intent—is a departure from the norm.

A few examples[14] are enlightening:

- *Torture.* December 30, 2005: U.S. interrogators cannot torture prisoners or otherwise subject them to cruel, inhuman, and degrading treatment. Bush's signing statement: The president, as commander in chief, can waive the torture ban if he decides that harsh interrogation techniques will assist in preventing terrorist attacks.[15]

- *Research information.* December 30, 2005: When requested, scientific information "prepared by government researchers and scientists shall be transmitted [to Congress] uncensored and without delay." Bush's signing statement: The president can tell researchers to withhold any information from Congress if he decides its disclosure could impair foreign relations, national security, or the workings of the executive branch.[16]

- *DOE whistleblowers.* August 8, 2005: The Department of Energy, the Nuclear Regulatory Commission, and its contractors may not fire or otherwise punish an employee whistle-blower who tells Congress about possible wrongdoing. Bush's signing statement: The president or his appointees will determine whether employees of the Department of Energy and the Nuclear Regulatory Commission can give information to Congress.[17]

The Constitution, however, gives Congress the power to make the laws, and it is the obligation of the President to ensure their faithful execution. In the historical understanding of separation-of-powers, it has been the U.S. Supreme Court[18] that is the final arbiter of what is and is not the law.[19] The Supreme Court—even its conservative members, who are sympathetic to the unitary executive theory—has rejected the extreme positions taken by the Bush Administration.[20]

Openness advocates see this fight not as merely some abstruse argument among constitutional lawyers, but as a secrecy issue because, while the statements themselves are available, any one statement may contain challenges to multiple provisions of laws and it is, thus, difficult for the public to know that the President intends to "faithfully execute" the laws as required by the U.S. Constitution (Article II, Section 3). It is also important to note that historically these statements have been used as public announcements, containing comments from the President, on the enactment of the law—not as an obfuscated carving away of the authority of the legislative branch and an affront to the public.

In June 2007, the Government Accountability Office (GAO) reported[21] it had found "multiple examples in which the administration has not complied with the requirements of the new statutes." GAO found 160 separate provisions that Bush had objected to in signing statements in appropriations acts for Fiscal Year 2006. Of the 19 provisions out of the 160 that GAO investigators followed, six—nearly a third—were not carried out according to law. Ten were executed by the executive branch. Some examples include the following:

- Congress demanded in its 2006 military spending law that the Defense Department break down its 2007 budget request to show the detailed costs of global military operations, such as the wars in Iraq and Afghanistan. The department ignored the order.

- The Federal Emergency Management Agency (FEMA) also ignored Congress's demand that it submit an expenditure plan for housing assistance and alternatives to the approaches that failed after Hurricane Katrina. FEMA told the GAO that it does not normally produce such plans.

Rejecting the GAO's Demands for Disclosure

The other constitutional doctrine sometimes invoked by the executive branch when asserting its power is the doctrine of executive privilege. Executive Privilege "refers to the assertion made by the President or other executive branch officials when they refuse to give Congress, the courts, or private parties information or records which have been requested or subpoenaed, or when they order government witnesses not to testify before Congress. The assertion is based on the constitutional doctrine of separation of powers, is always controversial, subject to interpretation, and often litigated."[22] The story of Cheney's citing this doctrine in his confrontation with the investigative and audit arm of Congress, the General Accounting Office—subsequently (and possibly consequently) renamed the Government Accountability Office—is a great example of a bare-knuckles fight. Unfortunately, it is one in which Congress apparently threw the fight.

On April 19, 2001, Representatives John Dingell and Henry Waxman launched joint requests to both the Vice President and the GAO—which acts on Congress's behalf with the Executive Branch—concerning the Vice President's National Energy Policy Development Group (NEPDG), its members, and its proceedings. The issue centered around the Federal Advisory Committee Act (FACA). Under FACA, if a person who is not an officer or employee of the government is a member of a government group, then the group's proceedings must be open to the public. It was generally suspected that the NEPDG included representatives of oil, coal, and other energy industries. This fight centered on identifying those participants. Just that, not what they said to the White House.

In response to the request, the GAO issued the first-ever demand letter to a sitting Vice President. GAO considered its statutory authority to do so clear.[23]

David Addington, Counsel to the Vice President, responded that the Energy Group was not subject to the FACA—although as a matter of comity he would provide some answers about the Energy Group's members, staff, and activities. Addington declared that GAO was seeking "to intrude into the heart of Executive deliberations, including deliberations among the President, the Vice President, members of the President's Cabinet, and the President's immediate assistants, which the law protects to ensure the candor in Executive deliberation necessary to effective government."[24] GAO argued that even assuming this claim was accurate, it still had the authority to make the requests it had made. In February 2002, GAO filed suit,[25] for the first time in its 81 years, against a federal official in connection with a records access issue.

It was clear, even this early in this administration, that executive privilege was an issue of central importance. As John Dean—who, as counsel to former President Nixon might be considered to know something about abuse of power—writes "not since Richard Nixon stiffed the Congress during Watergate has a White House so openly, and arrogantly, defied Congress's investigative authority." Dean rejects the argument that he sees Cheney as making, that GAO (and therefore the Congress, too) has no authority to seek the information it has requested.[26]

On December 9, 2002, U.S. District Judge John Bates, a Bush appointee and former deputy for Kenneth Starr, ruled against the GAO (*Walker v. Cheney*). The opinion reads:

> *The parties agree that no court has ever before granted what the Comptroller General seeks—an order that the President (or Vice President) must produce information to Congress (or the Comptroller General). Because the Comptroller General does not have the personal, concrete, and particularized injury required under Article III standing doctrine, either himself or as the agent of Congress, his complaint must be dismissed. Historically, the Article III courts have not stepped in to resolve disputes between the political branches over their respective Article I and Article II powers; this case, in which neither a House of Congress nor any congressional committee has issued a subpoena for*

> *the disputed information or authorized this suit, is not the setting for*
> *such unprecedented judicial action.*[27]

This decision, in essence, secures the Bush Administration's position that it has the right to withhold from Congress and the public any and all details of its policy-development meetings with nongovernmental people. It also potentially chilled any attempt by Congress to use the GAO to monitor the executive branch and allow the Congress to exercise its oversight authority on behalf (ostensibly, anyway) of the American people. As I have noted—frequently and repeatedly—good information must be available if the government is to be held accountable.

The suit culminated with the Supreme Court's nondecision in *Cheney v. U.S. District Court*,[28] and the D.C. Circuit's en banc ruling on remand,[29] siding with the Administration on the merits of the case. It is worth noting that it was the White House that petitioned the Supreme Court for a writ of mandamus vacating the district court's discovery orders. They asked the Court to direct the district court to rule on the basis of the administrative record, and order dismissal of the Vice President as a party.[30] The White House wanted it clear that they did not have to give up any materials.

Another probable reason the White House sought the vacating of the orders is that it is not clear that the Vice President *can* assert executive privilege. The Constitution vests the executive power in the President. "So long as the President remains healthy, the Vice President has no constitutionally assigned executive function. As far as the Constitution is concerned, the Vice President's role is legislative in nature: to preside over and break ties in the Senate."[31]

GAO initially considered appealing the district court's decision in *Walker v. Cheney*, but on February 7, 2003, after, as it discreetly[32] put it, "bipartisan outreach efforts to the Congress," GAO decided not to appeal the district court's decision.[33] In the Comptroller General's statement they noted that, although they believed "[the] district court's decision was incorrect," their continuing to pursue the access request "through the courts would have required significant time and resources over several years."

Moreover, they argued that "because the district court's decision in GAO's case did not reach the merits of GAO's audit or access authority, the decision in no way diminishes these authorities or the obligation of agencies to provide GAO with information. The court's decision is confined to the unique circumstances of the NEPDG case and does not preclude GAO from filing suit on a different matter involving different facts in the future."[34]

GAO's problems with the executive branch have continued. In May 2007, Comptroller General David Walker said[35] that "he wants Congress to grant him the authority to take sworn testimony from executive branch employees during oversight investigations." The particular casus belli is that in December 2006, GAO auditors asked the Department of Homeland Security for inspection reports "for federally funded jails housing foreign detainees to ensure that safety standards were being met." It took DHS "five months to turn over all of its records and did so only after senior department officials intervened."[36]

The issues here are the same as those in the health reform task force of about 500 health policy experts First Lady Hillary Clinton convened in 1993. It worked behind closed doors for more than six months. Remember that under FACA, if a person who is not an officer or employee of the government is a member of a government group, then the group's proceedings must be open to the public. The health care–reform panel had kept its proceedings private, so if the First Lady was not a government officer or employee, it had broken the law.

The issue is made complicated by the complex makeup of the task force. In addition to the First Lady, the other appointed members were cabinet secretaries and senior White House officials. The President also formed an interdepartmental working group to support the task force by gathering information and developing various healthcare options. The working group consisted of around 300 permanent federal employees drawn from the Executive Office of the President, federal agencies, and Congress; around 40 "special government employees" hired for a limited duration; and various consultants who attended some of the group meetings.[37] FACA does not apply to working groups of advisory groups—so the only question for the courts was whether any nongovernmental person (i.e., the First Lady) was on the highest-level task force.

The U.S. Court of Appeals for the D.C. Circuit held, in *Association of American Physicians and Surgeons, Inc. v. Hillary Clinton*, that the First Lady is indeed an officer or employee of the government, and FACA thus did not apply. Michael Dorf[38] notes that "under a well-established principle of legal interpretation, courts construe statutes in order to avoid difficult constitutional questions." For the D.C. Circuit, the difficult constitutional question had to do with executive privilege and separation-of-powers issues raised by the congressionally passed FACA:

> *Does executive privilege extend to conversations between Executive officials and persons outside the government? If so, then FACA*

unconstitutionally violates that privilege by requiring those conversa-
tions to be disclosed. Had the court ruled that the First Lady was
neither a government officer nor a government employee, it would
have had to decide the difficult constitutional question—for FACA
then would have required disclosure of deliberations between the
(non-government) First Lady and the executive branch government
officials on the commission.[39]

Presidential Records

In 1978, Congress, declaring that the official records of a former President belong to the American people, passed the Presidential Records Act of 1978.[40] The Act was to ensure that the official records of the President are preserved and made publicly accessible.

Under the Act, as amended in 1989, the U.S. government asserts complete "ownership, possession, and control" of all presidential and vice-presidential records. When a President's term in office is complete, the Archivist of the United States is required to assume custody of the records and to make them available to the public "as rapidly and completely as possible." Records containing national security classification, information relating to appointments to federal office, confidential communications between the president and his advisers, confidential financial or commercial information, or other records constituting a privacy concern may be withheld from public release by a president leaving office for up to 12 years.

At the end of the 12-year period, members of the public can submit a FOIA request to view any previously embargoed papers. At that point, access—prior to Executive Order 13233 (discussed below)—could be denied only if a former or incumbent president claims an exemption based on a "constitutionally based" executive privilege or continuing national security concern.

The first presidential records to come under the Act are those of former President Ronald Reagan. Those records should have become publicly available in February 2001. But for much of that year, their release was delayed by the second Bush Administration.

On November 1, 2001, President Bush issued Executive Order 13233 to govern the review of a former President's records for possible executive privilege claims. The executive order asserts an extremely expansive view of the scope of that privilege. It not only asserts the privilege for confidential communications with the President's advisers (recognized by Supreme Court precedent), but also[41] provides both a former President and the incumbent President an unlimited amount of time to review records to determine whether to object to their release to the public. It also empowers the incumbent President to order the Archivist to withhold access to the former President's records on grounds of privilege—even if the former President does not object to their being made public—and even in the absence of any claim that national security would be affected by public release. Previously, under the Presidential Records Act and before the E.O., the national Archivist was permitted to exercise discretion in such cases.[42]

It also extends, for the first time, the constitutional executive privilege to the Vice President. This raises a serious constitutional issue: does the Vice President have the same immunities and privileges as the President, especially those that aren't available for other executive officers, e.g., cabinet officials?[43] A related issue was raised in the previous chapter as to whether the Vice President can declassify information not classified by him (or her). Vice President Cheney—and President Bush—appear to think of him as co-President. Why is this important? There is no text in the Constitution to support this view and no mention of any powers inherent in the Vice Presidency. We have enough trouble with the President's assertions of expansive executive privilege; we don't need the Vice President chiming in.

The executive order also changed the FOIA process specified under the Presidential Records Act (PRA), and created a new barrier to access by requiring that researchers must assert a "demonstrated, specific need" for presidential records, even after the end of the 12-year embargo period. In contrast, the FOIA specifically does not require a requestor to provide a reason for the request.

On November 28, 2001, Public Citizen, a nonprofit public interest group, filed suit against the National Archives and Records Administration (NARA) and U.S. Archivist John Carlin to overturn E.O. 13233 and "to compel the release of presidential materials of former President Ronald Reagan that are in the custody of NARA and are being withheld in violation of the PRA."[44] In March 2002, the administration released 59,850 of the 68,000 pages from the Reagan papers originally identified by the Archivist. A remaining 155 pages were released that July. During the discovery process, however, approximately 1,500 additional pages of the Reagan papers were identified by NARA archivists.

In October 2002, the House Committee on Government Reform unanimously approved legislation first introduced by Representative Stephen Horn and co-sponsored by 44 other legislators that reinforced implementation of the Presidential Records Act of 1978. In a letter to the Committee, the White House attacked the bill as "unnecessary and inappropriate, and, more importantly, unconstitutional."[45] The administration claimed that the Reagan presidential records had been released, showing the bill is not needed.

And most of them had been . . . but the remaining pages that are still not released have to do with the Iran-Contra scandal—some of the participants in that have served as advisors not only to G. H. W. Bush but also to G. W. Bush.

According to the National Archives, the first segment of records for the G.H.W. Bush presidency were released in February 2005 and "representatives of former President Bush and incumbent President Bush have chosen not to assert any constitutionally-based privilege."[46] As of the most recent release of the G.H.W. Bush presidential library (in August 2006), a little over 60,000 pages (out of 40-million) pages had been released for public access.[47] It is hard to say what part of that is processing backlog and what is the impact of the executive order.

The 2002 bill went nowhere in that Congress and it was not revisited again until March 2007, when the House passed legislation (H.R. 1255) that would overturn the Bush executive order and clarify the Archivist's role in consideration of claims of constitutionally based privilege against disclosure. A partner bill has been introduced in the Senate.

September 11th Inquiry

In late 2001, a joint inquiry of the Senate Select Committee on Intelligence and the House Permanent Select Committee on Intelligence was impaneled and charged with making a full investigation into "[the] response of the United States Government including that of the Intelligence Community to international terrorism." The original three choices for the conduct of the inquiry had been for it to be undertaken by standing committees of Congress, by a special investigating committee, or by an independent commission. The Bush Administration initially opposed all the choices— calling them a distraction from the war on terrorism—but eventually they promised to cooperate with the joint inquiry.

The administration's notion of cooperation was not what most of us understand by the term. They declined to offer data about the provision of terrorism intelligence to Bush and, in the declassification process that preceded open hearings in September, they refused to release material indicating presidential awareness (even where the substance of the documents was known or was being declassified) and refused to let security or intelligence officials testify.[48]

In an interview with the *New York Times*, Alabama Republican Senator Richard Shelby, the joint committee co-chairman, remarked, "We were told that there would be cooperation in this investigation, and I question that. I think that most of the information that our staff has been able to get that is real meaningful has had to be extracted piece by piece."[49] Similarly, Shelby, asked on NBC Television, "Are we getting the cooperation we need?" Shelby then answered his own question: "Absolutely not."[50] In an October 20th Reuters interview, Senator Bob Graham, the other co-chair, said, "There's been a pattern in which information is provided on a classified basis, and then what is declassified are those sections of the report that are most advantageous to the administration."[51]

The President's daily briefs were an item of particular contention. Both Vice President Cheney and National Security Condoleezza Advisor Rice declared in 2002 that the President's daily briefs cannot see the light of day because declassification would reveal intelligence sources and methods. Cheney maintained that such documents have not been released in the past and seemed concerned that a poor precedent would be set now[52]—tying back to his belief, discussed earlier, that the executive branch has ceded too much of its rightful, unitary power.

There is disagreement with this characterization. John Prados[53] notes that the daily briefs are analytical, not operational, reports and that statements regarding sources can be easily deleted in the declassification process. As for the argument about setting precedent, a number of the President's daily briefs, as well as the predecessors of these documents (called president's intelligence checklists), have long been on the public record.[54]

In any event, in the hearings, the White House refused to permit open testimony by any intelligence agency chief or by the secretaries of state or defense. They also did not permit access to the President's daily briefs. Great cooperation! (It's sort of like their cooperation with Congress on the issues around the firing of U.S. Attorneys, and the hiring process/practices in the Department of Justice generally.)[55]

In Conclusion

What this chapter—and those that follow—illustrates too clearly is that the balance of powers on which our system of government relies can get dangerously lopsided. There are, of course, constitutional issues involved here—and constitutional scholars to address and argue them; I am concerned with the impact of access and accountability. Although the President is elected in a nationwide vote, the office is largely insulated from the public, in a way that neither representatives nor senators are. The President also controls (to a greater or lesser extent) the vast executive branch. For these reasons, the office can wreak much greater havoc on openness—and can evade accountability more easily. The balance of powers is the only real regulation we have when it comes to the assertions of executive power and authority we have seen in this chapter.

Notes

1 Circuit Judge Damon Keith, Opinion, U.S. Court of Appeals Sixth Circuit, August 26, 2002, in the case of *Detroit Free Press v. Ashcroft*. The opinion strongly affirmed a trial court ruling, finding across-the-board closure of immigration proceedings unconstitutional.

2 "Reps. Shays and Inslee Seek Reinstatement of Access to CRS Reports on Member Web Sites," letter to Representative Bob Ney, November 24, 2003. http://www.fas.org/sgp/news/2003/11/crs112403.pdf.

3 "The arrogance of power," ToledoBlade.com, December 22, 2003. http://www.toledoblade.com/apps/pbcs.dll/article?AID=/20031222/OPINION02/112210093/-1/OPINION.

4 William J. Clinton, "Memorandum on Use of Information Technology to Improve Our Society" White House, December 17, 1999. http://www.ombwatch.org/article/articleview/631/1/255?TopicID=1, http://govinfo.library.unt.edu/npr/library/direct/memos/elecgovrnmnt.html.

5 James Love, "The Clinton/Gore Administration and public access to government information" December 20, 1994. Posted on Taxpayer Assets Project—Information Policy Note, January 6, 1995. http://lists.essential.org/1995/info-policy-notes/msg00109.html.

6 Carl Malamud, "The Importance of Being EDGAR," media.org. http://www.mundi.net/cartography/EDGAR/.

7 Love, op. cit.

8 Patrice McDermott, "Withholding and Control: Information in the Bush Administration," *The Kansas Journal of Law and Public Policy*, Vol. XII, No. III Spring 2003, pp. 671-691.

9 Conversation at a public forum in 2006.

10 Dana Milbank, "White House Puts Limits on Queries From Democrats" *Washington Post*, November 7, 2003, p. A29.

11 OpenTheGovernment.org, "Secrecy Report Card 2006." http://www.openthegovernment.org/otg/SRC2006.pdf.

12 Joyce A. Green, "Presidential Signing Statements." http://www.coherentbabble.com/signingstatements/signstateann.htm.

13 Jennifer Van Bergen, "The Unitary Executive: Is the Doctrine Behind the Bush Presidency Consistent with a Democratic State?" FindLaw Writ, Monday, January 9, 2006 http://writ.news.findlaw.com/commentary/20060109_bergen.html.

14 "Examples of the president's signing statements" *Boston Globe*, April 30, 2006. http://www.boston.com/news/nation/articles/2006/04/30/examples_of_the_presidents_signing_statements/.

15 President's Statement on Signing of H.R. 2863, the "Department of Defense, Emergency Supplemental Appropriations to Address Hurricanes in the Gulf of Mexico, and Pandemic Influenza Act, 2006." http://coherentbabble.com/signingstatements/SSann2005.htm.

16 President's Statement on H.R. 3010, the "Department of Labor, Heath and Human Services, and Education, and Related Agencies Appropriations Act, 2006."

17 President's Statement on the Energy Policy Act of 2005.

18 Jennifer Van Bergen, op. cit. "The Administration's actions under this doctrine have become so prevalent that even conservatives on the Supreme Court who are sympathetic to the unitary executive theory have felt compelled to reject them. Last year, for example, the Court ruled that the President does not have absolute authority to detain enemy combatants without due process." And "Scholar says Bush has used obscure doctrine to extend power 95 times" *The Raw Story*, September 23, 2005. http://www.rawstory.com/news/2005/CanExecutive_Branch_Decide_0923.html.

19 "Separation of Powers and Checks and Balances," U.S. Constitution, FindLaw. http://caselaw.lp.findlaw.com/data/constitution/article01/01.html.

20 Jennifer Van Bergen, op. cit.

21 http://appropriations.senate.gov/News/2007_06_18_Text_of_GAO_Opinion_on_White_House_Signing_Statements.pdf.

22 C-SPAN, Congressional Glossary. http://www.c-span.org/guide/congress/glossary/exprivilege.htm.

23 General Accounting Office, Fact Sheet On GAO'S Access Case. January 31, 2002. http://www.gao.gov/accessfs.pdf.

24 John W. Dean, "GAO v. Cheney Is Big-time Stalling: The Vice President Can Win Only If We Have Another Bush v. Gore-like Ruling" FindLaw, Friday, February 1, 2002. http://writ.news.findlaw.com/dean/20020201.html.

25 http://www.gao.gov/press/gaostatement0222.pdf.

26 John W. Dean, op. cit.

27 Memorandum Opinion and Order. http://www.washingtonpost.com/wp-srv/onpolitics/transcripts/cheney_120902.pdf . The suit brought by Judicial Watch, *Judicial Watch, Inc., Plaintiff v. National Energy Policy Development Group*, Defendant., Civ. Action. 01-1530 (EGS) and the Sierra Club, *Sierra Club, Plaintiff, v. Vice-President Cheney, et.al.*, Defendant, Civ. Action. 02-631 (EGS), also were decided for the administration's positions. http://caselaw.findlaw.com/data2/circs/DC/025354B.pdf.

28 http://a257.g.akamaitech.net/7/257/2422/24june20041201/www.supremecourtus.gov/opinions/03pdf/03-475.pdf.

29 http://caselaw.lp.findlaw.com/data2/circs/dc/025354b.pdf.

30 http://caselaw.lp.findlaw.com/scripts/getcase.pl?court=dc&navby=case&no=025354A&exact=1.

31 Michael C. Dorf, "A Brief History of Executive Privilege, from George Washington Through Dick Cheney," FindLaw's Writ, Wednesday, February. 6, 2002. http://writ.news.findlaw.com/dorf/20020206.html.

32 The story around town was that their funding was threatened by powerful congressional Republicans.

33 http://www.gao.gov/nepdgchron.pdf.

34 Id.

35 Rebecca Carr. "GAO wants more power to do oversight: Comptroller general wants to be able to use subpoenas to pry information from reluctant agencies." statesman.com, May 5, 2007. http://www.statesman.com/news/content/news/stories/nation/05/05/5gao.html.

36 Id.

37 Minority Staff, Committee on Government Reform, U.S. House of Representatives, "Comparison of Vice President Cheney's Energy Task Force to President Clinton's Health Care Task Force" January 30, 2002. http://oversight.house.gov/documents/20040625095742-68735 .pdf.

38 Michael C. Dorf is the Isidor and Seville Sulzbacher Professor of Law at Columbia University School of Law. His dozens of scholarly articles and essays have appeared in leading law journals.

39 Michael C. Dorf, op. cit.

40 44 U.S.C. §2201-2207.

41 To the extent it would go beyond the privilege for confidential communications between the President and his advisors. Miriam Nisbet http://www.ala.org/ala/washoff/WOissues/ governmentinfo/laadmin.htm.

42 David Glenn.,"Legal Barriers Hamper Scholars' Access to Papers of Recent Presidents," *Chronicle of Higher Education*, March 9, 2007. http://chronicle.com/weekly/v53/i27/ 27a02101.htm.

43 Steve I. Vladeck, Associate Professor of Law at the University of Miami School of Law, on February 17, 2006 at 3:01, http://prawfsblawg.blogs.com/prawfsblawg/2006/02/ vicepresidentia.html.

44 Public Citizen Lawsuit, November 28, 2001 http://www.citizen.org/litigation/briefs/ FOIAGovtSec/PresRecords/articles.cfm?ID=6515.

45 Adam Clymer, "House Panel Seeks Release of Presidential Papers," *New York Times*, October 10, 2002. http://www.nytimes.com/2002/10/10/politics/10RECO.html.

46 National Archives and Records Administration, "Bush Presidential Records to be Released," February 18, 2005. http://www.archives.gov/press/press-releases/2005/nr05-40.html.

47 "Information on release of documents formerly withheld under Presidential Records Act restrictions P-2 and P-5." http://bushlibrary.tamu.edu/research/releaseddocuments.html.

48 John Prados, "Don't Ask, Don't Tell: The Bush administration is playing politics with the investigation of the 9-11 intelligence failures—and standing in the way of a full accounting." *The American Prospect* online. www.prospect.org/print-friendly/webfeatures/2002/09/prados-j-09- 23.html.

49 "Threats and Responses: Perspectives/Senator Richard C. Shelby; A Reaction to Sept. 11: 'This Is a Massive Failure of Intelligence,'" *New York Times*, December 8, 2002. p. A-1. http:// select.nytimes.com/search/restricted/article?res=F4081FF73D550C738DDDA00894DA404482.

50 Dana Milbank. "Barriers To 9/11 Inquiry Decried—Congress May Push Commission" *Washington Post*, Thursday, September 19, 2002, p. A14. Referenced in *Congressional Record*: September 19, 2002 (Senate) p. S8901-S8913.

51 "Sen. Graham Seeks to Declassify Key 9/11 Data," Reuters, October 20, 2002.

52 Dick Cheney on Fox News Sunday, Sunday, May 19, 2002. http://www.foxnews.com/story/0,2933,53155,00.html.

53 Interview with John Prados, National Security Archive, Senior Analyst July 16, 2004. Transcription by Scott Anderson http://www.echochamberproject.com/prados.

54 John Prados. " Don't Ask, Don't Tell," op. cit.

55 Id.

CHAPTER 8

MANIPULATING INFORMATION:

THE DANGEROUS CAPACITIES OF THE EXECUTIVE BRANCH

Summary

We need to be able to trust what our government tells us. Access is meaningless if you can't trust the source—and are not able to get all the information, rather than just what the government wants you to see or know about.

A 2006 Lichtman/Zogby Interactive poll found Americans across the spectrum are distrustful of their leaders, with three out of four (75 percent) saying they trust government less than they did five years ago.[1] According to a survey of 1,008 adults commissioned by the American Society of Newspaper Editors (ASNE) for Sunshine Week (March 11–17, 2007), concerns about federal secrecy are rising: 25 percent believe the federal government is either "very open" or "somewhat open," while 69 percent said it's either "somewhat secretive" or "very secretive." In a similar poll in 2006, 33 percent thought the federal government was open and 62 percent thought it was secretive.[2]

For a number of years, I have been following the efforts of the government to control or suppress information. This did not begin with the second Bush Administration, but it has certainly reached new depths since the 2000 elections. The scope and breadth of the secrecy, control, and manipulation exceed the tracking and analysis capacity of a single individual. So this chapter relies heavily on reports by other experts, key among them journalists. In it and the following chapter on the politicization of science, I have tried to give an overview, a snapshot, of the very overt control of information by the Bush Administration.

As Theodore Roosevelt once said, the office of the President is a "bully pulpit." Every President tries to shape public perception of the administration's policies and practices, every White House tries to control the direction of legislation, and every administration takes an interest in the scientific research being performed and published by the executive branch agencies. But the sense of what has come out of the G.W. Bush White House is misdirection and manipulation toward ideological and sometimes disturbing objectives (or so it seems to me, at least).

Propaganda

Of course, every administration tries to shape its public image by carefully crafting the information it produces and by working with the media. But when does that effort reach the status of what we call "propaganda?" I think that it did during the George W. Bush administration, and here are some stories of the kind of behavior that everyone interested in public dialogue— i.e., every member of the public—should be on the watch for. Included here are stories of scrubbing a government Web site, misleading Congress, stiff-arming the opposing Democratic party, and forcing conformity with conservative mores on some government grantees. As noted above, the selection is illustrative, not comprehensive.

Controlling Contacts

Before we look at these examples, though, let me take you back to Chapter 2, where I talked about online directories being removed from the originally proposed E-Government Act. At that point, September 11th was still very fresh in everyone's mind—and we did not fully know all the things the Bush Administration was (and would be) getting up to on controlling access to government employees—so we wrote it off to post-September 11 jitters. Well that may have been some part of it, but recently I learned[3] that it was really about controlling access to government officials and the officials' ability to talk to people outside government without the calls going through a public affairs office. Indeed, at least at OMB, a key official on access issues was not allowed to answer his own phone (for calls originating outside government, at a minimum) but had to wait for the public affairs office to answer it!

Controlling PR

Not coincidentally, the growth in federal PR staff has been significant during the second Bush Administration. Between September 2000 and September 2004, while the federal workforce grew 6 percent, the number of public affairs officials in executive branch agencies rose 9 percent, from 4,327 to 4,703, according to U.S. Office of Personnel Management statistics.[4] According to a 2005 report by *Newsday*, agencies with the biggest growth in PR staff are those that deal with urgent or controversial issues, such as war or the environment.[5]

The news media and others who routinely work and talk with government officials—such as public interest groups that work with government data—have frequently complained that the Bush Administration has tightened its control over messages and restricted access to public information. According to one expert, the White House appoints the departments' communications directors and talks with them daily.[6] A 2005 overview of the press practices of the Bush administration noted the following:

> *An emphasis on tighter news management has been building as each successive administration learns from the previous one. A rigid approach to staying on message and a clampdown on access for reporters and the public have been increasingly used by the executive branch, a trend that began to take shape during the Reagan administration, if not earlier. The current Bush administration has shown that the method can be perfected, with little to no downside for the White House.*[7]

In May 2007, staffers at McClatchy newspapers' Washington, D.C., bureau claimed it was now being punished for being one of the few major news outlets skeptical of intelligence reports during the run-up to the war in Iraq. Bureau Chief John Walcott and current and former McClatchy Pentagon correspondents said they have not been allowed on the Defense Secretary's plane for at least three years.[8]

Who Can You Believe?

Although the trend to control the spin on information about the administration may have followed a trend from previous presidents, the Bush Administration has taken control to new levels (at least since 1968)—not just increasing PR staff and tightening news management, but even paying pundits to promote its programs.

Thus in January 2005, we learned[9] that since 2002, two syndicated columnists (Maggie Gallagher and Mike McManus) and a commentator (Armstrong Williams) had been paid by government agencies, through public relations companies, to promote administration initiatives. Gallagher and McManus were paid by the Department of Health and Human Services to promote the President's marriage initiative. Williams was paid by the Department of Education to promote the "No Child Left Behind" education reform plan. The same month these payments were disclosed, President Bush stated the payments would stop.[10]

Also in 2005, we learned[11] that the federal government has been using a "well-established tool of public relations: the prepackaged, ready-to-serve news report." In all, at least 20 federal agencies, including the Defense Department and the Census Bureau, had made and distributed hundreds of television news segments since 2001. While federal agencies made clear to broadcasters the origin of the "news" segments, the reports were designed to fit seamlessly into the typical local news broadcast and often featured "interviews" with senior administration officials—in which questions were scripted and answers rehearsed. Critics—and any hints of mismanagement, waste, or controversy—were excluded. In most cases, the "reporters" were careful not to state in the segment that they worked for the government. Many of the reports were broadcast on local stations across the country without any acknowledgment of the government's role in their production.

Scrubbing Web Sites

In May 2002 a Department of Education (ED) memo concerning the Department's Web site instructed employees to remove all items dated earlier than February 2001 (i.e., prior to the beginning of the Bush Administration) unless the item

- Is needed for a legal reason;
- Supports No Child Left Behind or other Administration priorities and initiatives;
- Is important for historical perspective (i.e., statistical trends, the Nation at Risk report);
- Is important for policy reasons identified by an Assistant Secretary; or
- Is useful or valuable to parents, students, or educators and is consistent with the Administration's philosophy.[12]

This was, in essence, a test case for the transition from the first Web-based administration to the next. It did not set a good precedent. After meetings with concerned public access advocates (including the author), the department promised to list the documents of the Clinton Administration in an archive: "There are no plans for a wholesale elimination of anything on the site. Everything will be archived and available to our customers."[13] Some documents are archived, but there is no searchable "archive." If you know the title of the document, you might be able to find it, but if you are searching by subject—say for historical comparison—you are out of luck.[14] What the site now says is "ED publications are available throughout our website. New or recent publications may be ordered through ED Pubs. Older and out-of-print publications may be found in ED Publications in ERIC."[15] Good luck with that, if you don't already know what you are looking for, because the Department also did away with all the ERIC (Education Resources Information Center) resources.[16]

This site scrubbing was noticed. It is likely that similar removals (or obscurings) happened in other agencies. A new administration is fully within its rights to highlight its initiatives, but the public has a right to be able to easily find information from prior administrations; it is all government information and all paid for by tax dollars.

The Medicare Spin

In early 2004, Congress—and the public—learned[17] that the new Medicare drug benefit will cost about 35 percent more than Congress anticipated—about $540 billion over 10 years, instead of the $396 billion projected in the law that Congress approved in late 2003. Certainly, historians can point to numerous instances where the White House has been less than totally forthcoming about the true costs of programs. In this case they went beyond just shading the numbers, however.

When the bill was under discussion, President Bush had indicated willingness to spend as much as $400 billion for the drug benefits and other Medicare changes during the next decade. The Congressional Budget Office[18] (CBO) predicted the law would cost $395 billion. In late January 2004, after the legislation had passed, the White House said calculations provided by Richard S. Foster, a nonpartisan Department of Health and Human Services (HHS) official who had been Medicare's chief actuary for nine years, indicated the law would cost $534 billion. That provoked an outcry from Democrats and conservative Republicans concerned that the drug benefits would deepen the federal deficit. Internal documents and federal officials made clear that the White House had known of the higher cost estimates for months.[19]

Indeed, in March 2004, Foster said[20] that, in 2003, Bush administration officials threatened to fire him if he disclosed to Congress that he believed the prescription drug legislation favored by the White House would prove far more expensive than lawmakers had been told. Foster told the *Washington Post* that Thomas A. Scully, then administrator of the HHS agency that oversees Medicare, repeatedly told him in the spring and summer of 2003 that he would be fired if he complied with requests from Republican and Democratic lawmakers to provide cost estimates of aspects of the prescription drug legislation. The administration's practice of withholding budget predictions continued until the legislation was enacted in November.

The *Boston Globe* quoted an administration official, who spoke on the condition of anonymity, that "it is not unusual for the Congressional Budget Office, which estimated the cost of the bill Congress approved last November, to come up with different projections than the administration's analysts. The president's budget document will mention the budget office numbers, but the White House is required under law to use the projections developed by its Medicare actuaries."[21] Unfortunately, for the Congress and the American people, the numbers the White House gave Congress were a lie. The cost[22] is not the issue here, of course; the issue is consciously lying to Congress and threatening civil service employees who want to share truthful information. More on that in the next chapter.

Department of Defense Media

As I noted at the outset of this chapter, we need to be able to trust what our government tells us and to trust it when it is speaking for us. Access is meaningless if you can't trust the source. Issues of veracity, accountability to the American public, and trustworthiness have been particularly raised by U.S. action abroad in times of conflict. Of course, disinformation and manipulation in times of war did not begin with this administration. A familiar adage is "The first casualty of war is truth."[23] So, although most of this chapter focuses on the importance of government information being accurate and unbiased, I present these few examples as disturbing examples of foreign propaganda and, in one case, apparent violation of the DoD policy and an executive order on psychological operations (psy-ops). Why should we care if our government lies to foreigners? Because it is our country—or our ideals and our sense of ourselves as a people—that is undermined over time when lies are presented as true and objective.

- *The Pentagon Channel.* In 2004, the Pentagon created its own 24-hour television channel "to cut out the middle man—the national media—in covering news events at the headquarters of the world's most powerful military."[24] The Pentagon Channel marked the first time that the U.S. military has been able to provide its own programming to troops stationed inside the country. The American Forces Radio and Television Service (AFRTS) cannot legally provide programming to U.S.-based forces, because its content consists of recycled and live material from such commercial sources as Fox, CNN, and NBC. The Pentagon Channel contains 100 percent military content, with the goal of being a "pure conduit" of information for the troops. Although its primary programming includes DoD briefings and interviews with top defense officials, the channel also carries stories about the daily life and work of service members.

The intent to influence, if not control, hearts and minds is much more covert when it has been directed overseas.

- *Information War on the Air.* After September 11,[25] the White House set up a secret panel to coordinate information operations by the Pentagon, other government agencies, and private contractors, to counter anti-American sentiment in the Muslim world. In Iraq and Afghanistan, the military operates radio stations and newspapers, but does not disclose their American ties. Those outlets produce news material that is at times attributed to the "International Information Center," an untraceable organization. The United States Agency for International Development finances about 30 radio stations in Afghanistan and has also distributed tens of thousands of iPod-like audio devices in Iraq and Afghanistan that play prepackaged civic messages, but it avoids disclosing U.S. involvement.[26]

- *Information War on the Web.* The DoD, in 2005, was already running sites overseas that were aimed at people in the Balkan region in Europe and the Maghreb area of North Africa, respectively. CNN reported,[27] in February 2005, that the Department planned to add more sites on the Internet to provide information to non-U.S. audiences. The Pentagon maintained that the information on the sites is true and accurate. But in a contemporaneous memo,[28] Deputy Secretary of Defense Paul Wolfowitz insisted that the Web site contractor should hire only journalists who "will not reflect discredit on the U.S. government." CNN noted that, at first glance, the Web pages appear to be independent news sites. To find out who is actually behind the content, a visitor would have to click on a small link—at the bottom of the page—to a disclaimer, which

219

says, in part, that the site is "sponsored by" the U.S. Department of Defense.

- *Information War in Print.* And, finally, in late 2005, we learned[29]that a Pentagon contractor in Iraq paid newspapers to print "good news" articles written by American soldiers. According to Pentagon documents, the contractor, the Lincoln Group, says it planted more than 1,000 articles in the Iraqi and Arab press and placed editorials on an Iraqi Web site. Military officials told the *New York Times* that Army psychological operations units sometimes pay to deliver their message, offering television stations money to run unattributed segments or contracting with writers of newspaper opinion pieces.[30] In January 2006, we learned[31] that, according to a then newly declassified document, obtained by the National Security Archive under FOIA, the campaign may violate Pentagon policy.[32] While a preliminary investigation into the program in December 2005 concluded that it did not violate U.S. law or DoD regulation, the document,[33] (a secret directive on information operations policy dated October 30, 2003 and signed by Secretary Rumsfeld) states that "Psy-op is restricted by both DoD policy and executive order from targeting American audiences, our military personnel, and news agencies or outlets."[34]

In Conclusion

As I noted in the introduction to this part of the book, the work of journalists is key to the unearthing of government information and, perhaps more importantly at least now, exposing the misrepresentations and untruths of government. This chapter has shown clearly—once again—what happens when the Executive Branch plays fast and loose with the truth to suit its political ends and how the processes of news-telling and public affairs can be manipulated toward those ends. This is a story that could be told at some level about any administration, but G.W. Bush's has taken these tools to new depths.

The next chapter will look at a range of examples of regimentation of the facts. These, however, have much more directly to do with the work of government scientists and other government officials. The ends are the same, though, political and ideological manipulation.

Notes

1 Zogby International. "U.S. Public Widely Distrusts Its Leaders." http://www.zogby.com/search/ReadNews.dbm?ID=1116.

2 ASNE, "Federal Government Seen as Increasingly Secretive." http://www.sunshineweek.org/sunshineweek/scrippspoll07.

3 Conversation with Glenn Schlarman, a retired OMB official.

4 Tom Brune, "Cadre Grows to Rein in Message," *Newsday* - Long Island, N.Y., February 24, 2005, p. A22. http://www.newsday.com/news/nationworld/nation/ny-uspr204156187feb24,0,5203878.story.

5 Id.

6 Id.

7 Lori Robertson, "In Control," *American Journalism Review*, February-March 2005. http://www.ajr.org/Article.asp?id=3812.

8 Joe Strupp, "McClatchy's D.C. Bureau Claims It's Barred From Defense Secretary Plane" May 23, 2007, http://www.editorandpublisher.com/eandp/news/article_display.jsp?vnu_content_id=1003588819.

9 CBS/AP, "3rd Columnist On Bush Payroll," CBS News, January 28, 2005. http://www.cbsnews.com/stories/2005/01/26/politics/main669432.shtml; "Bush: Pundit payments will stop," CNN.com Politics. Thursday, January 27, 2005. Posted: 1:06 PM EST (1806 GMT). http://www.cnn.com/2005/ALLPOLITICS/01/26/paid.pundits/.

10 CNN, "Bush: Pundit payments will stop," op. cit.

11 David Barstow and Robin Stein, "Under Bush, a New Age of Prepackaged TV News" New York Times March 13, 2005. http://www.nytimes.com/2005/03/13/politics/13covert.html?ex=1268370000&en=c040ac38c7b344fa&ei=5090&partner=rssuserland.

12 Department of Education, Criteria and Process for Removing Old Content from www.ed.gov May 31, 2002.

13 eSchool News online. "Critics drub ED's plans to scrub its web site," January 1, 2003. http://www.eschoolnews.com/news/showstory.cfm?ArticleID=4157.

14 In what comes up if you search on "Archives," the only documents earlier than 2001 are Federal Register notices.

15 http://www.ed.gov/about/pubs/intro/index.html?src=gu.

16 ERIC—the Education Resources Information Center—is an internet-based digital library of education research and information sponsored by the Institute of Education Sciences (IES) of the U.S. Department of Education. ERIC provides access to bibliographic records of journal and non-journal literature indexed from 1966 to the present. http://www.eric.ed.gov/.

17 Susan Milligan, "Cost estimates rise to $540 billion for Medicare plan" *Boston Globe*, January 30, 2004. http://www.boston.com/yourlife/health/aging/articles/2004/01/30/cost_estimates_rise_to_540_billion_for_medicare_plan/.

18 CBO Fact Sheet. http://www.cbo.gov/aboutcbo/factsheet.shtm.

19 Amy Goldstein, "Official Says He Was Told To Withhold Medicare Data," *Washington Post,* Saturday, March 13, 2004. p. A01. http://www.washingtonpost.com/ac2/wp-dyn?pagename =article&contentId=A54524-2004Mar12.

20 Id.

21 Milligan, op. cit.

22 In February 2006, Dr. Mark B. McClellan, administrator of the federal Centers for Medicare and Medicaid Services, said the estimated cost over 10 years is $678 billion, down 8 percent from the earlier estimate of $737 billion for the decade from 2006 to 2015—but still more than 50 percent more than Congress was told by the Administration. Medical News Today online. http://www.medicalnewstoday.com/medicalnews.php?newsid=37177.

23 From "The first casualty when war comes is truth," attributed to Senator Hiram Johnson, remarks in the Senate, 1918. *The Macmillan Book of Proverbs, Maxims, and Famous Phrases,* ed.

24 Guy Taylor, "Pentagon Channel targets troops," *Washington Times,* December 27, 2004. http://www.washtimes.com/national/20041226-114855-2257r.htm. These are the words of the *Washington Times,* not (or at least not directly) those of Defense officials.

25 Jeff Gerth, "Military's Information War Is Vast and Often Secretive," *New York Times,* December 11, 2005.

26 Id.

27 Barbara Starr and Larry Shaughnessy, "Pentagon sites: Journalism or propaganda?" Politics, CNN.com. Saturday, February 5, 2005. Posted: 3:04 AM EST (0804 GMT). http:// www.cnn.com/2005/ALLPOLITICS/02/04/web.us/index.html.

28 Starr and Shaughnessy, op. cit.

29 Jeff Gerth, op. cit.

30 Jeff Gerth, op. cit.

31 Jeff Gerth, op. cit.

32 Mark Mazzetti, "IRAQ: Planted Articles May Be Violation," *Los Angeles Times,* January 27, 2006. http://corpwatch.live.radicaldesigns.org/article.php?id=13181.

33 Doctrine for Joint Psychological Operations. Joint Publication, pp. 3–53. http:// www.gwu.edu/~nsarchiv/NSAEBB/NSAEBB177/02_psyop-jp-3-53.pdf.

34 Associated Press, "Pentagon: Planting Stories in Iraqi Newspapers Was Within the Law." Published: October 19, 2006 5:15 PM ET http://www.editorandpublisher.com/eandp/news/ article_display.jsp?vnu_content_id=1003285543.

CHAPTER 9

POLITICAL SCIENCE

Science, like any field of endeavor, relies on freedom of inquiry; and one of the hallmarks of that freedom is objectivity. Now, more than ever, on issues ranging from climate change to AIDS research to genetic engineering to food additives, government relies on the impartial perspective of science for guidance.

—President George H. W. Bush
April 23, 1990

As I noted at the beginning of Chapter 8 it is not just access to the records or databases that makes government information useful and supportive of an informed public and our democracy. We need to be able to trust what our government tells us. Access is meaningless if you can't trust the source—and are not able to get all the information, rather than just what the government wants you to see, hear, or know about.

This chapter looks at our ability to learn the informed thought of government experts and their ability to speak about their research. More than ever in my memory, this sort of access has been put in peril.

The politicization of science[1] started shortly after the Bush Administration took office. Robert F. Kennedy, Jr., writing in *The Nation*,[2] points out that in October 2001 Interior Secretary Gale Norton falsely claimed, in response to a Senate committee inquiry on the effects of oil drilling on caribou in the Arctic National Wildlife Refuge, that the caribou would not be affected, because they calve outside the area targeted for drilling. Norton later explained that she somehow substituted "outside" for "inside." She also substituted findings from a study financed by an oil company for some of the ones that the Fish and Wildlife Service had prepared for her.

A mistake that anyone could make. That global search and replace can be dangerous.

A quiet erosion had begun, and it became an extensive undermining of government science and of scientific integrity.

Global Warming

I will begin with a discussion of the global warming issue because it is probably the best-known example of the Bush Administration's actions on scientific research and, arguably, one of the most important.

In February 2007, the Intergovernmental Panel on Climate Change (IPCC—the world's most authoritative group of climate scientists), in its first major report since 2001, said the likelihood was 90–99 percent that emissions of heat-trapping greenhouse gases like carbon dioxide, spewed from tailpipes and smokestacks, were the dominant cause of the observed warming of the last 50 years.[3] The Bush Administration has recently begun to take the issue of climate change seriously; in 2007, it has apparently admitted the validity of the scientific research on the human impact on that change, embracing the findings of the IPCC.[4] This does not, however, relieve the administration of its responsibility for delaying and suppressing science and scientists (as I discuss below) until the problem could no longer be ignored. In that interim, the administration has striven to undermine science and has, in the process, undermined trust in government.

Early Actions: 2002

The administration began its tenure by maintaining that there is still "considerable uncertainty" on the causes of global warming. Shortly after coming to office, the administration asked the National Academy of Sciences (NAS) to review the findings of the IPCC, and provide further assessment of what climate science could say about this issue. The NAS panel rendered a strong opinion,[5] in essence confirming the findings of the IPCC that human actions were probably the cause of global warming. In May 2002, the administration dismissed an Environmental Protection Agency (EPA) report on climate change that said that human activities are mostly to blame for recent trends in global warming; President Bush said[6] dismissively, "I read the report put out by the bureaucracy." In September 2002, the administration removed a section on climate change from the EPA's annual air pollution report, even though the climate issue had been discussed in the report in each of the preceding five years;[7] the decision to delete the chapter on climate change "was made by top officials at the Environmental Protection Agency with White House approval," according to White House officials.[8]

Changing NOAA Reports: 2005

In March 2005, whistleblower Rick Piltz, a senior associate from the government office that coordinates federal climate change programs (now known as the Climate Change Science Program) at the National Oceanic and Atmospheric Administration (NOAA), resigned because he did not want "to sacrifice the ability to speak freely." Piltz declared that political appointees were working "to impede forthright communication of the state of climate science" and tried to "undermine the credibility and integrity of the program."[9]

In early June 2005, the Government Accountability Project, a nonprofit, public interest organization and law firm representing Mr. Piltz, gave documents to the *New York Times* showing that Philip Cooney, White House Council on Environmental Quality (CEQ) chief of staff, "repeatedly edited government climate reports in ways that play down links between [greenhouse gas] emissions and global warming." According to the *New York Times* report,[10] Cooney, in handwritten notes on drafts of several reports issued in 2002 and 2003, removed or adjusted descriptions of climate research that government scientists and their supervisors, including some senior Bush Administration officials, had already approved. In many cases, the changes appeared in the final reports.

Mr. Cooney, significantly, had no scientific training. A lawyer with a bachelor's degree in economics, he would later be hired by Exxon Mobil after resigning from the CEQ in mid-June 2005. Before joining the White House staff, Mr. Cooney had been an oil industry lobbyist who worked as the head of the climate program at the American Petroleum Institute (API), the largest trade group representing the oil and gas industry. Exxon is a member of the API.

Some of Mr. Cooney's changes were arguably tendentious; given the Bush Administration's stance on global warming, one can only assume that such changes were intended to create doubt about scientific findings on cause and impact. For example, Cooney crossed out a number of sentences, including: "[Global] warming also will cause reductions in mountain glaciers and advance the timing of the melt of mountain snow peaks in polar regions," and wrote a note stating that the section "stray[ed] from research strategy into speculative findings." In an October 2002 draft of "Our Changing Planet,'" a regularly published summary of government climate research, Mr. Cooney changed the wording—and weight—of this sentence by inserting "extremely": "The attribution of the causes of biological and ecological changes to climate change or variability is *extremely* difficult." (Emphasis added.) He also made other such subtle but portentous changes as inserting "significant and fundamental" before the word "uncertainties." Indeed, one sentence in the draft originally read, "Many scientific observations indicate that the Earth *is* undergoing a period of relatively rapid change;" Mr. Cooney changed it to read, "Many scientific observations point to the conclusion that the Earth *may be* undergoing a period of relatively rapid change." (Emphasis added.) A not very subtle change.

Denying Access to NOAA Scientists: 2005

On September 19, 2006, Representative Henry Waxman released[11] internal Commerce Department e-mails on climate change that appear to show that the Department denied a October 2005 media request to interview Tom Knutson, a NOAA scientist who had concluded that global warming may lead to more dangerous hurricanes. The request was denied, the e-mails indicate, because of Knutson's viewpoint.

On March 28, 2007, House Science Subcommittee on Oversight held a hearing on "Shaping the Message, Distorting the Science: Media Strategies to Influence Public Policy."[12] On the following day, March 29, the Commerce Department (parent agency of the NOAA) issued a revised press policy,[13] which as Subcommittee chairman Brad Miller (D-NC) said, "is a good step, but it doesn't go far enough. We want a policy that is clearer on free speech rights and assures scientists the right of final approval for their official media materials after public affairs has edited them."

Silencing a Top NASA Scientist: 2006

In January 2006, a top National Aeronautics and Space Administration (NASA) climate scientist and longtime director of the agency's Goddard Institute for Space Studies, James Hansen, reported[14] that he was being silenced. He said the Bush Administration had tried to stop him from speaking out since he gave a lecture in December 2005 calling for prompt reductions in emissions of greenhouse gases linked to global warming (particularly from motor vehicles), and that officials at NASA headquarters had ordered the public affairs staff to review his coming lectures, papers, postings on the Goddard Web site, and requests for interviews from journalists. According to the *New York Times*, both Dr. Hansen and public affairs officers indicated that, after that speech—and the release of data by Dr. Hansen on December 15th showing that 2005 was probably the warmest year in at least a century—officials at NASA headquarters repeatedly phoned public affairs officers. Those officers relayed the warning to Dr. Hansen that there would be "dire consequences" if such statements continued.

NASA's press secretary, Dean Acosta,[15] said the calls and meetings with Goddard press officers were not to introduce restrictions, but to review existing rules. He said Dr. Hansen had continued to speak frequently with the news media. In one infamous call, however, George Deutsch, a recently appointed public affairs officer at NASA headquarters, rejected a request from a producer at National Public Radio (NPR) to interview Dr. Hansen. According to notes taken by a Goddard public affairs officer,[16] Mr. Deutsch called NPR "[the] most liberal" media outlet in the country. In that call and others, Mr. Deutsch said his job, as a White House appointee, was "to make the president look good."[17]

In March 2006, NASA Administrator Michael D. Griffin unveiled[18] new rules that govern the release of agency information to news media and the public. The new eight-page policy, written by an internal team of scientists, lawyers, public affairs specialists, and managers, states that NASA scientists are free to talk to members of the media about their scientific findings and even express personal interpretations of those findings. The policy also makes clear that scientists are not required to have a public affairs officer with them when they speak with members of the media, though Griffin emphasized shortly thereafter in comments broadcast to NASA employees that he believes such behavior is unwise.

Gagging Polar Bears: 2007

The Fish and Wildlife Service, responsible for protecting Arctic polar bears, in early 2007 barred two Alaska scientists from speaking about polar bears, climate change, or sea ice at international meetings. It announced that agency scientists must obtain a memorandum designating which official, if any, is allowed to respond to questions, particularly about polar bears, and include "a statement of assurance that these individuals understand the Administration's position on these issues." Fish and Wildlife Director H. Dale Hall denied that the memos were a form of censorship, saying they were part of a policy to establish an agenda and the appropriate spokesperson for international meetings. The agency has taken steps to evaluate whether the polar bear should be listed and has significant questions about scientific studies, including those dealing with when sea ice will melt and the effects on the bear, he said.[19]

In April 2007, the Supreme Court ruled 5 to 4 that the Environmental Protection Agency violated the Clean Air Act by improperly declining to regulate new-vehicle emissions standards to control the pollutants that scientists say contribute to global warming. Justice John Paul Stevens, writing for the majority, said "EPA has offered no reasoned explanation for its refusal to decide whether greenhouse gases cause or contribute to climate change."[20]

Agency by Agency

Agencies dealing with global warming are not the only ones that have felt the heavy hand of the Bush Administration. Here are some additional examples, arranged (more or less) by agency.

The National Academies on Bioterrorism: 2002

In October 2002, the National Academies of Science (NAS) had a run-in with the Bush Administration over publishing sensitive information.[21] According to an NAS spokesman, the U.S. Department of Agriculture (USDA) "tried to suppress" an NAS research report on the vulnerability of U.S. agriculture to bioterrorism. Researchers found that harmful foreign pests and pathogens are "widely available and pose a major threat to U.S. agriculture" and that the department has failed to plan a defense against a biological attack. USDA officials wanted the unclassified report withheld. Some at the NAS believe the agency really wanted to suppress the report's criticism. The NAS published the report anyway; even after the NAS removed details from the report, USDA officials continued to object, saying the report would endanger national security.

The USDA and Preclearance: 2002

In February 2002, USDA officials told top scientists in the department's Agricultural Research Service (ARS) to seek prior approval on all manuscripts pertaining to "sensitive issues." According to a Department memo,[22] these issues included:

> *Agricultural practices with negative health and environmental consequences, e.g., global climate change; contamination of water by hazardous materials (nutrients, pesticides, and pathogens); animal feeding operations or crop production practices that negatively impact soil, water, or air quality.*

The EPA on Benzene: 2002

In 2002, EPA scientists studied a process used in extracting oil and gas known as hydraulic fracturing, in which benzene is injected into underground formations. They found[23] that benzene could contaminate groundwater supplies in violation of federal drinking water standards. A week after reporting their findings to congressional staff members, however, they revised the data to indicate that benzene levels would not exceed government standards.[24] In a letter[25] to Representative Henry Waxman, EPA officials said the change was made based on "industry feedback."

HHS and Ideological Agendas: 2002

On October 21, 2002, 12 Members of the House of Representatives (11 Democrats and 1 Independent) wrote[26] to the Secretary of the Department of Health and Human Services (DHHS), Tommy Thompson, expressing concern about "a pattern of events at the Department of Health and Human Services suggesting that scientific decision-making is being subverted by ideology and that scientific information that does not fit the Administration's political agenda is being suppressed." In the letter, they detailed a "growing number of cases providing evidence that actions directly affecting public health are being driven by ideology rather than by science." Among these were expert appointments to scientific advisory boards going to individuals with specific ideological viewpoints rather than scientific credentials;[27] organizations that provide science-based programs to prevent pregnancy and sexually-transmitted diseases, but that disagree with the Administration's "abstinence-only" position, being singled out for discriminatory audits; scientific information on both the National Institutes of Health and the Center for Disease Control Web sites being removed, apparently because it did not fit with the Administration's ideological agenda.[28]

Interior and the World Heritage Committee: 2003

In 1995, the World Heritage Committee, with the agreement of the United States, placed Yellowstone National Park, a designated World Heritage site, on its lists of parks at risk and in need of international attention. In particular, it placed the park on the List of World Heritage in Danger, in response to specific threats it identified to the outstanding universal value of the park.[29] In April 2003, Deputy Assistant Interior Secretary for Fish and Wildlife and Parks Paul Hoffman wrote to the United Nations World Heritage Committee and requested that Yellowstone be removed from the list. "Yellowstone is no longer in danger,"[30] Mr. Hoffman said, citing a report written by Yellowstone Park staff. An early 2003 draft of that report[31] discussed problems that continue to threaten Yellowstone, including the degradation of water from mining toxins, a parasitic disease among native trout, and continued controversy over potentially diseased bison who stray outside park boundaries.

The final version of the report sent by the Interior Department to the United Nations World Heritage Committee does not include these ongoing concerns.[32] The Committee removed Yellowstone from the list, but required the United States to report back on several ongoing environmental threats and requested that the government involve independent organizations and scientists in its assessments.[33] The report to the World Heritage Committee, issued in January 2006, does discuss the potentially diseased bison, but has no mention of the other issues.[34]

Interior and Cattle Grazing: 2005

In mid-June 2005, the *Los Angeles Times* reported[35] that the Bush Administration altered a scientific analysis of the environmental impact of cattle grazing on public lands, removing a phrase warning that the new rules would have a "significant adverse impact" on wildlife. The bureau concluded, instead, that the grazing regulations are "beneficial to animals." The early version concluded, "The proposed action will have a slow, long-term adverse impact on wildlife and biological diversity in general." That conclusion was eliminated. According to two retired specialists, a government biologist and a hydrologist, Interior excised their warnings on the effects on wildlife and water, replacing them with language justifying less stringent regulations favored by cattle ranchers.

The new rules require federal land managers to conduct protracted studies before taking action to limit that access, reversing a long-standing agency policy that gave Bureau of Land Management (BLM) experts the authority to quickly determine whether livestock grazing was inflicting damage. The regulations also eliminated the agency's obligation to seek public input on some grazing decisions; public comment will be allowed but not required.[36]

Interior and the Lobbyists: 2007

In early May 2007, Julie MacDonald, a deputy assistant secretary at the Interior Department, resigned a month after the department's inspector general issued a stinging report[37] that said she violated federal rules by giving industry lobbyists internal agency documents and that she rode roughshod over agency scientists. Her resignation also came about a week before a House committee was set to hold hearings on political interference with biologists.[38] According to that report, Ms. MacDonald had heavily edited biologists' reports on sage grouse, a species whose habitat overlaps with vast parts of the Rocky Mountain West where oil and gas drilling and cattle ranching are prevalent. If the grouse were to be listed as endangered or threatened, it could have curbed those industries' access to federal lands; in the end, the species was not placed on the threatened or endangered lists. She also had demanded that scientists reduce the nesting range for the southwest willow flycatcher to a radius of 1.8 miles (from 2.1 miles), so that the protected range would not cross into California, where her husband has a ranch.[39]

Ms. MacDonald took what has become common practice in the second Bush Administration—altering the research of professional scientists to suit ideological concerns or the needs of major industries (and major party contributors)—and raised it to a new level. She also gave internal agency documents to industry lawyers and a lawyer from the Pacific Legal Foundation, all of whom frequently filed suit against the Interior Department over endangered species decisions. Indeed, in one instance, an Oregon environmental group discovered that a timber lobbying group, the American Forest Resource Council, had based part of its March 7, 2007, lawsuit against the Interior Department on an internal draft of endangered-species regulations, not on the rules actually in force.[40]

Case Study: Air Quality

Why should *we* care? What impact does bad or distorted science make?

For starters, if you want to be able to believe what the government tells you about the quality of your air, you should care.

Air in lower Manhattan post-September 11

In a 2004 article in *The Nation*,[41] Robert F. Kennedy, Jr. wrote about the quality of the science the EPA had provided related to the quality of the air in lower Manhattan following the attacks of September 11, 2001. Kennedy noted that on September 13, just two days after the terror attack, EPA had announced that asbestos dust in the area was "very low" or entirely absent; on September 18 the agency had said the air was "safe to breathe." An inspector general's report[42] released in August 2003 revealed that the EPA's data did not support those assurances and that its press releases were being drafted or doctored by White House officials intent on reopening Wall Street. In fact, said Kennedy, more than 25 percent of the samples collected by the EPA before September 18 showed presence of asbestos above the 1 percent safety benchmark. Among outside studies, one performed by scientists at the University of California, Davis, found particulates at levels never before seen in more than 7,000 similar tests worldwide. As reported by Kennedy, a study being performed by Mt. Sinai School of Medicine had found (as of 2004) that 78 percent of rescue workers suffered lung ailments and 88 percent had ear, nose, and throat problems in the months following the attack and that about half still had persistent lung and respiratory illnesses nine months to a year later.

Recently, it was reported[43] that New York officials say some 400,000 were exposed to Ground Zero dust and 71,000 have enrolled in a long-term health monitoring program for people with and without health problems. Most experts believe there are thousands of people still sick years after Ground Zero exposure.

A federal lawsuit by lower Manhattan residents accused Christine Todd Whitman (the EPA secretary at the time of 9/11) of jeopardizing their health by declaring that "[the] air is safe to breathe" at a time when, according to the EPA inspector general, a quarter of dust samples were recording unhealthy asbestos levels. A federal judge has refused to dismiss the lawsuit; that decision is being appealed. The lawsuit alleged that the EPA did not have sufficient information and lacked the monitoring data necessary to make the reassuring statements it issued. Indeed, the EPA's Office of the Inspector General eventually criticized[44] the agency's response, saying it did not have available data and information to support the September 18, 2001, statement that the air was safe to breathe and, at the urging of White House officials, gave misleading assurances that there was no health risk from the dust in the air after the towers' collapse.[45] On April 19, 2007, the court, in *Lombardi v. Whitman*, held[46] that EPA could not be held responsible for harm caused by misinformation, whether deliberate or not. The "pull of competing obligations"—EPA's mandate to inform the public about environmental dangers and the apparent conflicting duty of the federal government to keep peace and order—neutralized any claim that government action amounts to "deliberate indifference."[47]

Soot and dust

For the first time in its history, in 2006 the EPA rejected recommendations from its Clean Air Scientific Advisory Committee.[48] Although the EPA imposed stricter standards on particulates (such as soot) for the first time in a decade, it rejected the panel's recommendation for even stricter standards and also decided to exempt rural areas—as well as dust generated by agriculture and mining.[49]

The EPA's rejection of the recommendations was probably tied to the OMB's review of the proposed rule changes. Notably, the OMB—which reviews all proposed rule changes, and sometimes the underlying science—had, in a rulemaking docket, deleted references to a study concluding that low-income people could be more vulnerable to exposure to soot and dust, and a sentence asserting that the air quality rules "may have a substantial impact on the life expectancy of the U.S. population."[50]

Antibiotic-resistant bacteria in hog farm air

Prior to April 2002, Dr. James Zahn, a nationally respected microbiologist with the Agriculture Department's research service, had identified bacteria that can make people sick—and that are resistant to antibiotics—in the air surrounding industrial-style hog farms. His studies proved that billions of these "superbugs" were traveling across property lines daily, endangering the health of neighbors and their herds.[51] The *Des Moines Register* reported that USDA officials told Zahn not to publish the results of his study finding antibiotic-resistant bacteria in the air near hog confinements in Iowa and Missouri. He was also not allowed to present his findings at public or private meetings in the spring of 2002, including at a meeting of the Board of Health in Adair County, Iowa—apparently as a result of industry complaints. A short time later, Dr. Zahn joined the ever-growing list of government scientists resigning in frustration or disgust.[52] Similar findings were reported in 2005 in *Environmental Health Perspectives*, the peer-reviewed journal of the United States' National Institute of Environmental Health Sciences.[53]

NOAA on Sonar and Beached Whales: 2006

In January 2006, documents released pursuant to a FOIA suit by the Natural Resources Defense Council (NRDC)[54] showed[55] that a government investigator studying the stranding of 37 whales on the North Carolina coast in 2005 changed her draft report to eliminate all references to the possibility

233

that Navy sonar may have played a role in driving the whales ashore. The April 2005 preliminary report on the deaths by the coordinator of the National Marine Fisheries Service's stranding response program, Teri Rowles, described injuries to seven of the whales that "may be indicative" of damage related to the loud blasts of sound from active sonar and noted that one of the injuries—air bubbles in the liver of a pilot whale—had been reported in mass strandings in the Bahamas and Canary Islands associated with sonar activity.

Before the preliminary report was ordered to be released, NOAA released an updated report—by Rowles and others—that did not mention sonar. In a cover letter to that report, NOAA officials said the initial draft that mentioned sonar "contains early information that was later found to be inaccurate." However, in March 2006, the National Marine Fisheries Service issued its final report on the 2005 mass stranding of whales in North Carolina, identifying sonar operated by the U.S. Navy as a possible cause of the incident. The report also excludes most other causes.[56]

NOAA on Endangered Salmon: 2006

In May 2006, the *Washington Post* reported[57] that the administration, "having made it hard for federal scientists to talk publicly about global warming—appears to have decided that loose lips are also bad when they talk about salmon." In this instance, it was the headquarters of the NOAA, in its capacity as the agency responsible for protecting endangered salmon, that instructed its representatives and scientists that only three people in the entire agency, all of them political appointees, were now authorized to speak of salmon. No one in the western United States was to respond to media questions about salmon. The *Post* noted that the order was issued the day after an article appeared in that paper quoting federal scientists making positive statements[58] about two recent decisions—one by a federal judge, the other by federal scientists—that challenged previous Bush Administration policy about protecting salmon in the Klamath River. Was this censorship? No, of course not—according to the NOAA spokesman, the order came down because "some folks were trying to consolidate a little bit and make sure everything we were putting out was accurate and as up to date as possible."[59]

Controlling Scientists: Some Final Thoughts

While it is not uncommon for administrations to want a unified message on matters of policy, what does seem to be different in the second Bush administration is the suppression of outside speech. Take, for example, Indur M.

Goklany, assistant director of science and technology policy in the policy office of the Interior Department. Dr. Goklany, an electrical engineer by training, told the *New York Times* that in the Clinton Administration he was shifted to nonclimate-related work because he has, for 30 years, written in papers and books that it may be better not to force cuts in greenhouse gases because the added prosperity from unfettered economic activity would allow countries to exploit benefits of warming and adapt to problems. Dr. Goklany said, however, that he had never had to stop his outside writing, as long as he identified the views as his own.[60]

As we will see below, reports have documented a widespread perception—and evidence of—inappropriate political interference with employees of the federal climate science agencies and programs, as well as with journalists from national, mainstream outlets who cover their research. These reports have also found pervasive "unduly restrictive policies and practices" on the communication of "sensitive" (i.e., controversial) scientific information to the media, the public, and Congress. This is a sea change from previous administrations. It is not about government scientists making clear they are speaking only about views identified as their own; it is about the chilling of speech and controlling our right to have objective, not political, science from our government.

Getting Around Government Scientists

Controlling scientists directly isn't the only way to control scientific research. Sometimes, the political appointees simply outsource the "science" in order to get the desired result.

A case in point: in July 2003, the EPA's regional office overseeing the western Everglades decided to accept a study financed by a committee (the "Water Enhancement and Restoration Committee," WERC) that had been formed primarily by local developers and was chaired by the consultant for a golf course development. By no coincidence, I suspect, the EPA had denied this same golf course a development permit on the grounds that the development would pollute surrounding waters and destroy wetlands. In 2001, after the Estero Bay Agency for Bay Management and other watershed-watchdog groups asked for an EPA representative to review permits for Lee and Collier counties, the EPA had brought in a former water quality scientist for the Florida Department of Environmental Protection, Bruce Boler, and gave him the task of safeguarding the area's water quality. Mr. Boler said he was able to curtail much of the wetlands destruction when he first took the position by writing letters recommending denial for many of the proposed projects because they would pollute federally protected waterways. Less than three years later, Mr. Boler lost his job, forced out of his position, he said, as the federal government's top wetlands scientist for this region.[61]

The study by WERC contradicted everything known about wetlands functioning, including a determination by more than 25 scientists and managers at the Tampa Bay Estuary Program that, on balance, wetlands do not generate nitrogen pollution. In contrast, the developers' study concluded that wetlands discharge more pollutants than they absorb. There was no peer review or public comment. In approving this study, the EPA is giving developers credit for improving water quality by replacing natural wetlands with golf courses and other developments![62]

Another example: in November 2003, EPA[63] cut a private deal with a pesticide manufacturer to take over federal studies of a pesticide it manufactures. Atrazine, the most heavily utilized weedkiller in America, has been identified as a potential carcinogen associated with high incidences of prostate cancer among workers at manufacturing facilities. Testing by the U.S. Geological Survey regularly finds alarming concentrations of Atrazine in drinking water across the Corn Belt. The European Union has banned the chemical.

In 2003, scientists at the University of California, Berkeley, found that Atrazine—at one-thirtieth the government's "safe" three parts per billion level—causes grotesque deformities in frogs, including multiple sets of organs. And this same year epidemiologists from the University of Missouri found reproductive consequences in humans associated with Atrazine, including male semen counts in farm communities that are 50 percent below normal.[64] Iowa scientists are finding similar results in a related study.[65]

Did the Bush Administration ban Atrazine? No; it took the studies away from EPA scientists and gave control over federal research on this chemical and its effect— to the chemical's manufacturer, Switzerland-based Syngenta. Without irony, in an interview with the *Los Angeles Times*, a spokesperson for Syngenta offered one of the advantages of having the company monitor its own product: "This is one way we can ensure it's not presenting any risk to the environment."[66]

And Getting Rid of Them Altogether

If outsourcing individual projects is a good way for an administration to control science, then outsourcing entire jobs is an even better one. In January 2003,[67] the National Park Service announced it was preparing a first phase of contracting out reviews for about 1,800 positions, including biologists, archeologists, and environmental specialists. You should be concerned; the risk is that scientists who work for a contracting firm will be under pressure to produce the science that will allow the firm to keep its contract. And employees of such private firms do not have the civil service protections and the (sometimes quite minimal) protections of the Whistleblower Protection Act that federal employees do.[68]

This effort has been put on hold a number of times. For example, Senator Harry Reid (D-NV) and Representative Nick Rahall (D-WV) introduced the Park Professionals Protection Act in the 108th Congress, which would prohibit the Department of the Interior from conducting studies aimed at implementing any plan to privatize, divest, or transfer any part of the National Park Service, and would reallocate outsourcing study funds toward the operations and maintenance accounts of the Park Service. A similar effort was made in the Bereuter/Boyd amendment to the Fiscal Year 2004 Interior Appropriations Bill, which overwhelmingly passed the House with a vote of 362 to 57. It prevented funds from being used to implement privatization studies at the Midwest Archaeological Center in Lincoln, Nebraska, or the Southeast Archaeological Center in Florida.[69] But it is still the intent of the Bush Administration to declare the work of such civil servants not "inherently governmental" and, therefore, "commercial."

Even Non-government Information Is Not Safe

In 2004, the Centers for Disease Control and Prevention (CDC) published[70] proposed regulations to require review and approval of the Web site content of groups seeking grants. These regulations would also require that "accountable state, territorial or local health officials have independently reviewed educational materials" to rule out anything the local community might consider obscene.[71]

According to the *Wall Street Journal*,[72] the "Bush administration's revised CDC grant guidelines come in the wake of a conservative furor over provocative content in AIDS-prevention programs." In May 2004, they report, San Francisco's Stop AIDS Project failed to win renewal of a $225,000 CDC grant after "its workshops were criticized as being racy." A

STOP AIDS spokesperson noted, "The packaging was sexy so people would come. We were targeting people at high-risk for HIV on how to use a condom, how to negotiate safe sex, being honest about status, what the risks are with oral and anal sex, what to do in an anonymous situation."[73]

As early as April 2003, scientists who study AIDS and other sexually transmitted diseases (STDs) said federal health officials had warned them that their work may come under unusual scrutiny by the Department of Health and Human Services or members of Congress if its topics were politically controversial.[74] Speaking on condition of anonymity, the scientists said they had been advised they can avoid unfavorable attention by keeping certain key words—such as "sex worker," "men who sleep with men," "anal sex," and "needle exchange"— out of grant applications to the National Institutes of Health (NIH) and CDC. According to Dr. Alfred Sommer, dean of the Bloomberg School of Public Health at Johns Hopkins University, a researcher at that institution had been advised by an NIH project officer to change the term "sex worker" to something more euphemistic in a grant proposal about HIV prevention among prostitutes. He noted that "[the] idea that grants might be subject to political surveillance is creating a 'pernicious sense of insecurity' among researchers." In the past, he said federal financing of medical research had been largely protected from political influence.[75]

Direct Political Control

Not content with controlling only the science (by rewriting it) and the scientists, the White House acted in 2007 to be sure that all regulations that might result from the use of that science were subject to direct political control. On January 18, 2007, President Bush issued Executive Order 13422. According to the Congressional Research Service (CRS), the most important changes made to E.O. 12866 by E.O. 13422 fall into five general categories: (1) a requirement that agencies identify in writing the specific market failure or problem that warrants a new regulation, (2) a requirement that each agency head designate a presidential appointee within the agency as a "regulatory policy officer" who can control upcoming rulemaking activity in that agency, (3) a requirement that agencies provide their best estimates of the cumulative regulatory costs and benefits of rules they expect to publish in the coming year, (4) an expansion of Office of Information and Regulatory Affairs (OIRA) review to include significant guidance documents, and (5) a provision permitting agencies to consider whether to use more formal rulemaking procedures in certain cases.[76] A CRS report on the order concludes "The changes made by this executive order represent a clear expansion of presidential authority over rulemaking agencies. In that regard, E.O. 13422 can be viewed as part of a broader statement of presidential authority presented throughout the Bush Administration."[77]

In addition to submitting significant[78] guidance documents—policy papers that clarify or interpret existing rules—to OIRA for review, agencies must make available to public scrutiny tens of thousands of these documents. Public review of proposed rules is appropriate and needed; public review of guidance is intended to paralyze the regulatory system: "William Kovacs, vice president of environment, technology and regulatory affairs at the U.S. Chamber of Commerce, the nation's largest business lobby, said the chamber's complaint about guidance 'was one of the first issues we talked about' with John Graham, the administration's first regulatory czar at the OMB."[79]

Industry Influence

In all administrations (and all Congresses), groups—industry associations, public interest nonprofits, and others—compete to have their views and perspectives represented. This is what political scientists call "interest group politics." The business sector was much more successful during the 109th Congress and continues to be during the G.W. Bush administration. The interests of industry and business—i.e., responsibility to the bottom line and to investors of companies traded publicly—are not necessarily bad, but when it comes to health and safety concerns, they rarely coincide with the public interest.

A fundamental conflict between the business/industry sector and the liberal public interest community revolves around the role of the government in regulating businesses in order to protect public health and safety. Since the 1980s, with the Reagan-era Paperwork Reduction Act (PRA), this conflict has regularly focused on information—that collected by and that disseminated (or made available) by the government. One recent area of battle has been the Data Quality Act.

Impact of the Data Quality Act

The Data Quality Act is just two sentences directing the OMB to ensure that all information disseminated by the federal government is reliable. The Act directs OMB to issue guidelines for data quality according to four key terms—"quality," "objectivity," "utility," and "integrity"—and for other federal agencies to issue their own conforming guidelines.

A Data Quality Act (DQA) aimed at ensuring reliable data might seem like a good, reasonable bill on its face. So one might ask why it was slipped into and passed as part of the FY 2001 Consolidated Appropriations Act without congressional discussion or debate at any point along the way. The reason? Its authors intended to give regulated industries opportunities to gum up the work of government scientists and regulators.

The Data Quality Act was written[80] by the Center for Regulatory Effectiveness (CRE), an industry-funded, for-profit think tank. CRE has no members, but it receives, from time to time, financial support, services in kind, and work product from foundations, trade associations and private firms. Consequently, at any one time, CRE benefits from the input or advice of literally hundreds of small and large firms. It receives support from companies and trade associations "usually in the form of a monthly contribution to support the Center's activities."[81]

The CRE's advisory board consists of James B. MacRae, Jr., former Deputy Administrator, Office of Information and Regulatory Affairs (OIRA) at OMB during the Reagan and G.H.W. Bush Administrations; Jim J. Tozzi, former Deputy Administrator of OIRA from the Reagan through at least part of the Clinton Administration (and at OMB since the Nixon Administration); and Kenneth Glozer, former Deputy Associate Director of OMB. The key person among these is Jim Tozzi. A 2004 *Washington Monthly* article[82] is informative about his long-term commitment to what many have called regulatory "paralysis by analysis." In the 1990s, Tozzi's consulting shop, Multinational Business Services, took on the tobacco industry as a client. The industry was intent on battling the emerging scientific consensus that secondhand smoke was a danger to those who were over exposed to it. One strategy was to advocate standards for "good epidemiology" that would have made it almost impossible to conclude that secondhand smoke was dangerous. A good example of Tozzi's tactics: he "deployed a phalanx of lobbyists to his old haunts at the OMB to block the implementation of a government medical code, used for Medicare and Medicaid claims, that tracked secondhand smoke illnesses." Tozzi said that had the government been allowed to accumulate such statistics, tobacco firms "could have been subject to tons of legal actions saying, 'Look at all these illnesses caused by secondary smoke.'" During the mid- and late-1990s, as part of his work for Philip Morris, Tozzi circulated information and proposals concerning two pieces of legislation: "data access" language and a "data quality" bill, both of which were later incorporated as amendments to other pieces of legislation.[83]

The Data Quality Act is one point of what CRE calls "[the] federal information triangle." The OMB Office of Information and Regulatory Affairs is at the apex of the triangle, establishing the policy for both data coming into the government as well as data leaving the federal government, along with the mandates set forth in the Paperwork Reduction Act[84] and the Data Quality Act; the other two points are the Data Quality Act and an earlier "data access" law that allows interested parties to obtain, under FOIA, "all data produced" (including all the underlying data) by any publicly funded scientific study (including those conducted by private entities and nonprofits not subject to FOIA) that are used for making policy. The implementation of the data access statute by OMB and the affected agencies mitigated some of its potential for grinding government-funded research to a halt.

As far as the Data Quality Act is concerned, although by its terms it allows individuals as well as corporate interests to challenge government information believed to be inaccurate, the reality is that some have more resources to utilize it than others. And guess who?

A 2004 *Washington Post* analysis[85] of government records indicated that in the first 20 months[86] after implementation of the Act, it was used predominantly by industry. The *Post*'s analysis found 39 petitions with potentially broad economic, policy, or regulatory impact. Of these, 32 were filed by regulated industries, business or trade organizations, or their lobbyists. Only seven were filed by environmental or citizen groups. Some environmental groups were boycotting the Act, adding to the imbalance in its use. The *Post* found "petitioners are homing in on agencies whose mission is to protect the environment and public health. The most heavily petitioned are the Environmental Protection Agency, the Fish and Wildlife Service, the National Institutes of Health, and the Consumer Product Safety Commission."

Among the petitions noted in the *Post* analysis are the following:

- The American Chemistry Council and others challenged data used by the Consumer Product Safety Commission as it sought to ban wood treated with heavy metals and arsenic in playground equipment.

- Logging groups challenged Forest Service calculations used to justify restrictions on timber harvests.

- Sugar interests challenged the Agriculture Department and the Food and Drug Administration over dietary recommendations to limit sugar intake.

- The Salt Institute and the U.S. Chamber of Commerce challenged data that led the National Institutes of Health to recommend that people cut back on salt.

- The Nickel Development Institute and other nickel interests challenged a government report on the hazards of that metal.

Another example of how industry groups can use the Data Quality Act to subvert the congressionally mandated agency goals can probably be found in a story I told earlier in this chapter, in "Interior and the Lobbyists: 2007." In that story, I reported that the Interior Department had declined to put sage grouse on the lists of threatened or endangered species—which would have interfered with the oil and gas drilling and the cattle ranching prevalent in the grouse's habitat. I also reported that one of the Interior Department's deputy assistant secretaries had had to resign after the department's inspector general found that she had heavily edited scientific reports on sage grouse and had improperly given industry lobbyists internal agency data. It may well be that the agency's decision on the sage grouse in this case was influenced by a Data Quality Act challenge brought by an industry group, the Partnership for the West, which is a coalition of organizations that support a largely anti-environment agenda and receive support from corporations like Dow Chemical. This group asserted that reports favoring the listing of the grouse "overstate threats to the species and understate the exhaustive conservation efforts currently underway by federal agencies, eleven Western States, local working groups, private landowners and environmental groups." The petition also stated that listing the greater sage grouse as endangered would actually put the species at greater risk because it would undermine current conservation efforts.[87]

One example of using the act to *protect* the environment, by a Fish and Wildlife Service whistleblower and Public Employees for Environmental Responsibility (PEER), came in 2004. Andrew Eller (the whistleblower) and PEER challenged Fish and Wildlife under the Data Quality Act.[88] In March 2005, the agency acknowledged three violations of the Act, involving documents issued based on faulty assumptions and bad data collection practices on the home range of Florida panthers. As a result of the challenge, the agency said it would protect more varieties of habitat, such as prairie, wetlands, pasture and rows of crops where other animals feed, although not more acreage. The breeding population of panthers in 2005 was thought to be below the minimum needed to sustain the population.

The most recent DQA report concerns a lawsuit filed in February 2007, in a federal court in California. The suit claims that the DHHS and the

FDA are disseminating false and misleading information regarding the health benefits of marijuana.[89]

Uses of the DQA by environmental and other public interest organizations remain few and far between. This lack of use may well be due to a sense that, with this second Bush administration, such a petition is a waste of energy when there are so many other information battles to fight. When it feels like the vast majority of information coming out of the executive branch is filled with inaccuracies at best and lies at worst, where does one start?

If you think this sounds disaffected and depressed, just read on to see how "[the] bureaucracy" feels.

Scientific Discontent

The erosion of science that I've described in this chapter has been a subject of great concern and dismay among prominent elements of the scientific community. In February 2004, more than 60 influential scientists, including 20 Nobel laureates, issued a statement[90] asserting that the Bush Administration had systematically distorted scientific fact in the service of policy goals on the environment, health, biomedical research and nuclear weaponry at home and abroad. During the same week, the Union of Concerned Scientists (UCS)[91] issued a 38-page report[92] detailing the accusations of those scientists. This report is based on UCS' investigation of many of the allegations made in the mainstream media, in scientific journals, in overview reports issued from within the federal government,[93] and by non-governmental organizations.[94] Read together, the scientists' statement and the UCS report accuse the administration of repeatedly censoring and suppressing reports by its own scientists, stacking advisory committees with unqualified political appointees, disbanding government panels that provide unwanted advice, and refusing to seek any independent scientific expertise in some cases. Some of the reports' allegations mirror those I have listed here, but others go beyond my noninclusive listing. It's interesting reading, and I commend it to you.

This report was essentially dismissed[95] by an administration spokesman, who argued that the report consisted of a largely disconnected list of events that did not make the case for a suppression of good scientific advice by the administration. But the opinion of an emeritus professor of physics at Stanford and a senior fellow at the Hoover Institution might be worth listening to. Dr. Sidney Drell, who has advised the government on issues of national security for some 40 years and has served in Democratic and

Republican administrations, including those of Presidents Nixon and Lyndon B. Johnson, was not a signatory to the statement, but he said the overall findings rang true to him: "I am concerned that the scientific advice coming into this administration seems to me very narrow. The input from individuals whose views are not in the main line of their policy don't seem to be sought or welcomed."[96]

The UCS/PEER Survey on Scientists' Discontent

How widespread is the discontent in the scientific community? I've listed several examples above of distinguished scientists quitting government service in disgust. Also relevant is a 2004 survey conducted by UCS and PEER. This survey[97] was addressed to more than 1,400 US Fish and Wildlife Service (USFWS) biologists, ecologists, botanists, and other science professionals working in Ecological Services field offices across the country, and asked about perceptions of scientific integrity within the USFWS, as well as political interference, resources, and morale. Nearly 30 percent[98] of the scientists returned completed surveys, despite agency directives[99] not to reply—even on personal time.

The results,[100] released in February 2005, paint a troubling picture.[101] Over half of the responding scientists could cite instances where commercial interests induced the suppression of scientific conclusions. Almost half responded they had been instructed, for non-scientific reasons, to avoid making decisions that would protect species, and one in five admitted government officials told them to alter or remove scientific information from federal agency documents. Almost a third felt they were not allowed to do their jobs as scientists. Indeed, Roger Kennedy, former director of the National Park Service, told Robert Kennedy[102] that the alteration and deletion of scientific information is now standard procedure at Interior: "It's hard to decide what is more demoralizing about the Administration's politicization of the scientific process—its disdain for professional scientists working for our government or its willingness to deceive the American public."

EPA internal surveys reportedly have shown similar results. At a March 16, 2006, hearing to examine the proposed EPA Science and Technology budget for fiscal year 2007, PEER Executive Director Jeff Ruch presented testimony[103] pointing to EPA internal surveys showing a growing pessimism by agency scientists about the direction of EPA. Examples raised by PEER included giving corporate contributors direct influence over which research projects are undertaken by entering into a record number of joint ventures. Mr. Ruch also told the House Subcommittee, "Unfortunately, EPA has forbidden its own specialists from speaking without political clearance." He further noted that EPA's research program is plagued by suppression of findings for nonscientific reasons and lack of protection for its scientists.

The GAP Report on Scientific Censorship

On March 28, 2007, the House Science Subcommittee on Oversight held hearings on press office manipulation, focusing on censorship of climate science via agency press offices. At that hearing, the subcommittee heard from an investigator for the Government Accountability Project (GAP), a nonprofit whistleblower group. A just-published report[104] by GAP documents more thoroughly than any previous report the broad extent of White House-directed political censorship of agency scientists working on climate change. The investigation incorporated dozens of interviews and a comprehensive review of thousands of FOIA disclosures, internal documents, and public records.

GAP's report found a widespread perception of inappropriate political interference among employees of the federal climate science agencies and programs, as well as among journalists from national, mainstream outlets who cover their research. This perception is substantiated by evidence from inside sources, scientists' personal testimonies, journalists, and FOIA disclosures. GAP found no incidents of direct interference with climate change research; rather, "unduly restrictive policies and practices were located largely in the communication of 'sensitive' scientific information to the media, the public, and Congress."[105]

In this context, "sensitive scientific information" meant any science that did not support the administration's positions on global warming. GAP found a clear trend toward increasingly restrictive policies and practices unsupported by any official justification from the agencies and programs. GAP noted that these restrictive communication policies and practices were "largely characterized by internal inconsistencies, ambiguity, and a lack of transparency," and that although restrictions tended to target a small number of federal employees, the overbroad application of restrictive policies had a chilling effect on a greater number.[106]

Why are these restrictions becoming more pervasive than ever before? The evidence GAP found suggests that incidents of interference are often top-down reactions to science that has negative policy or public relations implications for the administration. More specifically, GAP noted that

Directives and signals from executive offices such as the Council on Environmental Quality, the Office of Management and Budget, and the Office of Science and Technology Policy are channeled through political appointees and younger politically-aligned career civil servants at lower-level press and policy offices. These communications largely take place off the record, frequently deviating from written policy guidelines and involving individuals with few scientific qualifications. Whereas low-level agency and program support staff are typically sympathetic to the scientists and their science, as one scientist noted, "the closer you get to Washington, the more hostile [they are to the science]." Despite supportive rhetoric, senior managers who are aware of the perception and even the incidents of interference largely fail to address them. To the contrary, they may be conforming to pressures from above to downplay politically-inconvenient science.

As GAP noted, the effect has been to misrepresent the science generated by federal climate science agencies and programs, in some cases, even at the expense of scientists' free speech and whistleblower rights. In most cases, "[the] policies and practices undermine the government's inherent obligation to disseminate the results of publicly-funded research."[107]

In Conclusion

So, where does this leave us? Essentially in a holding pattern—hoping Congress can do something to protect the integrity of science by and for our government and, if not, waiting for a new Administration. Not that we expect everything to be completely open with whoever wins the Presidency in 2008; as I said before, every administration wants to control the flow of information. The next administration will have to be held accountable, and inevitably there will be struggles.

Notes

1 For an alternate understanding of the politicization of science and its impacts, see Michael Gough, ed., Politicizing Science: The Alchemy of Policymaking. (Stanford, California: Hoover Institution. 2003. http://www-hoover.stanford.edu/publications/books/polscience.html#toc. That is his book; this is mine.

2 Robert F. Kennedy, Jr., "The Junk Science of George W. Bush" The Nation, posted February 19, 2004 (March 8, 2004, issue). http://www.thenation.com/doc/20040308/kennedy/2.

3 William K. Stevens "On the Climate Change Beat, Doubt Gives Way to Certainty," New York Times, February 6, 2007. http://www.nytimes.com/2007/02/06/science/earth/06clim.html?ex=1180238400&en=1bffeb87027c66f0&ei=5070.

4 Elisabeth Rosenthal and Andrew C. Revkin, "Science Panel Calls Global Warming 'Unequivocal,'" New York Times, February 3, 2007. http://www.nytimes.com/2007/02/03/science/earth/03climate.html?ex=1180238400&en=15046ca451afd265&ei=5070.

5 National Academy of Sciences, Commission on Geosciences, Environment and Resources, "Climate Change Science: An Analysis of Some Key Questions," 2001. Online at www.nap.edu/books/0309075742/html.

6 K.Q. Seelye, "President Distances Himself from Global Warming Report" New York Times, June 5, 2002, Late Edition—Final, p. A23, col. 1. http://select.nytimes.com/gst/abstract.html?res=F30715FA355E0C768CDDAF0894DA404482 (payment required).

7 Union of Concerned Scientists, "Climate Change Research Distorted and Suppressed" (This page is an excerpt from the 2004 UCS report "Scientific Integrity in Policymaking.") June 2005 update. http://www.ucsusa.org/scientific_integrity/interference/climate-change.html.

8 Andrew C. Revkin.,"With White House Approval, E.P.A. Pollution Report Omits Global Warming Section." New York Times, September 15, 2002. http://www.nytimes.com/2002/09/15/politics/15CLIM.html.

9 Andrew C. Revkin, "Bush Aide Edited Climate Reports" New York Times, National Desk, June 8, 2005, pg. A15. http://select.nytimes.com/search/restricted/article?res=F10710F6385C0C7B8CDDAF0894DD404482.

10 Id.

11 Committee on Government Reform Minority Office, "Rep. Waxman Releases Internal Commerce Department E-Mails on Climate Change," September 19, 2006. http://www.democrats.reform.house.gov/story.asp?ID=1107.

12 http://science.house.gov/publications/hearings_markups_details.aspx?NewsID=1736.

13 Department of Commerce, Administrative Order 219-1, March 29, 2007. http://www.commerce.gov/opa/press/Secretary_Gutierrez/2007_Releases/March/29_DAO_219_1.pdf.

14 Andrew C. Revkin, "Climate Expert Says NASA Tried to Silence Him," New York Times, January 29, 2006. http://select.nytimes.com/search/restricted/article?res=F30D13FF355B0C7A8EDDA80894DE404482#

15 And Deputy Assistant Administrator for Public Affairs at NASA.

16 Leslie McCarthy, citing handwritten notes taken during the conversation. Revkin, op. cit.

17 Ms. McCarthy agreed to the New York Times interview after Mr. Acosta, at NASA head-quarters, told the Times that she would not face any retribution for doing so. Revkin, op. cit.

18 Rick Weiss, "NASA Sets New Rules On Media: Employees May Discuss Findings, Agency Says" Washington Post, March 31, 2006; p. A10. http://www.washingtonpost.com/wp-dyn/content/article/2006/03/30/AR2006033001864.html.

19 Jane Kay, "U.S. accused of silencing experts on polar bears, climate change —Scientists told not to speak officially at conferences" San Francisco Chronicle, March 9, 2007.

20 Massachusetts v. EPA (05-1120). Robert Barnes and Juliet Eilperin, "High Court Faults EPA Inaction on Emissions" Washington Post, April 3, 2007, p. A01. http://www.washingtonpost.com/wp-dyn/content/article/2007/04/02/AR2007040200487.html.

21 William Matthews. "'Sensitive' label strikes nerve" Federal Computer Week, October 31, 2002. http://www.fcw.com/fcw/articles/2002/1028/web-info-10-31-02.asp.

22 USDA, "List of Sensitive issues for ARS Manuscript Review and Approval by National Program Staff—February 2002 (revised)." February 2002. Cited at http://democrats.reform.house.gov/features/politics_and_science/example_agricultural_pollution.htm.

23 EPA, "DRAFT Evaluation of Impacts to Underground Sources of Drinking Water by Hydraulic Fracturing of Coalbed Methane Reservoirs, 5–14." (EPA 816-D-01-006) August 2002, Copy at http://democrats.reform.house.gov/features/politics_and_science/example_oil_and_gas.htm.

24 EPA, "Calculations for Estimating Fracture Zone Concentrations for Three Scenarios," September 18, 2002, cited in a letter from Representative Henry A. Waxman to EPA Secretary Christine Todd Whitman, October 8, 2002 http://www.house.gov/reform/min/pdfs/pdf_inves/pdf_enviro_epa_hydraulic_oct_8_let.pdf).

25 Letter from Rep. Henry A. Waxman to EPA Secretary Christine Todd Whitman (Oct. 8, 2002) (online at http://www.house.gov/reform/min/pdfs/pdf_inves/pdf_enviro_epa_hydraulic_oct_8_let.pdf.

26 http://oversight.house.gov/features/politics_and_science/index.htm.

27 http://oversight.house.gov/features/politics_and_science/example_abstinence.htm.

28 Id.

29 National Park Service, World Heritage Committee Report. http://www.nps.gov/yell/planyourvisit/world-heritage-committee-report.htm.

30 Administration, "Yellowstone Staff at Odds on Park Threats," Los Angeles Times, June 26, 2003.

31 Yellowstone Park Staff, Yellowstone National Park Site Report to the World Heritage Committee (2003). http://greateryellowstone.org/YNP_site_report.html.

32 Department of the Interior, Yellowstone National Park Site Report to the World Heritage Committee. February 2003. http://greateryellowstone.org/DOI_site_report.pdf.

33 "Park Will Be off List; World Panel Still Worried," Billings Gazette, July 2, 2003.

34 Yellowstone National Park, "Report to the World Heritage Committee: Status of Key Issues," January 2006. http://www.nps.gov/yell/planyourvisit/upload/whcreport01-06-2.pdf.

35 Julie Cart, "Land Study on Grazing Denounced" Los Angeles Times, June 18, 2005. http://www.organicconsumers.org/Politics/grazing062105.cfm. Also Editorial: Doctored science, Part II Sacramento Bee, June 21, 2005, http://dwb.sacbee.com/content/opinion/v-print/story/13102118p-13946902c.html.

36 "BLM Publishes New Grazing Regulations to Improve Management of Public Lands Grazing," http://www.blm.gov/grazing/final/AD42FinalClean062106.pdf.

37 Office of the Inspector General, Department of the Interior. Investigative Report on Allegations against Julie MacDonald Deputy Assistant Secretary, Fish, Wildlife and Parks. http://www.doioig.gov/index.php?menuid=2&viewid=-1&viewtype=REPORT&pgid=391&rpttype=special.

38 http://science.house.gov/publications/hearings_markups_details.aspx?NewsID=1736.

39 Felicity Barringer, "Interior Official Steps Down After Report of Rules Violation" New York Times, May 2, 2007. http://select.nytimes.com/search/restricted/article?res=F00E10FF3B5A0C718CDDAC0894DF404482.

40 Id.

41 Robert F. Kennedy Jr., op. cit.

42 Office of Inspector General, Environmental Protection Agency, "EPA's Response to the World Trade Center Collapse: Challenges, Successes, and Areas for Improvement," Report No. 2003-P-00012, August 21, 2003. http://www.epa.gov/oig/reports/2003/WTC_report_20030821.pdf.

43 Amy Westfeldt, "Whitman to Testify on 9/11 Health Issues" Associated Press, May 18, 2007. http://www.washingtonpost.com/wp-dyn/content/article/2007/05/18/AR2007051801388.html.

44 Office of the Inspector General, "EPA's Response to the World Trade Center Collapse: Challenges, Successes, and Areas for Improvement," Report No. 2003-P-00012 August 21, 2003. http://www.epa.gov/oig/reports/2003/WTC_report_20030821.pdf.

45 "WNBC.com Judge Blasts Ex-EPA Chief for 'Conscience-Shocking' Actions After 9/11" February 3, 2006. http://www.wnbc.com/politics/6689847/detail.html.

46 United States Court of Appeals for the Second Circuit, Docket No. 06-1077-cv. Argued: November 27, 2006; Decided: April 19, 2007.

47 http://www.kscourts.org/ca10/cases/1998/06/96-2297.htm.

48 Juliet Eilperin, "EPA Cuts Soot Level Allowable Daily in Air," Washington Post, September 22, 2006, p. A03. http://www.washingtonpost.com/wp-dyn/content/article/2006/09/21/AR2006092101616.html.

49 Bill Lambrecht, "Scientists See Clean Air Decision as Latest Snub" St. Louis Post-Dispatch, Washington Bureau, February 26 2006.

50 Michael Hawthorne, "War over clearing the air: In sharp rebuke, scientists say proposed EPA standards don't do enough to protect public." Chicago Tribune, March 8, 2006. http://www .electricityforum.com/news/mar06/NewEPAstandardsunderfire.html.

51 Kennedy, op. cit.

52 "Ag Scientists Feel the Heat," Des Moines Register, December 1, 2002. Cited at http:// democrats.reform.house.gov/features/politics_and_science/example_agricultural_pollution.htm.

53 Amy Chapin, Ana Rule, Kristen Gibson, Timothy Buckley, and Kellogg Schwab, "Airborne Multidrug-Resistant Bacteria Isolated from a Concentrated Swine Feeding Operation" Environmental Health Perspectives, Vol. 113, No. 2, February 2005, http://www.ehponline.org/ docs/2004/7473/abstract.html.

54 In the U.S. District Court for the Southern District of New York, Natural Resources Defense Council, Inc. v. National Marine Fisheries Service and the U.S. Department of Commerce. June 1, 2005. http://www.nrdc.org/media/docs/050601.pdf.

55 Marc Kaufman, "Reference to Sonar Deleted in Whale-Beaching Report" Washington Post, January 20, 2006, p. A09. http://www.washingtonpost.com/wp-dyn/content/article/2006/01/ 19/AR2006011902990.html.

56 Natural Resources Defense Council, "Proposed Sonar Training Range Threatens Whales, Marine Life along Carolina Coast" http://www.nrdc.org/media/pressreleases/060113.asp.

57 Blaine Harden, "Questions About Salmon Are Directed Upstream," Washington Post, Wednesday, May 31, 2006, p. A17. http://www.washingtonpost.com/wp-dyn/content/article/ 2006/05/30/AR2006053001057.html.

58 Id. "Brian Gorman, spokesman in Seattle for NOAA Fisheries, commented optimistically on the effect of the two decisions: "People may look back on this past week and say that is when things really turned around for fish in the Klamath. A senior biologist from the U.S. Fish and Wildlife Service made a similarly positive statement."

59 Id.

60 Revkin, op. cit. New York Times January 29, 2006.

61 Chad Gillis, "EPA water quality expert for Lee, Collier loses his job" Naples Daily News, October 19, 2003. http://web.naplesnews.com/03/10/naples/e7399a.htm.

62 Gillis, op. cit.

63 Kennedy, op. cit.; and Emily Green, " Regulators to Let Maker Test Chemical Levels" Los Angeles Times, November 1, 2003, p. A.19.

64 "Low Sperm Count, Quality in Rural Areas Tied to Herbicides, Pesticides." EHPonline, June 17, 2003. http://www.ehponline.org/press/swan2003.html.

65 Shanna H. Swan, et al., "Semen Quality in Relation to Biomarkers of Pesticide Exposure" Environmental Health Perspectives, September 2003, Vol. 111, No. 12. http://www.ehponline .org/docs/2003/6417/abstract.pdf.

66 Green, op. cit.

67 Julie Cart, "70percent of Jobs in Park Service Marked Ripe for Privatizing," Los Angeles Times, January 26, 2003.

68 Public Employees for Environmental Responsibility (PEER), "Citing cost overruns and potential side effects, Congress severely restricted the Bush Administration efforts to outsource National Park Service and U.S. Forest Service jobs during the 2004 fiscal year. Those restrictions, however, lapsed this past October and now the Bush Administration is again pushing its 'Competitive Sourcing' initiative." May 10, 2005 http://www.peer.org/news/news_id .php?row_id=524.

69 National Parks Conservation Association, "Privatization of National Park Service Jobs." http://www.npca.org/media_center/fact_sheets/privatization.html. Last Updated: March 4, 2007.

70 Federal Register, Notices June 16, 2004, Vol. 69, No. 115, pp. 33823-33826. http://a257.g .akamaitech.net/7/257/2422/06jun20041800/edocket.access.gpo.gov/2004/04-13553.htm.

71 Id.

72 Marilyn Chase, "Administration Limits Content of AIDS Efforts Seeking Grants," Wall Street Journal, June 21, 2004, p. B4.

73 Joyce Nishioka, "Governing Sexuality: Bush's HIV-prevention policies place ideology before science," American Sexuality Magazine, September 5, 2007. http://nsrc.sfsu.edu/MagArticle .cfm?Article=392&PageID=134&SID=4489683F48264189724D5914A6823637&DSN=nsrc_ dsn.

74"Certain Words Can Trip Up AIDS Grants, Scientists Say." The Body, April 18, 2003. http:// www.thebody.com/content/policy/art29778.html.

75 Id.

76 Curtis W. Copeland, Specialist in American National Government—Government and Finance Division, "Changes to the OMB Regulatory Review Process by Executive Order 13422" Congressional Research Service, February 5, 2007. http://www.fas.org/sgp/crs/misc/ RL33862.pdf.

77 Id.

78 An impact of $100 million or more on the economy.

79 Cindy Skrzycki, "Bush Order Limits Agencies' 'Guidance,'" Washington Post, January 30, 2007, p. D01. http://www.washingtonpost.com/wp-dyn/content/article/2007/01/29/ AR2007012901818.html.

80 For the uninitiated, much legislation is originally drafted by outside groups, including public interest groups. This author had a strong hand in drafting the original E-Government Act, for instance.

81 http://www.thecre.com/about.html.

82 Chris Mooney, "Paralysis by Analysis: Jim Tozzi's regulation to end all regulation" Washington Monthly, May 2004. http://www.washingtonmonthly.com/features/2004/ 0405.mooney.html.

83 Id.

84 I refer the reader back to Chapter 2, for the discussion of the Reagan-era PRA.

85 Rick Weiss, "'Data Quality' Law Is Nemesis of Regulation," Washington Post, Monday, August 16, 2004, P. A01. http://www.washingtonpost.com/wp-dyn/articles/A3733-2004Aug15 .html.

86 For a compendium of the ongoing uses and abuses of challenges under the Data Quality Act, see http://www.ombwatch.org/article/archive/231. The site contains a link to a docket of data quality requests submitted to federal agencies.

87 OMB Watch, "Sage Grouse Recommendation Follows Data Quality Challenge." http:// www.ombwatch.org/article/articleview/2568/1/231?TopicID=1.

88 John Heilprin, Associated Press writer, "Agency: Data on Endangered Panthers Flawed" Los Angeles Times, March 22, 2005, 6:16 AM PST.

89 OMB Watch, "Medical Marijuana Lawsuit Uses Data Quality Act." http://www.ombwatch .org/article/articleview/3743/1/231?TopicID=1.

90 Restoring Scientific Integrity in Policymaking" http://www.ucsusa.org/scientific_integrity/ interference/scientists-signon-statement.html.

91 The Union of Concerned Scientists (UCS) is an alliance of more than 200,000 citizens and scientists. UCS members are people from all walks of life: parents and businesspeople, biologists and physicists, teachers and students. http://www.ucsusa.org/ucs/about/.

92 Union of Concerned Scientists, Reports and Research, "Scientific Integrity in Policymaking: An Investigation into the Bush Administration's Misuse of Science." http://www.ucsusa.org/ scientific_integrity/interference/scientific-integrity-in-policy-making-204.html.

93 The Executive Summary gives the example of the House Committee on Government Reform, Minority Staff, Special Investigations Division, "Politics and Science in the Bush Administration," August 2003.

94 The Executive Summary gives the example of the Association of Reproductive Health Professionals, "Preserving Core Values in Science," 2003; Defenders of Wildlife, "Sabotaging the Endangered Species Act: How the Bush Administration uses the judicial system to undermine wildlife protection," December 2003.

95 James Glanz, "Scientists Say Administration Distorts Facts" New York Times. February 19, 2004.

96 Id.

97 Union of Concerned Scientists, "Survey Questions and Results." http://www.ucsusa.org/ scientific_integrity/interference/us-fish-wildlife-service-survey.html. Page last revised: August 10, 2005.

98 The survey was sent to 1,410 scientists, out of whom 414, or 29.4 percent, responded to the survey.

99 Directives not to reply to survey. http://www.ucsusa.org/scientific_integrity/interference/ us-fish-wildlife-service-survey.html.

100 Union of Concerned Scientists, "Survey Questions and Results," op. cit.

101 "Junk Science is the Law of the Land: Routine Censorship of Scientists Is Endangering the Nation's Wildlife." Frontline Newsletter, April 7, 2005, Vol. 150 http://ga4.org/guardians/notice-description.tcl?newsletter_id=3225803#Junk.

102 Robert F. Kennedy, Jr., op. cit.

103 Public Employees for Environmental Responsibility, "EPA Dumbing down its Research — Shrinking Environmental Research Budget Siphoned Off to Other Tasks," Press release, March 16, 2006. http://www.peer.org/news/news_id.php?row_id=661.

104 Tarek Maassarani with contributions from Jay Dyckman (National Coalition Against Censorship), "Redacting the Science of Climate Change; An Integrative and Synthesis Report," Government Accountability Project, March 2007. http0://www.whistleblower.org/doc/2007/Finalpercent203.28percent20Redactingpercent20Climatepercent20Sciencepercent20Report.pdf.

105 Id., Executive Summary, pp. 1- 2 .

106 Id.

107 Id.

Afterword

A Republic:

How to Keep It

"Well, Doctor, what have we got—a Republic or a Monarchy?"
"A Republic, madam, if you can keep it."

—Benjamin Franklin[1]

It was hard to find a stopping point for this book, in particular the second part of it. It seems that every day brings a new affront to access to information and to accountability. But this particular telling of the story has already gone on too long. A colleague wanted me to call this section "A Prologue to a Farce," playing on the oft-quoted statement by James Madison: "A popular government without popular information or the means of acquiring it, is but a prologue to a farce, or a tragedy, or perhaps both."[2] I think, though, that we still do have the means of acquiring the information to hold our government accountable, so I have chosen the somewhat more hopeful Benjamin Franklin.

It should be apparent to the reader by now that our problem is not lack of policy. There are a number of important laws on the books. These laws, such as the Freedom of Information Act, the Paperwork Reduction Act (at least the 1995 reauthorization thereof), and the E-Government Act of 2002, were passed to make government more open and more accountable to the public. Why, then, are we in the state we are?

One part of the explanation is—as we have seen in this book—the implementation of the laws. Sometimes that implementation has gone reasonably well; take, for example, the revisions to (OMB) Circular A-130 in 1994. But guidance from OMB, or the Department of Justice in the case of the FOIA (when that guidance has been aimed at openness, unlike the Ashcroft Memorandum), does not necessarily translate into practice that promotes openness at the agency level. This is not meant as an attack on the civil servants of this country, many of whom dedicate their careers to providing what is determined to be appropriate access to government information. The problems do not, for the most part, lie with the career civil servants; they lie with the political appointees and our elected officials.

Another part of the explanation is that we have been afraid since September 11th—and that fear has been used to political ends. An interesting and thought-provoking book[3] came into my hands as I was thinking about this final section of this book. In it, the author looks at the concept of political fear—"a people's felt apprehension of some harm to their collective well-being—the fear of terrorism, panic over crime, anxiety about moral decay—or the intimidation wielded over men and women by government and groups." The author argues that fear has a politics that we often ignore or misconstrue, "making it difficult to understand how and why fear is used. We blind ourselves to the real-world conflicts that make fear an instrument of political rule and advance, deny ourselves the tools that might mitigate those conflicts, and ultimately ensure that we stay in thrall to fear." Examples of this use (one might go so far as to say manipulation) of fear can be seen in critical infrastructure information, the proliferation of "sensitive but unclassified" types of control markings,[4] and reclassifications (and refusals to declassify) information. And, of course, the more direct suppressions and manipulations of information exercised by the White House.

I believe, though, and know from my own daily experience, that perhaps the largest part of the explanation of the state we are in is that it is just hard to keep track of all it and to make government—Congress, the executive branch, and even the courts[5]—pay attention. It is hard enough for those of us for whom this is our life's work. We are a dedicated community, but small—even counting the journalists for whom these issues are a beat, and we are not enough.

So what is to be done? The 2006 elections were a good start. The new Congress has indicated that they clearly received the voters' message about corruption and ethics and have taken some important steps forward in that regard. Of course, even there, the devil will be in the details of implementation and accountability. Is this a harbinger of greater congressional and government transparency and accountability overall? That is up to us.

I am assuming here that this book has outraged you and convinced you that you need to do something to protect—and strengthen—your access to government information. A first step is to connect with organizations that are engaged on the issues of access to government information and work with them. These groups exist at both the national level and the state level. A partial list is provided at the end of this chapter. Many, if not most, of these organizations work collaboratively on legislative and executive branch concerns and are a good way to keep track of what is happening and to become engaged. While we are the "usual suspects" that government hears from on these issues, our voices are not the ones they ultimately listen to. Those are yours.

A critical, sometimes difficult, part of this step is to think outside your comfort level when looking for allies. One of the mantras in the District of Columbia lobbying and advocacy[6] world is "No permanent friends; no permanent enemies." While that is not completely true—we do have permanent friends even if we don't work together on every issue—you cannot write off legislators and other organizations and causes as possible friends on issues such as openness. As another adage says, "Politics makes for strange bedfellows." It should be apparent by now to any reader that access to information is always a political affair. It is not, however, a partisan one. The effort to ensure passage of legislation to implement much-needed procedural reforms to the Freedom of Information Act, the OPEN Government Act (S. 849), is a good example of the non-partisan nature of this. Advocates span the right to the left and we are working together in unison in this effort. We don't necessarily agree about the roles or scope of the federal government, but we all believe in holding it accountable.

The events leading up to the final passage of S. 2590, the Federal Funding Accountability and Transparency Act, provide another good example. The bill was originally conceived by OMB Watch,[7] on whose wish list it had languished for years. The sponsors of the bill, Senators Tom Coburn (R-OK) and Barack Obama (D-IL), are not names that would have jumped to mind as partners—and they brought different views of government and its role to their collaboration. On April 6, 2006, Senators Coburn, Obama, Tom Carper (D-DE), and John McCain (R-AZ) introduced the bill requiring the Office of Management and Budget to make information on federal contracts and grants publicly accessible through a searchable Web site.

The legislation garnered wide right-left support. In June 2006, the Project on Government Oversight (POGO) and a right-left list of other organizations sent a letter of support,[8] noting that

> *Advocates from all points on the spectrum of opinion share the common notion that transparency of and public access to government information is vital to the health of our political system. ...Budget watchdogs can support the legislation because it would reveal duplicative or superfluous federal funding. Environmentalists can support it because it would detail exactly how much federal money goes to organizations and practices they deem to be ecologically harmful. Traditional values groups can support the legislation because it would allow them to track funding for causes they hold to be inimical to their own.*

Despite its widespread support, amassing an impressive group of cosponsors including both the Senate Majority and Minority leaders, and being unanimously approved by the Homeland Security and Government Affairs Committee in late July 2006, the bill ran into unexpected resistance. Two Senators placed anonymous secret holds on the transparency legislation, preventing it from passing quickly.

The blogosphere was outraged and bloggers from across the political spectrum and public interest and watchdog groups teamed up to launch an effort to expose the mystery senator or senators. Eventually this effort uncovered two senators who placed holds. The obstacle was eventually removed after increased public pressure on Senate Majority Leader Bill Frist led him to bring the bill for a vote despite the hold.[9]

This was one good example of both working across ideological lines and use of new technology. It also had an amusing side. As the *Washington Post* reported in October 2006, when President Bush signed the bill, he was flanked by the bloggers who had led the charge. Soon afterward, OMB Deputy Director Clay Johnson III spent an hour with the bloggers. After spending that hour with the bloggers, he and OMB Director Rob Portman appeared at a luncheon to talk about OMB's government performance push. As the *Post* reports, Portman also talked about the blogger fest, saying, "Clay asked them, 'Gee, since you're so good at this, can you help us on some of our other initiatives?'" He invoked the bloggers several times as weapons in his fight for government performance and accountability reforms, proposing that it would be a "no-brainer" to get the "blog community" to support a bill that required that a government "employee had to be minimally successful to get a raise."[10]

Technology has a role to play, but it needs follow-through and engagement. As I noted at the outset of this book, technology itself is not the answer, although it can be a potent tool. It is an old adage that information is power; it is, nonetheless, true. It is also true that power is not lightly given up—it usually must be wrested out of the hands of those holding it. And once power is taken, it must be used. There are some potentially transformative new uses of technology happening—wikis on congressional committees, wikis on the Presidency, wikileaks, "mashups" using public information, for example—that are all about sharing information. Their potential for transformation will, though, remain just that—potential—unless members of the public use that information to work for and demand change, and more access to more information.

A second, and deeply important, step toward protecting and strengthening the public's access to government information is to connect with your elected officials—at every level of government. Let them know that you care about access to the information created by or for government, about openness and accountability at whatever level of the official to whom you are speaking—from the school board to candidates for President in 2008. Share information with your officials and become a source for them to know what people like you—librarians, parents, senior citizens, students, members of the public—care about, and a source for good, solid information about your community and your causes (whether they be health care, taxpayer rights, environmental, or whatever else). Thank them when they do something good—and let them know you are watching and will hold them accountable when they are not so accommodating. Stay in there for the long haul, because that is what this is.

I consider this White House all but[11] a total loss in terms of any impact the public can have. Congress may have a shot at forcing greater accountability out of the executive branch, but for the rest of us, it would be a better use of time to get the candidates for election in 2008 on record on issues of access and openness.

Finally, support your local (and national) newspapers and libraries. The former can be[12] your lifeline for objective, deeply and broadly informed information about your government—local, state, and federal. The latter are the safety net for our republic and the place anyone can go to "arm themselves with the power which knowledge gives."[13]

The elected—and appointed—branches of our government have central roles in ensuring its openness and accountability. But, ultimately, it is up to us, the American public, to keep our republic. I hope you will join my colleagues and me in this fight.

Access to Government Information Organizations

American Association of Law Libraries: http://www.aallnet.org

American Booksellers Foundation for Free Expression: http://www.abffe.org

American Library Association: http://www.ala.org/ala/issues/issuesadvocacy.htm

American Society of Newspaper Editors : http://www.asne.org

Association of American Publishers: http://www.publishers.org

Association For Community Networking: http://www.afcn.org

Association of Research Libraries: http://www.arl.org

Bill of Rights Defense Committee: http://bordc.org

Californians Aware: http://www.calaware.org

Center for American Progress: http://www.americanprogress.org

Center for Democracy and Technology: http://www.cdt.org

Center for National Security Studies: http://www.cnss.org

Center for Progressive Reform: http://www.progressivereform.org

The Center for Public Integrity: http://www.publicintegrity.org/default.aspx

Common Cause: http://www.commoncause.org/site/pp.asp?c=dkLNK1MQIwG&b=186966

Electronic Frontier Foundation: http://www.eff.org

Electronic Privacy Information Center: http://www.epic.org

EnviroJustice: http://www.envirojustice.org

Environmental Defense: http://www.environmentaldefense.org/home.cfm

Essential Information: http://essentialinformation.org

Federation of American Scientists: http://www.fas.org/sgp/index.html

First Amendment Foundation: http://www.firstamend.org

Florida First Amendment Foundation: http://www.floridafaf.org

Free Expression Policy Project: http://www.fepproject.org/index.html

Friends Committee on National Legislation: http://www.fcnl.org/index.htm

Fund for Constitutional Government: http://www.fcgonline.org/home.html

Good Jobs First: http://goodjobsfirst.org

Government Accountability Project: http://www.whistleblower.org/template/index.cfm

Humanist Society of New Mexico: http://nm.humanists.net

Human Rights First: http://www.humanrightsfirst.org

Illinois Community Technology Coalition: http://www.ilctc.org

Indiana Coalition for Open Government: http://indianacog.org/main.php

Institute for Defense and Disarmament Studies: http://www.idds.org

The James Madison Project: http://jamesmadisonproject.org

League of Women Voters: http://www.lwv.org

Liberty Coalition: http://libertycoalition.net

Mine Safety and Health News: http://www.minesafety.com

Minnesota Coalition on Government Information: http://www.mncogi.org

National Coalition Against Censorship: http://www.ncac.org

National Coalition for History: http://historycoalition.org

National Committee Against Repressive Legislation: http://www.ncarl.org

National Freedom of Information Coalition: http://www.nfoic.org

National Security Archive: http://www.gwu.edu/~nsarchiv

National Security Whistleblowers Coalition: http://www.nswbc.org

New Jersey Work Environment Council: http://www.njwec.org

Northern California Association of Law Libraries: http://www.nocall.org

NPOTechs: http://www.npotechs.org/drupal

OMB Watch: http://www.ombwatch.org

PEN American Center: http://www.pen.org

People For the American Way: http://www.pfaw.org/pfaw/general

Project On Government Oversight: http://www.pogo.org/index.shtml

Public Employees for Environmental Responsibility: http://www.peer.org

ReadtheBill.org: http://www.readthebill.org

ReclaimDemocracy.org: http://www.reclaimdemocracy.org

Reporters Committee for Freedom of the Press: http://www.rcfp.org

Society of American Archivists: http://www.archivists.org

Society of Professional Journalists: http://www.spj.org

Southeastern American Association of Law Libraries: http://www.aallnet.org/chapter/seaall

Special Libraries Association: http://www.sla.org/content/SLA/advocacy/index.cfm

Sunlight Foundation: http://www.sunlightfoundation.com

Taxpayers for Common Sense: http://www.taxpayer.net

Transactional Records Access Clearinghouse: http://trac.syr.edu

U.S. Public Interest Research Group: http://www.uspirg.org

Washington Coalition for Open Government: http://washingtoncog.org

Working Group on Community Right-to-Know: http://www.crtk.org

Notes

1 The response is attributed to Benjamin Franklin—as he left Independence Hall on the final day of deliberation of the Constitutional Convention of 1787, when asked by a certain Mrs. Powell of Philadelphia what kind of government had been bestowed on the country as a result of the Convention's four-month effort—in the notes of Dr. James McHenry, one of Maryland's delegates to the Convention. McHenry's notes were first published in *The American Historical Review*, Vol. 11, 1906, and the anecdote on p. 618 reads: "A lady asked Dr. Franklin Well Doctor what have we got a republic or a monarchy. A republic replied the Doctor if you can keep it." When McHenry's notes were included in *The Records of the Federal Convention of 1787*, ed. Max Farrand, Vol. 3, Appendix A, p. 85 (1911, reprinted 1934), a footnote stated that the date this anecdote was written is uncertain. http://www.bartleby.com/73/1593.html.

2 Letter to W.T. Barry, August 4, 1822.

3 Corey Robin, *Fear: The History of a Political Idea.* (Oxford: Oxford University Press, 2004.)

4 At a count of well over 100 across the government, according to communications from the Information Sharing Environment program in the Office of the Director of National Intelligence.

5 To whom too little attention has been given, including in this book.

6 "Lobbying" has a very particular legal meaning in terms of the tax code; advocacy covers a much broader range of activities and includes work not related to specific legislation.

7 True to its history of innovative uses of technology to provide meaningful access to government data (and showing the government that it is not, as often claimed, just too complicated and difficult), starting with the Toxic Release Inventory (TRI) on its RTK NET in 1989 in support of the Emergency Planning and Community Right to Know Act (EPCRA), http://www .rtknet.org/aboutrtknet.php, OMB Watch has created and launched FedSpending.org http://www.fedspending.org/. At the same time, the Center for Responsive Politics also launched two databases on Congress and money (Congressional Personal Financial Disclosure, http://www.opensecrets.org/pfds/overview.asp including information on where Members are investing money, and Travel, http://www.opensecrets.org/travel/index.asp).

8 "An Open Letter to the United States Senate: Support a Full Accounting of Federal Grants!" http://www.pogo.org/p/government/gl-060601-federalgrants.html.

9 "Spending Transparency Bill Passes Senate, House Approval Imminent," OMB Watch, September 12, 2006. http://www.ombwatch.org/article/articleview/3581/1/86?TopicID=1 and Paul Blumenthal, "Transparency Issue Unites Right and Left Blogs," In Broad Daylight. Sunlight Foundation, August 28, 2006. http://www.sunlightfoundation.com/node/1085.

10 Elizabeth Williamson, "OMB Welcomes Help From Anti-Pork Bloggers" *Washington Post*, October 4, 2006, p. A23. http://www.washingtonpost.com/wp-dyn/content/article/2006/10/03/AR2006100301313.html.

11 President Bush did sign the Federal Funding Accountability and Transparency Act and did issue an executive order on procedural reforms to the implementation of the Freedom of Information Act—some would say to enrage the public about the use of tax dollars (and so support cutting taxes) in the former case and to forestall passage of legislation in the latter.

12 Although, unfortunately, more and more print newspapers are having their news supplanted by entertainment—and believers in the central, First Amendment, role of the press in our democracy supplanted by bottom-line driven stockholders or investors—and you may need to let them know that you really do want a *news*paper, not infotainment.

13 James Madison to W.T. Barry, August 4, 1822.

INDEX

A

Academic research, 13-14

Acosta, Dean, 227

Addington, David, 201

Administrative Procedures Act, 66

Aeronautical information, 139, 226–227

Afghanistan, 219

AFRTS. *See* American Forces Radio and Television Service

Aftergood, Steve, 145, 180n

Agency for International Development, 219

Agency web sites
  audit of, 29
  information regulation, 27–28, 216–217

Agricultural Research Service, 228

AIDS-prevention programs, 237–238

AIPAC. *See* American Israel Public Affairs Committee

Air quality, 231–233

Aircraft Owners and Pilots Association, 139

American Chemistry Council, 241

American Embassy, Baghdad, 149–154

American Forces Radio and Television Service, 219

American Forest Resource Council, 231

American Israel Public Affairs Committee, 163, 172

American Petroleum Institute, 225

American Society of Access Professionals, 71, 85

American Society of Newspaper Editors, 213

Anderson, Jack, 171–173

Anderson, Kevin, 172

H

I

J

K

L